GRANDMOTHERS, MOTHERS, AND DAUGHTERS

Oral Histories of
Three Generations of
Ethnic American Women

TWAYNE'S
ORAL HISTORY SERIES

Donald A. Ritchie, Series Editor

PREVIOUSLY PUBLISHED

Rosie the Riveter Revisited: Women, The War, and Social Change
Sherna Berger Gluck

Witnesses to the Holocaust: An Oral History
Rhoda Lewin

Hill Country Teacher: Oral Histories from the One-Room School and Beyond
Diane Manning

The Unknown Internment:
An Oral History of the Relocation of Italian Americans during World War II
Stephen Fox

Peacework: Oral Histories of Women Peace Activists
Judith Porter Adams

FORTHCOMING TITLES

Life on the Homestead: Interviews with Women of Northwestern Colorado, 1890–1950
Julie Jones-Eddy

Between Management and Labor: Oral Histories of Arbitration
Clara H. Friedman

CORINNE AZEN KRAUSE

GRANDMOTHERS, MOTHERS, AND DAUGHTERS

Oral Histories of
Three Generations of
Ethnic American Women

TWAYNE PUBLISHERS · BOSTON
A Division of G. K. Hall & Co.

Twayne's Oral History Series No. 6

Copyright 1991 by G. K. Hall & Co.
All rights reserved.
Published by Twayne Publishers
A division of G. K. Hall & Co.
70 Lincoln Street
Boston, Massachusetts 02111

Copyediting supervised by Barbara Sutton.
Book design and production by Janet Z. Reynolds.
Typeset in Baskerville by Huron Valley Graphics, Ann Arbor, Michigan.

First published 1991.
10 9 8 7 6 5 4 3 2 1

The paper used in this publication meets the minimum requirements
of American National Standard for Information Sciences—Permanence
of Paper for Printed Library Materials, ANSI Z39.48-1984.∞™

Printed and bound in the United States of America.

Library of Congress Cataloging-in-Publication Data

Krause, Corinne Azen.
    Grandmothers, mothers, and daughters : oral histories of three
generations of ethnic American women / Corinne Azen Krause.
        p.   cm.—(Twayne's oral history series : no. 6)
    Includes bibliographical references and index.
    ISBN 0-8057-9105-1 (alk. paper)
    1. Minority women—United States—Cross-cultural studies.
2. Mothers and daughters—United States—Cross-cultural studies.
3. Intergenerational relations—United States—Cross-cultural
studies.   4. Ethnicity—United States—Cross-cultural studies.
5. Women, Jewish—United States—Interviews.   6. Italian American
women—Interviews.   7. Slavic American women—Interviews.
I. Title.   II. Series.
HQ1410.K73   1991
305.48'8'0973—dc20   90-46014
                                                                    CIP

Contents

Foreword   vii
Acknowledgments   ix
Introduction   xi

  1. Historical and Geographical Background   1

Italian Families

  2. Michelena Gaetano Profeta, Josephine Fastuca, and
      Joanna Dorio   17
  3. Anna Casatelli Yorio Pizzuto, Lydia Pofi, and
      Judith Flack   50

Jewish Families

  4. Sylvia Sacks Glosser, Naomi Cohen, and Cathy Droz   79
  5. Eva Rubenstein Dizenfeld, Belle Stock, and Ruth Zober   112

Slavic Families

  6. Mary Miroka Laver, Elsie Firka, and Joanne Gereg   145
  7. Mary Grajewski Sypniewski, Eva Carey, and
      Mary Lou Olmo   178

Conclusion   207
Notes and References   213
Bibliography   219
Index   226

Foreword

Memory depends largely on perception. Where we stand affects what we see, what sense we make of it, and what we later recall. Most readers of oral history recognize that the race, class, gender, and ethnicity of interviewees (and to some degree of those who interview them) will necessarily shape their personal narratives. In *Grandmothers, Mothers, and Daughters,* Corinne Krause demonstrates that even within the same family different generations offer dissimilar versions of a shared history. Involved here is more than intergenerational conflict, for despite contrasting life-styles and aspirations, these women reveal the deep bonds and persistent values inside each family. Their stories suggest how family members experience the same events and react to the same individuals in widely varying ways, depending on their age, attitudes, and expectations. This experiment in multigenerational oral history invites each generation to speak for itself, from its own vantage point, treating seriously and sensitively the differences of opinion among them.

Oral history may well be the twentieth century's substitute for the written memoir. In exchange for the immediacy of diaries or correspondence, the retrospective interview offers a dialogue between the participant and the informed interviewer. Having prepared sufficient preliminary research, interviewers can direct the discussion into areas long since "forgotten," or no longer considered of consequence. "I haven't thought about that in years," is a common response, uttered just before an interviewee commences with a surprisingly detailed description of some past incident. The quality of the interview, its candidness and depth, generally will depend as much on the interviewer as the interviewee, and the confidence and rapport between the two adds a special dimension to the spoken memoir.

Interviewers represent a variety of disciplines and work either as part of a collective effort or individually. Regardless of their different interests or the variety of their subjects, all interviewers share a common imperative: to collect memories while they are still available. Most oral historians feel an additional responsibility to make their interviews accessible for use beyond their own research needs. Still, important collections of vital, vibrant interviews lie scattered in archives throughout every state, undiscovered or simply not used.

Twayne's Oral History Series seeks to identify those resources and to publish selections of the best materials. The series lets people speak for themselves, from their own unique perspectives on people, places, and events. But to be more than a babble of voices, each volume will organize its interviews around particular situations and events and tie them together with interpretive essays that place individuals into the larger historical context. The styles and format of individual volumes will vary with the material from which they are drawn, demonstrating again the diversity of oral history and its methodology.

Whenever oral historians gather in conference they enjoy retelling experiences about inspiring individuals they met, unexpected information they elicited, and unforgettable reminiscences that would otherwise have never been recorded. The result invariably reminds listeners of others who deserve to be interviewed, provides them with models of interviewing techniques, and inspires them to make their own contribution to the field. I trust that the oral historians in this series, as interviewers, editors, and interpreters, will have a similar effect on their readers.

DONALD A. RITCHIE
Series Editor, Senate Historical Office

Acknowledgments

I began oral history research on the topic of immigrant and ethnic women in 1975, and many people have contributed to this book, which is the result of that research. I owe a profound debt of gratitude to the Institute for Pluralism and Group Identity of the American Jewish Committee, which sponsored "Women, Ethnicity, and Mental Health," the study on which this book is based. I am equally indebted to the Maurice Falk Medical Fund, which funded the study. I extend sincere thanks to Irving M. Levine and Joseph Giordano of the American Jewish Committee and to Philip B. Hallen and Betty Klimchok of the Falk Fund for their personal support of the project. I am indebted to many individuals for help on the project, especially Professor Francesca Colecchia of Duquesne University and the late Bosanka Evosevic. Both scholars worked with me at every stage of the research. Joanna Dorio, Katie Hall, Rosalie Hazin, Natalie Klein, Joanna Karaczun, and Joan Shaffer conducted interviews. Shirley Angrist, then Professor of Sociology at Carnegie-Mellon University, organized statistical analyses of the interviews. Sandra Romanow Levine, Marilyn Russell, Raimi Slater, and Lori Santo provided superb secretarial and interviewing assistance. Mary Jane Welsh did the statistical analysis. I sincerely thank the 225 women who contributed their tape-recorded oral histories to the study.

I especially thank Professor Wendell Wray of the Graduate School of Library and Information Services at the University of Pittsburgh. He taught me much of what I know about oral history, encouraged and supported my work over the years, and made me aware of the oral history series undertaken by Twayne Publishers. For their support and encouragement I thank Ann Eastman of the Women's National Book Association, Arthur Eastman of Virginia Polytechnic Institute, David Cohen of Queens College, and Sherna Berger Gluck of California State University at Long Beach. Sydney Weinberg of Ramapo College in New

Jersey. I am indebted for suggestions made by Professors Maurine Greenwald of the University of Pittsburgh and Paula Hyman of Yale University. Thanks to the Maurice Falk Medical Fund for support in preparation of the manuscript of this book.

I thank Judy Bennett and Mary Jo Zeidler who prepared the map of Pittsburgh neighborhoods, and I thank Carol Bleir and Belle Stock for bibliographical research. I am most grateful to Helen Wilson, Faye Leibowitz, and Bart Roselli of the Historical Society of Western Pennsylvania for their willing cooperation. Marie Zini and the staff of Carnegie Library of Pittsburgh have my sincere gratitude for generous and time-consuming research and photo searching. I thank Anna Mae Gorman Lindberg and S. Raymond Rackoff for historical photographs. I am grateful to Father Edward McSweeney, Archivist of the Diocese of Pittsburgh, who provided lists of ethnic churches in the Pittsburgh area, and to Professor Leonard Plotnikoff of the University of Pittsburgh, who provided specific information I requested.

I thank Professors Lois Fowler, David Fowler, Thomas Morton, and Richard Schoenwald of Carnegie-Mellon University, Sima Godfrey and Paul Krause of the University of British Columbia for reading and commenting on the manuscript. I thank my husband, Seymoure, my three daughters—Barbara, Kathy, and Diane—my son, Norman and daughter-in-law, Ann, and many good friends whose interest, support, and helpful suggestions have helped shape this final version.

I am deeply indebted to my editors, Donald A. Ritchie, Associate Historian, United States Senate, and Anne M. Jones, Executive Editor of Twayne Publishers. Donald Ritchie read and critiqued each version of this manuscript and offered constant support. Anne Jones patiently answered my many questions and gave generous encouragement over the months of preparation of this book.

I extend my deepest thanks to the people most centrally responsible for this book—the eighteen women whose oral histories make up the body of the volume. All recorded oral histories for the original study; all surviving women were reinterviewed in 1988 and 1989. I thank them sincerely for their generous cooperation, for photographs, and most of all for the gift of their oral histories.

Introduction

I have been interested in women's and ethnic history since I began to teach in the 1960s. From my first month in the classroom, I recognized the need for more information about women in history. The same was true for American ethnic groups. In the 1960s and 1970s, history curricula in the high schools and colleges where I taught mentioned only briefly the fact that our nation is the product of diverse cultures brought to these shores by generations of immigrants of both sexes.[1] Because of my personal commitment to women's history and to ethnic history, I organized "Women, Ethnicity, and Mental Health," the oral history study on which this book is based. I wanted to bring new knowledge of immigrant and ethnic women into the mainstream of history. The oral histories in this book show indeed that women of various backgrounds, their names virtually unknown, have acted as a force in history.

I began my research in 1975. The timing was crucial, for I wanted to document the lives of immigrant women who were part of the mass migration from southern and eastern Europe between 1880 and 1920. Many immigrants of the early twentieth century were alive, well, and willing to share their life stories. I believed that recording their experiences and those of their daughters and granddaughters would contribute to better understanding the complex phenomenon of ethnicity. I was interested in the changing roles of women. I wanted to understand the behavior and attitudes of women who were part of traditional ethnic cultures and to examine areas of change and continuity over three generations in America. I wanted to explore areas of conflict between immigrant women and their American-born daughters. As I listened to three generations of women talk about their lives, it became clear that continuity and change in behavior and attitudes were affected by class as well as by gender and ethnicity. The complex interaction of all three factors—ethnicity, gender, and class—influenced women's behavior, choices, and attitudes over the generations.[2]

My research was sponsored by the Institute for Pluralism and Group Identity of the American Jewish Committee, the nation's oldest human relations agency, headquartered in New York. The study was funded by the Maurice Falk Medical Fund of Pittsburgh. Two hundred twenty-five oral history interviews were recorded and analyzed. The American Jewish Committee published the results of the study.[3]

Oral history's research approach proved particularly suitable for exploring female experiences and female values.[4] Psychologist Carol Gilligan, in her provocative book *In a Different Voice*, identifies interpersonal relationships, networks of intimacy, responsibility toward others, and avoidance of hurting others as particularly female values.[5] The study's informally structured, open-ended interview format encouraged women to discuss such issues in their own words.

Gilligan found that in contrast to men, who tend to think and act autonomously, women tend to think and act within a social context.[6] For the women who recorded the oral histories in this book, the most significant social context was the family. The central place of the family has given women a unique role in history. The life cycle of women demonstrates a sequence that centers on family and in this respect differs both qualitatively and quantitatively from that of men. In spite of contemporary trends that tend to blur strictly divided gender roles, for most men work continues to provide "the primary base" for life in society.[7] For most women, including women who work, the primary base is family. The life cycle of women is commonly described in biological terms related to family—*childhood, menses, marriage, pregnancy, childbirth, menopause, empty nest*.[8] In traditional history, such sex-specific topics have hardly been explored, and for this reason the oral history interviews paid particular attention to female experiences.

Women's issues identified in the oral histories extended beyond life-cycle events to food, relationships, and work/family conflicts. Food was a subject that arose again and again in women's oral histories. Women discussed holiday meals, ethnic foods, the feeding of children, and the serving of husbands. In another context, I asked one grandmother if she raised her children any differently from how she was raised. Her response, "I fed my children fruit," illustrates the prominent place that food held in the thoughts of many women and the relative absence of attention to child-rearing methods, especially among the grandmothers. Women were always planning the next meal or the next trip to the grocery store. Grandmothers, mothers, and daughters also talked a great deal about relationships with children and with parents. Oral histories identified areas of intergenerational conflict, hinted at concealed conflict, and suggested efforts to heal conflict. These histories also spoke of genuine love and caring between generations. Maintaining close bonds was very important to these grandmothers, mothers, and daughters. Work was a frequent topic, and women spoke of work in the context of family, bringing to the issue a distinctly female frame of reference. For virtually every woman interviewed, family was a primary concern.

I chose to study women of Italian, Jewish, and Slavic heritage because these were the three largest nationality groups that immigrated to the United States at the turn of the twentieth century. Uprooted from familiar people and places, immigrants had to find new ways of coping with life. Acculturation began with arrival in the United States. For some, accommodation to America was limited to learning enough of the language and laws to get along. A much larger number adopted American behavior in language, citizenship, work, and recreation while maintaining associations—marriage, friendships, clubs, organizations—almost exclusively within the ethnic group. For a few, assimilation was nearly complete; they relinquished ethnic behavior, values, and social ties. Various stages of transition from traditional to modern American culture can be identified.[9] Most immigrants and their children felt a sense of peoplehood with others who shared the same history and values. For many of them, the ethnic group acted as a "buffer against a strange and hostile society." And ethnicity continued to provide a source of personal well-being, a way of identifying one's place in society for many descendants of immigrants. In this sense, ethnicity has fulfilled a basic psychological need to belong.[10] At the close of the twentieth century, the process is being repeated by recent immigrants from Asia, Latin America, and eastern Europe.

In the original oral history project, three generations of women in seventy-five families (twenty-five Italian, twenty-five Jewish, and twenty-five Slavic) recorded oral histories. To identify persistence and change over generations as precisely as possible, the sample was limited to adult daughters (minimum age twenty-five), their mothers, and their maternal grandmothers. Eligible families were located through local institutions and organizations, such as schools, churches, and community centers. When an appropriate family was identified, I telephoned the middle-generation woman and invited her to participate. Once she had decided affirmatively, in most cases her mother and her daughter readily agreed as well. Letters of invitation and explanation followed the initial telephone contact. Respondents were assured of anonymity for the original interviews; each cassette was identified by a code. Once three generations of women in a family had agreed to participate, an assigned interviewer (one of a staff of eight) made appointments and interviewed the respondent privately at her own home. Interview time averaged two and a half hours. Following the interviews, bound transcripts were mailed to each participant, who called in corrections to be made on the office copy.

Several women have died since giving their oral histories. In preparation for this book, I recontacted the surviving women, and each had the opportunity to update her oral history, summarizing significant events of the intervening years. Each signed a deed of gift granting permission to print her oral history. Pseudonyms have been used for the women in chapter 6.

Each three-generation set of oral histories formed a chapter in the history of immigration and Americanization; each told of change and continuity. For this book I have edited eighteen of the oral history interviews into autobiographical narratives. Although all of the original 225 oral histories provided valuable insights into women's history, the eighteen in this book were chosen because they represent diversity in culture, class, and gender-related experiences. In addition, they touch on themes common to many participants in the original study. More important, however, the oral histories printed here reflect the overriding message of the study: women's lives do make a difference. What each grandmother thought and said and did affected how her daughter and granddaughter lived their lives.

This book is not an unbiased sample of immigrants and their children. The process of selection in itself skewed the sample to women who were known in their communities. And the selection was skewed toward successful families, for this was a self-selected population. A degree of satisfaction with one's life was probably a factor in deciding to record an oral history. Related to this point is the fact that the oral histories recorded the experiences of upwardly mobile women. This aspect does not invalidate the results, however, for sociologists have found that modifying trends in behavior and values usually occur first among upper and middle classes and are then followed sometime later by similar trends in the working-class population.[11] A caveat that applies to oral history and to all open-ended qualitative research methods is that respondents sometimes forget and sometimes say what they think the interviewer wants to hear. Then too, there is a human tendency to hide the unpleasant, either by design or by convenient failure to remember. Nor were all the respondents equally informative or equally open and frank. Language presented further inconsistencies. Some women expressed themselves articulately; others did not. Although I have tried to capture the tone and personality of each woman, in several instances I have changed the wording slightly to clarify meaning. In spite of these shortcomings, the oral history process has captured the spirit and personalities of immigrant and ethnic women. This is the way eighteen grandmothers, mothers, and daughters remembered their experiences. Their words attest to the fact that the lives of women have historical significance.

CITY OF PITTSBURGH AND HOMESTEAD
SELECTED ETHNIC NEIGHBORHOODS
1910 - 1977

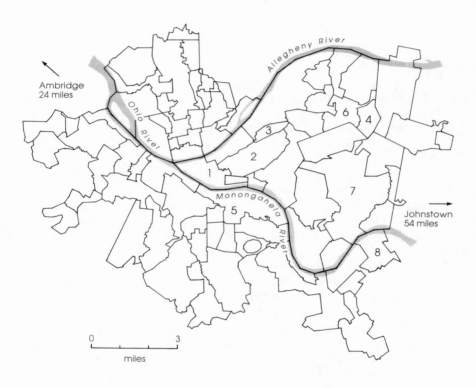

1. DOWNTOWN
2. HILL DISTRICT
3. POLISH HILL
4. LARIMER

5. SOUTH SIDE
6. EAST LIBERTY
7. SQUIRREL HILL
8. HOMESTEAD

ONE

Historical and Geographical Background

The story told in *Grandmothers, Mothers, and Daughters* began with the greatest migration in human history. In the century between 1820 and 1920, this migration brought to America more than thirty-five million European immigrants.[1] Profound political and economic changes in Europe set off this unprecedented movement of peoples. The immediate causes were the end of the Napoleonic wars and a rapidly industrializing economy developing in England and Western Europe. Before 1880, immigrants from northern and western Europe predominated. Then, in the 1880s a significant change occurred: in a single decade, the number of immigrants from southern and eastern Europe multiplied more than fivefold. By 1896, Italians, Jews, and Slavs—the largest of the nationality groups known collectively as the "new immigration"—accounted for 80 percent of all immigrants to the United States. Between 1880 and 1930, more than three million Italians, two million Jews, and one and a half million members of the various Slavic groups (one million of them Poles) left Europe to make permanent homes in the United States of America.[2]

Italians and Slavs came chiefly because economic changes in eastern and southern Europe had severely disrupted traditional peasant economies. The lives of eastern European Jews were further disrupted by political change in the Russian Empire. In its wake came legal restrictions and a wave of anti-Jewish riots that prompted a mass migration of Jews from all of the territories controlled by the Russian Empire.[3]

In the United States, industrialization and urbanization were proceeding at a rapid pace; coal and steel were in great demand to supply the fuel and the raw materials of economic growth. As the steel industry expanded, Pittsburgh, Pennsylvania, surged to the forefront of industrial and urban development. By 1910, that city led the nation in value of manufactured products. Pittsburgh was intensively industrialized in

1910; the giant enterprises started by Carnegie, Frick, Heinz, and Westinghouse were leaders in world industry.

Heavy industry shaped the work environment, and Pittsburgh offered jobs to immigrants. The economy, however, suffered periodic fluctuations, which meant unpredictable layoffs and variations in the semi-weekly pay envelopes of wage earners. Workers had virtually no power over their jobs. The failure of the Homestead Strike in 1892 had given unrestricted control over work to employers and, in effect, postponed labor organization until the 1930s.[4]

The uncertainty of male employment heightened the importance of women's role in the family economy. In Pittsburgh, women had the burden of managing household budgets with meager and unpredictable amounts of money. Women also had a difficult time supporting themselves or supplementing family income, for iron and steel and machinery did not generate the kinds of suppliers and businesses that employed large numbers of women. Those who were employed in industry, according to a 1907 volume of *The Pittsburgh Survey*, earned half the wages of men in comparable jobs.[5]

Most breadwinning women had jobs as domestics. They worked in laundries or restaurants or private homes. Domestic service was the largest single employer of women in the United States until 1930; in Pittsburgh, because of the male-oriented industrial economy, most working women held domestic service jobs until 1940.[6]

The immigration experience and the Pittsburgh industrial environment shaped the lives of the "grandmothers," the oldest generation of women who recorded oral histories for this book. Grandmothers of all ethnic backgrounds shared a great deal of common history. They remembered hardworking parents, responsibilities at home, and the difficulties of adjusting to a new society. As adults, the grandmothers managed on tight budgets; they earned money in the limited ways available to them. Keeping house was made more onerous by the city's dirt and smoke, which was all but impossible to clean. Women scrubbed houses and clothing to remove the ground-in dirt of the smoky city.[7] They survived and raised families and dreamed of a better life.

Then, in the 1930s, the Great Depression struck hard at this city of steel and its workers; employment and production declined drastically. Total unemployment at the low point, in August 1932, reached almost 40 percent and remained at more than one-third unemployed in 1935.[8] Depression dampened the hopes of many of the grandmothers and limited their expectations for their children. History and environment created a generation of stoic women who, within the restricted avenues open to them, took charge of their lives and did what they had to do to survive.[9]

Their daughters, the "mothers" of this oral history study, grew up during the depression and shared the experience of living in a bicultural world. They were pulled in different directions by old-world traditions at home and by modern American customs at school, at work, and on the street. As young women became more Americanized, differences between themselves and their parents became ever more difficult to bridge. Many felt ashamed of their parents, particularly of unfashionable mothers who could not speak English.[10] School provided these younger women with skills and with knowledge of American society; romantic movies fed their daydreams. The depression and their environment, however, limited their opportunities.

World War II was the pivotal event that shaped the lives of the second generation. In 1941, the United States joined the world conflict. War introduced the children of immigrants to an awareness of life beyond home and neighborhood. World War II stimulated the economy while it called men to military service and opened job opportunities to women. Industry, hospitals, and government asked for the labor of women. Women took wartime jobs; women joined the military. Others married servicemen and traveled with them; still others waited at home. Wartime experience broadened horizons and gave to women a vision of change and of choice.[11] After the war, women left wartime jobs to marry and raise families. Although their lives had been transformed only briefly, the changes set off by the war were profound and permanent. Many of the "mothers" generation achieved a sense of intrinsic strength and effectiveness through their wartime experiences.[12] Later, reinforced by the women's movement, they supported new roles and opportunities for their daughters.[13]

After World War II, the consumer-oriented economy kept living standards high. In Pittsburgh, the "Renaissance," a joint effort of private industry and government, cleaned up the smoke, installed flood control, razed the Lower Hill district, and rebuilt downtown Pittsburgh. Even as recession plagued the steel industry, optimism about the economy prevailed.

Most of the "daughters," the third generation to record their oral histories, were part of the baby-boom generation born between World War II and 1960. Television brought the world into their living rooms. They learned to read with Dick and Jane and were spurred by *Sputnik* to study science. They watched Neil Armstrong walk on the moon and wrote class papers about outer space and the intriguing possibilities of computers. The civil rights struggle and the war in Vietnam dramatized inequities and violence and contradicted the American ideals of freedom and equality that these young women had been taught in school. They were the young adults of the sixties. Some of them seemed unaware that students across the country were rebelling against traditional standards and mores. Others participated in the rebellion to varying degrees. Almost every young woman made a concerted effort to choose her own direction and determine her own life-style. The search for self and meaning gave this generation its unique place in American history. In the 1970s the women's movement touched all their lives. The oral histories of the "daughters" reflect the impact of contemporary ideas and events on aspirations, opportunities, and economic circumstances; they also document the persistence of certain deeply imbued cultural values and the bonds that continue to connect daughters with mothers and grandmothers.

ITALIAN WOMEN

Italian immigrants brought with them a strongly family-centered culture. Indeed, family and family welfare took precedence over the individual, and loyalty to family superseded all other allegiances, including individual ambitions.[14] The very definition of the word *family* had a distinct meaning to many Italian immigrants. *Family* referred to an extended network of relatives, and family responsibility extended to nieces and nephews, aunts and uncles, even great-aunts and great-uncles and their children and grandchildren.

Gender roles were strictly defined in the Italian family. The ideal Italian man was the authority and head of the family, the provider and protector of all its members.[15] Being an Italian woman carried with it a great deal of responsibility. The traditional role of the Italian female was that of nurturant, supportive "center of the family."[16] Being an Italian woman also implied motherhood. The Italian mother was known for the "unconditional" and "noncontingent" quality of love that she lavished on her children, particularly her sons.[17]

Traditionally in Italian culture, preparation for womanhood began in early childhood. For some little girls, family responsibility began as soon as they were old enough to hold a baby or to stand on a stool to wash dishes. Eight-year-old children were kept home from school to care for younger siblings.[18] Girls were raised for marriage and motherhood, and chastity and virtue were prerequisites for the role. As a result, girls were strictly chaperoned and kept close to their homes.

Although virginity was very important, sex was a taboo subject—a view that translated into lack of sex education at home and strong opposition to such education in the schools. Girls were frequently unprepared for menstruation; women were unprepared for childbirth. Italian immigrants even opposed the presence of male doctors at births.[19] Sexual topics, fraught with superstition and half-truths, were discussed only in whispers.[20]

Related to the values placed on chastity and on women's role as mother was suspicion of all activities outside the home. Parents did not consider schooling important; it seemed irrelevant to the domestic role of women.[21] In fact, many parents viewed the public school, the settlement house, athletics, and all outside activities as threats to traditional family life. Josephine Fastuca dropped out of high school because her parents would not allow her to attend swimming class. They considered it immodest, even disgraceful, to undress and be seen in a bathing suit.

Single women of every immigrant background were expected to work and to contribute to the family economy. Italian immigrants, however, worried that mingling with strangers in the workplace could compromise southern Italian cultural ideals. Moreover, a woman's "going out to work" could be interpreted as a failure by her father to fulfill his function of family provider and protector. Among immigrant women in Pittsburgh, the Italians were least likely to work outside their homes. No doubt this situation was due to lack of acceptable work opportunities in Pittsburgh, for in the cities of New York and New England, participation in the labor force was higher among Italian women than among immigrant women from most other countries.[22] For many families, however, the wage earned by a single woman was a necessity, and she frequently found work considered compatible with Italian values, as in a family business or a business owned by a relative. Sometimes an employed man secured a job for a single female relative at the place where he worked; presumably, he acted as chaperone.[23]

Married Italian women seldom worked outside their homes, but many worked for a family business or sewed at home. Work at home, regardless of hours and skills involved and regardless of whether money changed hands, was viewed not as "work" but, rather, as a normal extension of the woman's homemaking role. It was within Italian tradition that Michelena Profeta washed and ironed towels for her husband's barbershop and that Josephine Fastuca worked as unpaid secretary and bookkeeper for her husband's forging business.[24]

Conflict between traditional values and modern American behavior widened the generation gap in every ethnic group. And in each group, disagreement tended to focus on distinct issues. The role of women was one conflict-ridden issue among Italian-Americans.

JEWISH WOMEN

Jewish immigrants brought with them not only their religion, based on Torah and Talmud (the first five books of the Bible and rabbinic commentaries), but also a culture rich with traditions that had developed over eighteen hundred years in Jewish communities from Palestine to eastern Europe. Values and behavioral patterns, though altered, continued to influence Jewish life in America.

In traditional Judaism, gender roles were clearly defined. Historically, the highest position to which a Jewish man could aspire was that of a rabbinic scholar who prayed and "learned" in the synagogue. The highest position a woman could achieve was that of the wife of a scholar. This was the ideal, but seldom the reality, of eastern European life. Few men devoted their days to study; most worked to support their families. Women were responsible for the management of the household, for bringing sons to Torah (religious study), and for the socialization and "domestic" education of their daughters. For the Jewish woman in traditional society, fulfillment came from the achievements of her sons and from the propitious marriages of her daughters.[25]

The Jewish wife was expected to be a helpmate to her husband, and earning money was a traditional part of her "helping" role.[26] In eastern Europe, the Jewish woman was often the breadwinner, especially in the changing nineteenth-century economy that no longer demanded the goods or services offered by the Jewish man. Women ran little shops and market stalls, raised chickens and geese, sold eggs, baked bread, stuffed and sewed pillows and quilts.[27] Women also made dresses and hats and delivered babies.[28]

In Pittsburgh, Jewish immigrant women worked in stogie (cigar) factories and sweatshops and at sewing machines stitching men's work clothes. Eva Dizenfeld stripped tobacco in a Hill District sweatshop when she was nine years old. Most women left their jobs when they married, for like immigrants from every country, Jews rapidly adopted the standards of the American middle-class family. Except in times of extreme need, the father earned the livelihood and the mother stayed home. Many Jewish women felt that it would shame their husbands if they worked outside their homes. There was no shame, however, in working in a husband-wife business, as Dizenfeld did for more than fifty years. This practice was frequent among Jewish women; such work was considered an extension of household responsibility, and the mom-and-pop store was a ubiquitous fact of Jewish immigrant life.[29]

Jews saw education as the key to a better life, and for many of the immigrant generation, educating sons was a primary goal. Frequently daughters of immigrants went to work to help pay for the educations of their brothers.[30] By the second generation in America, however, Jewish women were completing high school; by the 1970s, equal numbers of Jewish males and females were enrolled in higher education.

Change, in the form of improvement of life from generation to generation, was part of Jewish immigrant thinking. Sociologist Marshall Sklare writes that "Jewish parents see their children as a continuation," almost an extension of themselves. They experience their children's success, status, and learning as their own and expect their children to progress from the level they themselves have achieved.[31]

In spite of higher educational levels and increased opportunities for women, many immigrant Jewish parents, like generations before them, repeated a medieval prayer on the birth of a daughter: "May she sew and spin and weave and be brought up to a life of good works." Jewish women's organizations have given contemporary expression to the traditional value placed on good works, and the oral histories contain many references that show the persistence of the tradition.

SLAVIC WOMEN

In Europe, the traditional Slavic family was patriarchal and women were held in low esteem. A new bride usually moved into her mother-in-law's home, where she was subject to the other woman's authority. A Slavic woman could achieve status only through her dowry, her children, or her husband's position.[32] Indeed, so undervalued were women in traditional Slavic culture that contemporary literature barely mentioned women. By contrast, in the United States the position of women within the Slavic family rose dramatically. Imbued in Slavic tradition were certain values that contributed both to the stability of the Slavic-American family and to the enhancement of the position of women.

Family roles centered on the home. A young married woman's position was immediately higher in the United States, for she was manager of her own household, rather than a dependent in her mother-in-law's house. Moreover, in her home she and her husband worked equally (although at different tasks) in the care and maintenance of the house. A woman's status was furthered by economic contributions to the household earned either by keeping boarders or by holding down an outside job.

In Slavic immigrant families, single daughters were expected to work and contribute to family income. Schooling was not important because families saw no practical use for education.[33] Families encouraged daughters to take domestic-service jobs because the experience taught housekeeping skills, which were highly valued in a prospective wife. And since the status of the entire family reflected the reputation of each family member, it was essential that a single woman maintain a "good reputation," both to attract a husband and to enhance the standing of the family.[34]

The work ethic was strong in Slavic culture. Manual labor was highly valued, and men and women respected a "good worker," male or female. In her oral history, one Serbian immigrant reported this tribute paid her by her dying husband: "Milka, I don't have to worry about you or the children, because you're such a good worker." Another woman's in-laws opposed their son's marriage to her because she was "too thin to be a good worker." A long history of hardship and work to ensure survival has given to work a very special value. To many people of Slavic heritage, work "is both a gift and sustenance."[35]

ETHNIC NEIGHBORHOODS

When immigrants arrived in Pittsburgh, they tended to settle close to others from the same parts of Europe, sometimes from the same town. In almost every block, one group predominated. In immigrant enclaves Italians, Jews, and Slavs developed ethnic neighborhoods. Urban historian Roy Lubove writes, "The significance of this phenomenon of ethnic cohesion and differentiation [in Pittsburgh] cannot be exaggerated."[36] The very topography of the city encouraged ethnic concentration, for hilly terrain and deep hollows formed boundaries separating one area from another.[37]

Ethnic neighborhoods multiplied in Pittsburgh and in outlying towns in the Pittsburgh industrial area. The neighborhoods described in this chapter are representative of Pittsburgh's many ethnic settlements. This is the environment in which most of the grandmothers of this book settled and raised their families. Many clusters of Slavic and Italian settlement were recognized by the Diocese of Pittsburgh, which established one hundred ethnic parishes in the city and in surrounding towns. Seventy-eight of the one hundred were Italian (twenty) or Slavic (fifty-eight). Polish and Slovak churches numbered, respectively, twenty-six and twenty-two of the fifty-eight Slavic parishes.[38] In contrast to multiple Italian and Slavic immigrant settlements within the city's boundaries, eastern European Jewish immigrants settled close to one another in a single area, the Hill District. By 1920 there were twenty-five synagogues in the Hill, each one organized by men from a particular province or town of eastern Europe.[39]

Italian neighborhoods in the city were located mostly in the northeastern sections. Bloomfield, an Italian neighborhood since the turn of the century, remained stable and predominantly Italian into the 1980s. Most Italian immigrant neighborhoods changed, however, over the years. The North Side, for example, where the Profeta/Fastuca family lived, was home to a large settlement of southern Italians and the site of the Regina Coeli Church. Yet between 1950 and 1970, the population of the district fell from more than fifteen thousand to five thousand and changed from 85 percent white to 70 percent black residents. Most of the Italian families, like the Fastucas, moved to suburbs to the south and east of the city.

Frequently the move to the suburbs involved several households of extended-family members, all of whom moved to the same suburban neighborhood.[40]

The East End is a large area made up of several residential neighborhoods; the hub is a mixed commercial and residential area called East Liberty. In the immigration years, working-class Italian immigrants settled in East Liberty and in adjoining Larimer, which had been home to Italian stonemasons and craftsmen since the nineteenth century. Italian workmen constructed the major railroad bridge in the area and the Meadow Street Bridge, which connects East Liberty and Larimer. Our Lady Help of Christians Church was constructed in 1892 to serve the Italian parish.[41] When Anna Pizzuto moved to East Liberty in 1921, the neighborhood contained streets on which every house was occupied by former residents of the same Italian town. In 1930, some two-thirds of the 6,286 persons in one census tract (12D) were born either in Italy or to foreign-born parents in the United States.

The Kingsley House Settlement, originally established in the Strip in 1892, relocated first to the Hill District and then, following the Italian immigrant community, to the East Liberty/Larimer neighborhood. The settlement provided classes, dances, social services, and a camp outside the city for mothers and children. Pizzuto and her children were among hundreds of Italian working-class women and children who enjoyed social and recreational programs at Kingsley House.[42]

After World War II, Italian residents began to leave East Liberty for newer neighborhoods and for suburbs outside the city. One popular new city neighborhood was Stanton Heights, an area of moderately priced houses west of East Liberty. Stanton Heights attracted young families, many of them of Italian and Jewish heritage. The blocks near Our Lady Help of Christians Church remained home, however, to many children and grandchildren of Italian immigrants, including Pizzuto's daughter Lydia Pofi and her husband, as well as their married son, who lived with his family on a neighboring street.

Jewish immigrants from eastern Europe crowded into the Hill District, an area that extends from downtown Pittsburgh two miles to the east. Outside the Hill District, which was home to approximately 90 percent of the city's Jewish immigrants, Jews also lived above or in back of small shops on the commercial streets of almost every outlying mill town.[43] For Jewish people who lived outside the city, the Hill was the center for shopping, socializing, and worship. Small-town storekeepers bought their merchandise from Jewish wholesalers in the Hill District. Even when they moved out of the immigrant district to newer neighborhoods, Pittsburgh's Jewish population never dispersed throughout the city; instead, they remained concentrated and clustered.

Tradition, history, and religion had conditioned Jews to live together with their coreligionists in a community. In eastern Europe, every Jewish town, large or small, had a community council that regulated various aspects of life.[44] Rabbi Gershon Cohen, chancellor of the Jewish Theological Seminary in New York, points out the significance of the community in raising Jewish children: "The community educated [children] . . . in the street, in the marketplace, in the synagogue, in the house of study, in the assembly hall."[45] In Pittsburgh, the community educated immigrant children also in settlement houses, Jewish "Y"s, orphanages, Hebrew schools, and Sunday schools.

In the Hill, Jews joined organizations enthusiastically. Jewish youth joined athletic teams, formed Jewish "Y"s, and organized clubs that they named after community leaders whom they chose as role models. In the daytime, Jewish children crowded the schools and libraries; in the evening, Jewish adults crowded night-school classes.

Despite the vitality of Jewish life in the Hill District, the neighborhood was an immigrant ghetto, and as soon as they could afford to live elsewhere, Jews moved away. Jewish people wanted bathrooms and backyards; they wanted to be Americans, not immigrants. And they wanted a better life for their children.[46] To move east was to move up, and Jews moved eastward to Oakland, East Liberty, and Squirrel Hill.

Gradually, Squirrel Hill replaced the Hill as the center of Pittsburgh Jewish settlement. By 1963, 64.3 percent of Pittsburgh's Jewish households were in Squirrel Hill, and 98.0 percent were located in Oakland, East End, and Squirrel Hill.[47] Except for Sylvia Glosser, who lived in Johnstown, all the Jewish women who recorded oral histories for this book lived in Squirrel Hill or East End at some point in their lives. By 1963, Jews had left the outlying towns, and 14 percent of Pittsburgh-area Jews were living in suburbs. Jewish synagogues, institutions, and community center relocated to Squirrel Hill, which to the present has remained Pittsburgh's center of Jewish life.

Pittsburgh is unusual in the stability of its ethnic neighborhoods.[48] The Pittsburgh Jewish experience reflects the stability enjoyed by many of the city's ethnic neighborhoods.

Slavic immigrants established ethnic neighborhoods in Pittsburgh and in mining and steel-manufacturing towns to the east and west of the city. Within the city of Pittsburgh, the South Side was and has remained the largest Slavic neighborhood. Polish Hill, east of downtown, winds its way downhill almost to the south bank of the Allegheny River and is today home to many older Polish Americans and their adult children. Homestead, located five miles east of downtown Pittsburgh on the south bank of the Monongahela River, was the site of the Carnegie Steel Company (after 1901, part of United States Steel Corporation [USX]) and home to thousands of Slavic immigrants who came from various states of the Russian, Austro-Hungarian, and Ottomon empires. The Slavic immigrants represented eleven nationality groups that are related linguistically and culturally and that are "similar in personality and family dynamics."[49] Poles constituted the largest Slavic group in the city of Pittsburgh, and Slovaks constituted the largest Slavic group in Homestead.

Slavic men came to America intending to take money back to Europe, either to buy property or to pay off mortgages on land their families had worked for years. As migrant workers became permanent immigrants, the goal of owning land—a goal peasants had cherished for generations—was transferred to home ownership in the United States.[50] This factor has, in all likelihood, contributed to the stability of Slavic ethnic neighborhoods.

Homestead expanded rapidly as the steel industry grew. In 1900, 12,554 people lived in the town; by 1910, the population had reached 18,713.[51] Slavic immigrants accounted for a large proportion of the increase. In Homestead, Slavic immigrants founded a variety of organizations. They built schools and churches, printed newspapers, and formed athletic and recreational organizations for the youth of the community. They established fraternal and mutual benefit societies with separate organizations of men and women.

Multiple ethnic churches attest to the importance of religion among Slavic immigrants. Whereas in 1896 Homestead had no Slavic churches, by 1907 the town had Polish, Slovak, and Lithuanian Roman Catholic churches; a Slovak Greek Catholic church; a Hungarian Reformed church; and one or two Slavic Protestant missions.[52]

Margaret Byington studied Homestead for the *Pittsburgh Survey,* an exhaustive study made between 1907 and 1914. She spent a year among the immigrants, and her account of Homestead presents a portrait of the mill town from the perspective of a middle-class social reformer. In spite of the bias implicit in her frame of reference, Byington has provided us with an invaluable historical document. She describes the typical housing pattern behind the mill as follows:

[T]hrough a narrow passageway you find yourself in a small court, on three sides of which are smoke-grimed houses, and on the fourth, low stables. The open space teems with life and movement. Children, dogs, and hens make it lively under foot; overhead long lines of flapping clothes must be dodged. A group of women stand gossiping in one corner, awaiting their turn at the pump, which is one of the two sources of water supply for the 20 families who live here. Another woman dumps the contents of her washtubs upon the paved ground, and the greasy, soapy water runs into an open drain a few feet from the pump. In the center a circular wooden building with ten compartments opening into one fault, flushed only by this waste water, constitutes the toilet accommodations for over one hundred people. Twenty-seven children find in this crowded brick-paved space their only playground; for the 63 rooms in the houses about the court shelter a group of 20 families.[53]

Mary Laver and her daughter, Elsie Firka, who lived for many years in such a courtyard, saw their neighborhood in a different light. Laver recalled the friendliness and warmth of living in a communal setting in which "nobody was better than anybody else."[54]

That neighborhood no longer exists. It was part of a six-block area that was razed in 1941 to accommodate a massive wartime expansion of the Carnegie Steel Company. Eight thousand workers and their families who formerly lived on City Farm Lane and Heisel, Ann, and Dixon streets had to leave their homes to make room for the new mills.[55]

In Slavic immigrant households, women played a significant economic role. They managed the wages brought home by husbands and sons, and to supplement family income, they kept boarders. Of a total of fifty-six hundred Slavic men employed in the Homestead mill in October 1907, almost eleven hundred were single men who boarded in homes managed by women. Keeping boarders, an occupation common to women in all immigrant groups, was most widespread among Slavic women. In one Homestead area of 239 households, 102 had lodgers.[56]

The steel industry and the town suffered during the depression. Then, with World War II came vast expansion of the steel mills and peak employment of twenty thousand people manufacturing steel. After the war, however, the steel-based economy began a gradual decline that was paralleled by a steady migration outward of the population. Yet despite periodic recessions and the declining population, steel companies and workers did not acknowledge the seriousness of problems in the industry until the crisis of 1982. By 1984, employment at the Homestead works had fallen to twenty-four hundred workers. On July 25, 1986, after more than a century of operation, USX, formerly United States Steel Corporation, permanently closed the last of the mills at its Homestead works. A rising exodus of young people gave evidence of profound change in the economy of Homestead and the entire Pittsburgh area.

The end of the era of steel manufacturing affected the entire industrial area. The population of Ambridge, where Eva Dizenfeld lived for fifty years, fell by 30 percent between 1940 and 1960; the population of Johnstown, where Sylvia Glosser lived, fell by 12 percent during the same period. Pittsburgh developed a postindustrial economy dependent on growth in education, medicine, and biotechnology as the city's leading industries. Further changes in the economy can be expected, and, in all likelihood these will be accompanied by increasing work opportunities for women.

History, world events, modern America, the neighborhoods of Pittsburgh, class, ethnic culture—all shaped the experiences and attitudes of three generations of women of Italian, Jewish, and Slavic background. The oral histories on the pages that follow tell fascinating tales of what it meant to be an ethnic woman in Pittsburgh, Pennsylvania, in the twentieth century.

Italian Families

TWO

Michelena Gaetano Profeta, Josephine Fastuca, and Joanna Dorio

Three generations of women in an Italian-American family with origins in Sicily tell of extended family, dominant fathers, strictly segregated sex roles, and gradual accommodation to contemporary American society. The oral histories say a great deal about mother-daughter relationships and about having and raising children. They tell, too, of the double responsibility of work and family within the home.

Michelena Gaetano Profeta immigrated to the United States in 1905 at the age of fifteen to enter a marriage arranged by her father to Vincent Profeta, a barber in Pittsburgh.

The Profetas' eldest child, their daughter Josephine, married Joseph Fastuca, a tradition-bound Italian immigrant who dominated and supported an eighteen-member extended-family household.

Joanna, the third child and only daughter of Joseph and Josephine Fastuca, was born in 1931 and grew up in a restricted, sex-segregated traditional household. Even as an accomplished professional nationally recognized in her field, she lived in a home rigidly controlled by her traditional Italian father. After her marriage to Robert Dorio, her life focused first on children and then, after 1980, on work and changing mother-daughter relationships.

Michelena Gaetano Profeta,
1890–1982
May 7, 1975, Interview

I was born in Italy in Della Rosa, in Sicily, on November 19, 1890. I had just one sister. My mother died when I was eighteen months old. I lived with my grandmother, my mother's mother. My father lived in the same town, and I saw him every Sunday. My grandmother was nice to me. She loved me and my sister, too. We slept all three in the same bed. I prayed all the time. I had no mother; everybody had the mother, and I feel bad. Not happy at all. Sometimes I cried. I had lots of friends, and all the children played hide-and-seek and jump rope.

Every Sunday we were going to church first, about eleven-thirty, and after church, going home. My grandmother cooked pasta—every night pasta, every night. I ate pasta *fagolli* and pasta with cauliflower, and pasta with broccoli, pasta with lentils, and every night she changed the pasta.

I went to school four years. They make you work hard in school. Then I went to learn to sew. A lady taught the classes. I learned pretty good. I think I [was] ten years old. See, the lady made suits for the men. She gave me thirty cents a week pay. Just like here, people ordered suits. There was no factory. She had the sewing in her house and had five or six girls sewing. She cut the suit, and we learned how to sew. I save my money and I buy something with my sister in town. I bought milk for me because I liked milk. My grandmother didn't need my money. Her son— my uncle—supported her.

I had lots of aunts and uncles. I saw them every Sunday. When I lived with my grandmother we went every Sunday to eat with her son. My uncle loved my grandmother, and he was real nice to me and my sister. He was the best one in the world. My father didn't come much. If he gave a penny, she [his second wife] got mad.

My grandmother got awful sick and went to live with her son, my uncle. Then she died. I went to live with my father.

Her father arranged a marriage to Vincent Profeta in Pittsburgh, Pennsylvania.

My aunt, my mother's sister, lived in New York, and she came to Italy and took my sister back to New York with her. My sister asked me to come, and I wanted to go. I wanted to be a dressmaker. I sewed, and I wanted to stay with my sister in New York and sew in New York. The house I lived in with my grandmother in Italy belonged to my mother, me, and my sister. When I came here, my sister sold the house and sent me money for my part of the house.

I didn't want to marry. I am telling you the truth. I didn't want to get married. "No, no," I told my father. He said, "I can't help you. The man sent the money for tickets for me and you, and I'll pay him back, and you marry him."

I was fifteen and eight months when I got married. I did not see my husband. I didn't know who he was. He said he knew me. He remembered me because my hair was wavy, and he saw me making spaghetti with the hand and he liked the way I moved my hand, and he came to my grandmother's house all the time. He knew me; I didn't know him. I was nine years and he was eighteen. How could I look at him? I didn't remember him at all.

I came the Fourth of July and married the last Sunday in July, the thirty-first of July, 1905. I came; I was twenty-seven days engaged and got married.

The kindness of her mother-in-law helped Profeta to cope with her new life.

My mother-in-law had Angeline, Giovannina, Carmella, Frank, Edward, and Vincent—six children. Five people lived in my husband's house with me—my husband, me, my husband's mother, my husband's brother, my husband's nephew. His father was dead a long time. I did dishes when I lived with my grandmother. Then when I went to my father, I went to learn the sewing. In the house, I dried dishes, and that's all.

I got married. I learn quick. I learn everything. I learn to make spaghetti, iron, wash. In one year married, I learn everything. My mother-in-law liked me. She taught me nice. She was good to me, very good to me. Yes. Summertime [before the wedding], I slept with the [little] boy. And after I get up, I didn't know how to fix the bed. She come, said, "Don't worry about it." She showed me. And in the summertime, when I ironed the shirt, I burnt the cloth sometimes. She said, "No worry, you'll learn it."

I was fourteen years old when I started my period. At that time I lived with my father and I had a stepmother. She told me what it was. I wasn't afraid. I had no trouble at all. Sure I knew when I was pregnant; my monthly didn't come.

But nobody told me about babies. My husband said, "You have baby when you see it coming, just coming." My sister didn't have a husband like mine. Nobody told her. When she had first baby, she had a midwife too, and she told the midwife, "When do you cut my stomach?" She thought you have to cut the stomach for the baby [to] come out.[1]

I had a lot of blood and they called the midwife. My mother-in-law took care of me. She took [care of] all the rest of the babies real nice at home. For one month after the completion of the baby I was in bed. Josephine was very little. I went to look at her and I was shaky. The midwife said, "Mother, are you tired?" After a month the baby looked just like a baby doll—little hands, little head. Now she grew to be a nice big woman.

After two years I had my son, Joe; after two and a half years, I had my daughter, Lucy; another two years I had my son, Sam. And my husband's mother and my husband's brother and my husband's nephew lived with me.

When I had my babies, I took care of them just like an old lady. I take care very good, you'd be surprised! My mother-in-law told everybody, "In one year, she learned everything. She learned to wash; she learned to iron; she takes care of the baby." Oh, I was crazy about my baby, especially the first one.

I played with my babies. And the rule was, no going out very much when they were little girls and little boys. When big, that's all right, but never going out theirself. They didn't play with other children. No. Lots of play at home. I took care of [a neighbor's] little girl for her mother, and that girl played with my children. I used to buy a baby doll and play at home.

Responsibilities included doing the laundry for her husband's barbershop. Although work at home was considered an extension of homemaking in the Italian tradition, Profeta's words reveal that she did not really accept this chore as part of her housekeeping responsibility. Unusual in this family was the fact that the husband did the cooking.

I cleaned and washed and ironed. My husband cooked the dinner. He was a good cook. But he didn't clean up! My mother-in-law was old. I couldn't expect her to clean and do dishes.

I had lots of jobs. Job of the wash, job making beds, job to wash the towels in the barbershop, and iron. And to make clothes for my kids. I washed two hundred barbershop towels every week and had to iron them with my hands, with an iron, not with a mangle. My husband had a barbershop [in front of the house], and he used one towel for every customer. I had my mother-in-law with me till Josephine was fifteen years old, and I washed clothes for my brother-in-law, Frank, and for my nephew, Joe. Of course, they had no mother, no father, so they lived with us.

Every night my husband liked to go to a show. How could I go every night and leave my children? I left them sometimes to my mother-in-law.

When children are small, once in a while is all right, but not every night. Every night my husband went to a show, and left me by myself. One time a week I went with him. I would feel a little bad when I would leave my children. Sunday, we finished eating and I didn't clean the table or wash the dishes. He cooked and there was lot to clean up. We went out to the show. Then he'd buy a comic book or something else for the children. Sometimes he'd bring me to a restaurant. Every Sunday we would go to Avalon Park. Me, my husband, my children. They'd play, run around, buy something, go on slides.

I go with my husband all the time to baptisms, dances, weddings, shows. All people are Italian and we all talk Italian. Lots of Italian people were coming with family, friends, or relations. They all would come to one place, to one street. We lived with all Italians.

My kids went to Catholic school. I never went once. I never would go in the school with my kids—never went once. I didn't talk English. I didn't go to church. Then when my Lucy was about fifteen years old, she started to go to church and I would go to church with her every Sunday. I go to church now one time a year, just Easter Sunday, and make communion at church. All my children went to church school, but not to church. I went to church when somebody was baptized, and when somebody married, and when my boy was engaged.

My husband was the boss of the family. He had the money. He would buy me everything, and of course, he was home all the time. He had to do all the buying. See, he talked a little bit English. I wasn't talking at all. The neighbors were mostly Italian. All Italian people talking Italian. Now I feel so bad that I don't speak good English. I spoke Italian to the children. They all talk good Italian. My mother-in-law talked Italian, and the children talked Italian. We talked Italian in the house. I had no best friend; I had no friends at all, just me and the family.

My husband is a very nice man. He would buy me lot of things—lavalieres, bracelet, ring, everything. But he had a little bit fast temper. I kept quiet, not because I was scared, because I was used to this in my country. Nobody was afraid, because he was never bad with the children. He was a very good father. I talked to him about the children and he always fixed it up. He would not make a fight. Yes, my husband was very nice with the children. He didn't play very much, because people from the old country have to act stuck-up, not play.

Italian tradition was reflected in the very different standards of behavior that the Profetas had for their girls and for their boys. Profeta's attitude toward her daughter's education was the polar opposite of that toward her son's education. It was no exaggeration to say "The girls were at a real disadvantage."[2]

I had my first girl, Josephine, my son Joe, my daughter Lucy, and my son Sam all in school. Josephine finished grade school and went to high school two years. All the time they asked her to go swimming and put [on] a swimsuit. I did not like her to put on a swimsuit; her father would not allow her to put on a swimsuit and go in the water. She was ashamed to tell this to her girlfriends. She couldn't go swim; she would not go to school. So she quit.

I was glad she didn't go. I was glad she started work in Kaufmann's warehouse. My son Joe, he didn't want to finish high school. Joe was a smart boy and I wanted him to be a lawyer. He told me he didn't want to go to school anymore, and I took a big knife and said, "I put this in your chest if you don't go to school." Honest to God, I put it in the wall! And my husband went to talk to the principal, and he said, "Mr. Profeta, I can't help it. He won't go to school." But he liked to work. He learned to be a barber. I sent my daughter Lucy to business school and she got a job in City Hall. The youngest boy didn't want to go to high school. He went to trade school and he learned machine shop, and he did plumbing machine shop. He had lots of jobs.

I wanted my daughters to marry and be happy, that's all. Josephine was not allowed to go out with a boy. I had to go. My husband and I would go out with them, but with the second girl, Lucy [six years younger], no. She would go out with the boyfriend [unchaperoned]. Times change. And my son Joe would not go out [unchaperoned] with his girl; her father and mother would go with him. And my other son, he would go out with the girl, like Lucy. Times changed, that's all. When my daughter Josephine was going with her husband, my husband used to say to him, "When I'm not home and when my wife not home, you no stay here with my daughter." When he was in the house, I watched from the dining room and the hall. I watched what he did, and my mother-in-law said to me, "You bad. Leave go the kids what they want to do. He just going to kiss her." But I watched. Till they got married, I watched.

Profeta's memories of Christmas were associated with gifts for the children; her memories of the Great Depression were associated with food.

Christmas, I made a nice Christmas in the house. The children all would have presents, new dresses, new shoes for all four—thank God, everything. Before the holiday we had no tree. We had lots of things in the house; we would buy everything and hide it in the kitchen. All the girls would get a baby doll, and maybe a baby-doll dress, and furniture for the baby. My daughter Lucy had everything and the boy got a little pony, a rocking horse.

The depression was oh, bad. I remember starting to eat [ersatz] bread flour. It was called flour, but I couldn't eat it. Lots of people used dark flour during the depression. My husband didn't make much money. Before he was making good money. Then after the depression, things got better. And my son came to work for my husband.

Incidents from more recent times suggest that Michelena Profeta was more receptive to modernization than was her husband, who died in 1966. Money she had saved from the sale of the family house in Italy paid for the first family car.

I went to Atlantic City with Josephine. Josephine wanted to go in the water, and my son-in-law said, "If your mother is going in the water, you can go in the water, but if your mother's not going, you're not going." I didn't bring a bathing suit; I never went swimming in my life. To make my daughter happy, I rented the suit, and that's the way I went in the water, and that was first time.

When we sold the big house, I went to New York. I went to see my sister in New York. I love my sister; I wanted to see her. We never fight. My daughter Josephine, with her four-year-old, and my son Joe and his baby, about one year old, and I go see my sister, my uncle, my father, and my cousin, and I stayed about two weeks. I went another time to New York when my uncle died. I went on the train, and my sister came to the station to meet me. And another time I went to Geneva Lake.

I bought our first car when my son Joe was eighteen or nineteen years old [1927]. The first money I had in America was in a bank. My sister-in-law had a car, and my son said, "Everybody buys a car; why don't you buy a car?" So I got the money at the bank and I went out to buy a car for my children. Then my son said he wanted to go out by himself, but the girls didn't want to stay home. So Joe would take one night for his friends; my daughter Lucy would take another night. Lucy ran the car, and she was only sixteen years old. What do you think? Sixteen years and she got the license, and every night was going out driving with the machine!

My husband did not drive. I tried to run the car, but I made a wreck going jump into the wall. I tried once, but my husband, no—he would not try at all.

Now my granddaughters and my grandson like to go to college. I like everybody to go. I like the life better now. I like the way Joanna does with her children. My other granddaughter works too hard. I think she should stay home when she wants. I tell her to look at other job.

Michelena Gaetano Profeta died in August 1982 at age ninety-two.

Josephine Fastuca,
1906–1987
May 12, 1975, Interview

I was born in 1906 on Reedsdale Street on the North Side in Pittsburgh, Pennsylvania. My father was a barber and my mother was a housewife. I went to Conroy School, which was a public school.

I remember when we had parent-teachers meetings, my mother would never come, because she could not speak the language, and that was very disappointing for me. So when my children were growing up, I made sure that I was there. My children went to the same school that I did.

We had a big family in our house. We had a nephew of my father's, his brother's son, because the parents were dead. And my grandmother was living with us, and she had grandsons with her. And then we had my father's single brother, and that was the complete family.

We ate dinner together, and my mother naturally did the washing and ironing for all of them, and my grandmother would do most of the mending. She would set us on her knee and she would tell us stories, which we enjoyed very much, about the saints and different folklore from her village. She was from Italy.

One responsibility that I didn't like was ironing the barbershop towels. That was my job [laughter]. I tried to get out of it [laughter] as many times as I could, but I didn't succeed. That was one job that I had to do. I never did any cooking, because in our house, you see, my dad did the cooking. He loved to do the cooking. He even made homemade noodles and all different kinds of food. In fact, I think he was a gourmet cook, really. Since he had the barbershop, he had time on his hands sometimes, and he prepared most of the meals. Of course, my mother had a hard time cleaning afterwards, because men [laughter] aren't very neat when they cook!

Frequently daughters provided information that their mothers had not mentioned. It was not always possible to tell whether the information was omitted purposely or simply not remembered. Michelena Profeta told us that she learned to sew and wanted to be a seamstress. Her daughter Josephine remembered that her mother did sew professionally at home. Josephine Fastuca also recalled family gatherings, particularly music and food and holiday celebrations.

My mother never worked outside. She did sewing, though. She sewed if there were any women that wanted dresses made, or something like that. She would do that, besides sewing our clothes.

Sometimes my dad would play cards with his friends, and the men would put a small amount of money in the kitty. When they were through, they would go out and buy ice cream for the women and pitchers of beer for the men. And they would spend that money in the kitty.

On the holidays we would get together with the relatives. My father's sisters and brothers would come. Most of the time we had them at our home and we would eat our meals together. On Sundays we would go to church in the morning and then the family would gather together to have dinner and to play guitars and mandolins, and dance, mostly waltzes and polkas.

Do you want to know anything about the foods? We would have breaded veal, and we would have meat rolls in sauce and, naturally, spaghetti in tomato sauce. And sometimes we would have a roast and we would have different greens.

We had a grapevine in our backyard and we made wine at home. My father used to go to Penn Avenue [wholesale produce district in Pittsburgh] and buy the grapes by the crate. Then [the adults] would go down in the basement, where we had our own grape crusher. And they would squeeze the grapes. They would put a big container at the bottom and get as much out of it as they could. We all helped do that.

For Easter and for Christmas we would bake cannoli. I don't know if you know what they are or not. They are round shells, and we would fill them up with ricotta mixed with honey. Or else we would have the cake we call *cassatta*. That has the cake on the bottom, and then the ricotta in the middle with mixed fruits, and then another layer of cake on top, and then they would glaze it. Sometimes they poured rum through it. And we would have that for Christmas. And then they baked fig cakes with figs and nuts in them, and sometimes we would have fritters that we would deep-fry. This was sweet and we would put confectioners' sugar on top.

When I was small, we did not have a Christmas tree. That was American; I saw the tree first in school. When I started to understand it myself, then I got after my parents to get a Christmas tree. Yes, and to buy presents for my brothers and sister, and hide them. Over in Italy, they didn't put Christmas stockings up. They would put their shoes on the doorstep, and then the fairy or Santa Claus or whatever they believed in would leave them presents alongside.

We celebrated St. Lucy's Day, which the people from our town in Italy believed in. St. Lucy was a saint to take care of your sight. This was in Della Rosa, Italy, and we kept that up, here. On that day we wouldn't eat anything made with flour. We wouldn't eat any noodles or anything made with flour. We would eat beans. We'd eat rice and meat and potatoes, but no bread that day.

I remember some other customs we had. If someone was sick or if there was trouble in the family, the woman of the house would pray and then promise that she would walk to church on her knees, from her home on her knees, if He would grant this grace. Then at other times, she would promise some of her jewelry, like earrings or a pin. When that prayer was granted, she would go and pin this jewelry onto the saint's robe.

My grandmother had a necklace with little trinkets on it to keep bad luck away. She would wear it around her neck. There were different saint things that were supposed to keep evil away from you. We used the doctor for all the children's illnesses, but I remember that they [the older people] used to lance people in the back and this was supposed to take the poison out. Then they had leeches, and they believed when the leeches died, they were dying from the poison they took out of the sick person. My grandmother believed in that. She had her own cures. In fact, when my husband had tonsillitis, the doctor told me to put ice bags on his neck. My mother-in-law got so upset—"What are you trying to do with him? Kill him? You're supposed to put hot stuff on, not cold stuff!" I said, "That's what the doctor ordered!"

Fastuca did not argue with or disobey her father. Too ashamed to admit at school that she wasn't allowed to swim, she saw no way to cope with the situation except to leave school. She acknowledged that she had accepted and internalized the family values.

I quit high school when I was about sixteen. When I was going to high school I was doing really well, and we had swimming lessons, and my father was the type that wouldn't allow me to go swimming. He wouldn't allow it. So, as a result, I quit school. I said, "If I can't do that, I will quit school." Because I was embarrassed. He didn't think it was right for girls to swim, because you had to undress and all that.

We didn't feel the restrictions so much, because the whole street where we lived—six, seven, eight blocks—we were all Italians and we all more or less did the same thing, and if there were restrictions, we sort of grew up with them.

We wouldn't even walk home with a boy from school—we would get into trouble. Instead, we would just go for a walk with another girl; then we had to be home at night. We never went out at night. We didn't go on dates.

After I quit school I worked at Kaufmann's [department store] at the book department, typing. Now here is an incident that happened when I went for my first job. I left looking for a job, and I had an understanding with my mother that I would call her whatever the results were. So I got a job just for a few days, stuffing envelopes. So about noon I said, "I think I will call my mother and tell her about this." Then one girl said, "Oh, what do you want to call your mother for? She knows by this time probably that you're working." So I forgot about it. I came home, and I got off the streetcar. I found my father, my cousin, my uncle, and everyone else [laughter] at the car stop, and I said, "What is this?" "Oh," they told me, "your mother has been calling the hospital; she has been calling the police stations; she has been calling everyone to find out what has happened to you." [Laughter] I had to call my mother every time I was five minutes late, because she would get hysterical.

When I was working, I was going to night school at night. I was taking up bookkeeping and typing and shorthand. I'd get together with the girls for lunch. One time I told my parents I'd go to a movie after work, so they said, "All right." My girlfriend brought two fellows with her, one for herself and one for me. I said, "No, I don't think I'll go; I think I'll go home." My parents asked, "What happened?" and I told them, "The other girl brought a boy over and I thought maybe you wouldn't want me to go." That was it. That was the way I felt about it. I really followed what they suggested, because it wasn't that they really restricted [me from doing what I wanted]. What they restricted was what I believed in. That was the way it should be and that was the way it was.

When Josephine was seventeen, Joseph Fastuca, twenty-nine, asked for her hand in marriage. This was done indirectly, according to Italian tradition; Joseph Fastuca's brother spoke for him. With no more information about sex and childbirth than her own mother had possessed nineteen years earlier, Josephine Profeta married Joseph Fastuca.

My husband knew my family. Sometimes we would go to the movies, and I would see him and would say hello. And in fact when he had a shop near our house, I used to play jacks on his doorstep. He saw me and he liked me. He told me about this later, after we got together.

When I got married, the way it came about was that my husband's brother went to my father's brother to tell him about his brother's intentions. And then my father's brother came to my father and told him that my husband would like to ask for my hand in marriage because he had seen me.

Then [Joseph] came to visit with his brother, and after they left, my parents said, "Well, what do you think?" And I said, "Well, I don't know. He looks all right. I don't know. I don't know."

Then he started to come down and we'd go out. Of course, we were accompanied by my parents. Not only did they have to take me; we had to take them along. If we went to the movies, we would take them to the movies. If we went to visit friends, they'd come along. If we went for a walk, they would walk ten paces behind, but I mean they were there! And that was the way it should be, because we all did the same thing on that street. It wasn't as if I was tempted by seeing another person do something else.

I knew him about six months when we were married. I was going to be eighteen in May [1924], and I married him in April, before my birthday. He was born in Italy, and he was twenty-nine years old.

My husband bought my wedding gown, and he bought my going-away suit. In fact, when we were engaged, he bought me a necklace and earrings. They used to buy gold for the girl, everything, like earrings, necklaces, and bracelets, and all for an engagement, and then they would buy the gown and the going-away suit.

I'll tell you about the honeymoon. My husband's relatives came here from Chicago, so we went back with them. That was our honeymoon. We went back with them to their house in Chicago. So we were there for a while, and my husband's family decided to surprise us, so they all came to Chicago. Coming back, there were about fifteen of us! Together! They don't ask permission or anything. They decided to surprise us [laughter]! How did they know we were going to like the surprise? It doesn't matter—that's the way they do it!

When I was married, I didn't know what was involved. Afterwards, I was a little upset about that too. Why didn't anybody tell me anything?

I was ready for menstruating. One of my girlfriends started menstruating before and she told me about that. Of course, when we got together we would talk about that, and a little bit about birth. One time we were sitting together talking, and the cat had kittens. Oh, you sort of got the idea, but you really—you never put it all together. I couldn't put it together. In fact, when I was pregnant I used to worry and think, "How is it going to be born?"

I even asked my mother-in-law. "Well," she said, "It's going to come from where it entered." She sort of made me understand it—that was the way it was going to be born.

I had my first child about a year and a half after I was married. I took that in stride. I had another one the next year, and I had my girl after five years and my youngest boy four years later. I had all my children at home; the doctor came to deliver them. My mother had a midwife. It was my grandmother, my father's mother, who would take care of the birth. Except for me, they had a doctor, because there were complications and they had to operate on me.

I never thought about birth control or anything like that. Not at the time, but after we got our fourth, yes, my husband took care of that. We didn't have any more after four. We felt that we couldn't give more children what we wanted to give them. And besides, we had those other children to take care of; my sister-in-law had four children, and we supported them.

The household included three nuclear families. Joseph Fastuca was undisputed head of the extended family. When Josephine Fastuca said "he," she referred to her husband.

We lived in an eighteen-room house. My husband's mother died five years after our marriage, and we divided the house. His brother took six rooms, and we took six rooms. My sister-in-law used to live up on the third floor when she was married, so after she was widowed we kept her up there and we supported her and her children. We all lived in that house. There were twelve children in the house.

Most of the week we stayed home, or we'd go to a movie once or twice a week. On Saturday he wanted all of us to be ready at noon, and then we would take off. We'd go for a ride, and sometimes I would ask him where we were going and he would answer, "You'll find out when we get there!" And, believe it or not, we'd land on the lake, or Ocean City, or someplace like that, and then the next day we'd start back, that's all. We'd take sandwiches with us for the car. In the summer, we'd go to live on the lake for a week or two weeks. Then we started to go to Ocean City. We have been going there, I would say, about forty years, and to this date we still go there. And we'd take one of our nieces or nephews with us every time we went, one or two of the other children.

Each family had their meals separately in their own apartment. Christmas we would all be over on my side of the house, and then for New Year's we would have it at my brother-in-law's side of the house.

Everybody got along, but they had their squabbles. Then we would separate them and put them in different rooms, and would tell them, "When you feel that you can get along together, we'll let you out to play." That was it!

Housework and work for her husband's business were interwoven in Fastuca's life. She was sole secretary/bookkeeper/office manager for a substantial business. This work was fully within Italian tradition. She worked at home and was unpaid.

My husband had a forging shop, and it was at the rear of our house. He was an apprentice in Italy. The way I understand it, he went to school in the morning, and then from noon to two o'clock he would go to the forging shop, and then go back to school from two to four o'clock. This is the way he learned his trade. Then he came here and he had different jobs, and he couldn't get used to the fast pace, which was so much faster here than it was there. He changed different jobs and then finally he decided he would go into business for himself. He was only eighteen years old, and he's been in business since. With a loan of five hundred dollars he bought his equipment, and he made bits for coal mines in his own shop. [Bits were bolts that held up the roof of the coal mine where the miners were digging.] His business grew, and he used to supply all the coal mines. During the war he made parts for airplanes.

I used to take care of all his paperwork, his telephone answering, secretarial work and keeping his books, sending out bills and letters and things like that. I did all of that. To tell the truth, I couldn't enjoy it, because I was really busy with four children and I'd have to do most of my housework at night. Ironing I'd have to do at night, and washing I'd have to do at night. I had no one to help for a long time. Then after things started to pick up, I'd have someone come in twice a week to do housework. Yes, I did that for about thirty-five years.

World War II was a busy time for our business. We had more work than we could handle at that time. We were making pumping tools for the government. The government men would come over and give us the specifications and check things. In fact, they wanted to lend my husband money to make a bigger factory, and he didn't want it. He wanted to do it on his own. He felt, "I'll do it my way."

Fastuca recognized the clash of cultures between her traditional Italian husband and her American children. Although she often disagreed with her husband, she never defied his wishes. Daughter Joanna was most affected by her father's old-world standards, for her every movement was restricted. Her brothers, on the other hand, were free to do as they pleased; their misbehavior, even breaches of the law, were tolerated with a "boys will be boys" attitude. Josephine Fastuca indulged her sons, and she spoke more extensively about them than about her daughter.

It was important to my husband that [the children] marry the same. It bothered him—lots of things bothered him—if it was a man from a different town; if they weren't of the same class; if they had a little bit more money; if they had a little less. All these things bothered him because we had certain customs. In other words, [the boy's family and girl's family] had to match. Now if there was a little less on one side or a little more on the other side, there was friction.

There were many petty grievances. Of course, sometimes I'd have to interfere. He was a little more strict than I was, because he came from Italy when he was sixteen or seventeen years old, and he never left any of that behind him. He sort of held onto their traditions—their ways—you know. And me, I was a little different. I was born here and grew up here, and felt the difference that I didn't want my children to go through the same thing. So I would interfere sometimes.

One time, when Joanna wanted to start to date—oh, she was about twenty-one, and he was still making a fuss that she couldn't go out. I said, "Look, don't fuss about it. She has to get out with someone, because if she doesn't, how is she going to find someone to marry? They don't come to your doorstep today like they did before." Right! The first time she wanted to go to school in Chicago in the summer, to Northwestern University after college. She was going with two girlfriends in a car, and he wanted us to follow her with our car until she got to her destination. I had to fight that a little bit. I said, "No!" and said how ridiculous she would feel with her friends. And so he gave in.

The boys would tell me about their dates. They wouldn't tell him, but they would tell me. And they would buy the girls flowers, and I would put them in the refrigerator for them. And if they'd buy the girls presents, I'd wrap them for them, and things like that.

My children had a lot more freedom growing up than I did. One time when they were small a bunch of boys got together and they went to the car yard, where trains stop. They got cases of pop, and they went to some boy's house and they were going to have a good time, and the police got them and took them all to jail [laughter]. So they called us to come and get them, and that was about all.

One other thing. My brother-in-law once found everything stripped in a house that he owned. Bathtubs were taken out; toilets were taken out. We never found out until they were grown up that our kids did it. They helped a gang of boys strip that house. All the boys in the neighborhood would get together. You don't know what boys are doing when they are away from the house, and we thought for sure our boys weren't doing anything, but you never know [laughter]!

My nephews used to sell newspapers, and one of them used to come home and say that people wouldn't pay him. Well, we found out that he was taking the money and buying candy, and then going back to the people and saying, "You didn't pay me." Finally we realized he was lying—my husband punished him for that. Another time one of the boys got into trouble, and he said to the policeman, "You take me home, because if I go home myself my uncle will beat me." The policeman came home with him, and when my husband came out, he said, "Oh, it's you, Mr. Fastuca, forget it!"

Education was very important to my husband. Oh yes, he would say he'd die if his children didn't have an education. He would die very unhappy. I wanted it too, but I think with the one who didn't want to go to college, I would have given up sooner, if it was left to me. But my husband kept at it, and he went, and later he appreciated it. My husband wanted my oldest to be a mechanical engineer, because he always had in mind the business. He wanted the second one to be a metallurgist. He wanted the youngest to be a doctor. He called him "Doctor," made remarks such as "Here is my little doctor," and made a sign "Doctor" for the desk he used during vacations when he worked at the business.

The youngest son did not want to become a doctor but was afraid to tell his father. Josephine Fastuca intervened, and as a result, the son, with his father's approval, changed to law.

Fastuca concluded her oral history with some observations that show she changed with the years to accept and adapt to contemporary society.

Now my husband and I like to go to the opera and to the symphony and to movies. I read, and I crocheted four tablecloths, one for each of my children, and gave it to them.

Life is different for my children. Today parents have to bend a little to keep their children in line, because if they don't, they may lose them altogether. The young people have the attitude, "If you don't like it, I'll leave." And we don't want that to happen, so we sort of bend a little. You go as far as you can one way, but you don't put your foot down. When we went for Mother's Day dinner, my son said, "You know, I'm ashamed to see the kids walk in." They are not that bad. It's just that their hair is a little long. It bothers him, but he doesn't put his foot down. He sort of goes along with it, but he doesn't like it. That's the difference. We used to put our foot down, and that was it. Today it's a little different. I told him, "Don't worry about it. They will grow out of it." In fact, I used to be like that with my boys. My husband would put his foot down a little more, but me, more or less I would try to go along with them, because I felt they have to go through a certain period and if they don't go through that period, they can't grow up.

We made some mistakes. We never told our children our worries. We never told them about the taxes. We never worried them about anything, and I don't think this is too good, because they had a hard time adjusting because they never had responsibility. Everything hit them when they got out of school and got a job, and as soon as they got a job they thought about getting married, and they had to support a home, and it hit them too fast. I think you should tell children when hard times hit. Children can understand; you'd be surprised how they cooperate when you tell them.

I think that's where the difference is. Today they tell the children what's going on, and I think that's good. They sit around the table and discuss their concerns with them instead of trying to keep everything away from them.

So far we've been lucky. All of our grandchildren are very nice. They're still small, and I don't know what's going to happen, but they are nice children, and I'm happy about that.

Joseph Fastuca died in 1978 at age eighty-three. Josephine Fastuca died October 17, 1988, at age eighty-two.

Joanna Dorio,

b. 1931

November 21, 1975, and December 28, 1988, Interviews

I was born in Pittsburgh on August 4, 1931. We lived on the North Side in Pittsburgh, and we had an eighteen-room house. In that house there were three families—our family, my father's brother and his family, my father's sister and her family—and each of us had six rooms. Twelve children were raised very much like brothers and sisters rather than cousins, and we all shared everything in that house.

Each family had its own kitchen, and each family ate in its own home. But the great thing about that was if you didn't like what was served at your house, you could always run upstairs or go to the front of the house and have dinner with the other family and find maybe you liked what they were having better. The mothers shared laundry facilities, and, of course, the mothers helped each other raising the children. There were always baby-sitters available, because we could always count on one of our aunts to baby-sit if our parents had to go somewhere.

In our immediate family I had three brothers, two of them older than I, and I had one brother that was younger. There was a big difference in the way boys and girls were treated. There was definitely that idea that a girl is different than a boy, and I remember many times being upset about something and my mother would say, "Well, remember now, they're boys and you are a girl, and they can do things that you are not allowed to do." This used to make me so angry because I never could understand what difference it made, but these were the rules.

Sometimes mothers and daughters remember events differently. Josephine Fastuca recalled doing housework at night; her daughter Joanna remembered her working at the typewriter at night. Fastuca said her sister-in-law was a widow;

Dorio said she was divorced, and later explained that the couple did not divorce but separated for life.

Our business was behind our home while we were growing up and through my high school years. So my father was always there; my mother served as his secretary. My mother worked very hard. She would take care of the house during the day. She would have to stop her housework to do typing for him, and in the evening she would spend hours and hours at the typewriter plus taking care of us. We were never neglected. She did all the cooking and so on, so my mother worked very hard. My father would run back and forth from the factory to the office, which was in our home, so we saw him all the time. He had breakfast, lunch, and dinner with us.

My father was the "godfather" of the family. His brother never seemed to make it in business. His sister was divorced, and in those days Italian women did not go out to work, so her family was my dad's responsibility. He was a real disciplinarian. He was born in Italy, and he had many old-world ideas which my mother, who was born here, did not have. For example, I was not permitted to go to girl-boy parties, and I was not permitted to date alone until I was twenty years old.

A network of supporting relatives provided a warm and loving environment of extended family.

It was really great for the holidays. With twelve children in the house, it was an awful lot of fun. Christmas Eve we would have everyone living in the house over to dinner at our house. We would have a typical Italian dinner with lasagna, pizza, that sort of thing. Then after dinner we would go into our living room and open all the gifts, and after all of the cousins had opened gifts there, we would open the door connecting with my aunt's living room. We would go in there and open gifts under their tree. The families separated when I was in high school, and each bought a house for themselves. Then we would all meet at our house again for Christmas Eve dinner, and we would open gifts at our house; then we would drive over to my uncle's house and open gifts over there; then we would all drive over to my aunt's house and open gifts over there. Then, Christmas Day we would meet again for dinner together about one o'clock. If anyone had to go off to the in-laws, they would do it later in the evening.

We always got together for Easter dinner. When we were still in the big house, the baskets were interchanged, so that we would all be running through eighteen rooms looking for our Easter baskets and the Easter eggs. That was something I always looked forward to. Even though each woman had her own kitchen, for the holidays they would all get together in one kitchen and prepare the food. I remember the cookies and cake particularly. There were Italian cakes in the shape of baskets and dolls, and the dolls each had a hard-boiled egg for the stomach. The mothers would fold the arms of the pastry over the stomach, and each one of us would find one of these in our Easter basket.

We went to the Regina Cielo Church, which was an Italian Catholic church, so that we did have Italian priests. My father did not go to church with us. My father was strictly Italian in that sense—the Italian men in those days were disillusioned with the church. It was almost a conflict of power between the Italian priests and the Italian families in a church of that kind. My grandfather was that way too. The men didn't believe in the priest's authority. They would send us to church, but they did not want the priest to tell them how to raise us. I remember that just out of spite, my father did not have me baptized until I was twelve years old. Because the priests were pushing, and he was going to show them that he was the authority in our home and he would decide when I would be baptized.

Dorio articulated the dilemma of a generation of Americans who grew up feeling "between two worlds."

I was very proud of being an Italian, and I loved the Italian customs. However, many times when I would be shopping with my parents, I would be very embarrassed when they would speak Italian. I remember turning to my mother and saying, "Speak English. We are in the United States. I don't want you to speak Italian when we are outside the home." I would be very embarrassed about it. I guess that I always felt between two worlds, because many of my friends didn't come from a foreign family as directly as I did, so that they were in my eyes more American than I was. I wanted to be very American, but I didn't want to lose my Italian heritage either.

When I was in high school, I wasn't even allowed to go ice skating or roller skating, because boys were there and you just didn't go where boys were. I remember I had to go to the movies with my parents, and even in the movies it was always very funny, because my father always made sure that I sat between him and my mother. At sixteen, when you are still going to the movies with your parents, it can be a little bit embarrassing, but this is the way he wanted it and this is how we did it. I did most things with girls. He never objected to having my friends over, and he never objected to my going to my girlfriends' homes. However, anything that involved boys was strictly out.

I went to a public elementary school. Then in ninth grade I went to

Our Lady of Mercy Academy. There were restrictions in school too. They were just as bad as my father in those days, what with the uniform, and "Don't roll up your sleeves!" "Don't wear lipstick!" "Don't smoke!" They always had a student council member on every streetcar to give you demerits if they found you with lipstick while in uniform, because that would be a disgrace to the uniform.

I never was allowed to work, and I wanted to work in the worst way. I remember at the academy, they asked the girls to serve as volunteer ushers at the Syria Mosque [concert hall]. I wanted to do that because I loved the opera and I loved the symphony, and I thought this was a good way to see it for nothing. But I was not permitted to take that job, because no daughter of his was going to work! Even though this was volunteer work, it was work away from home among strangers.

I was not permitted to go to my prom, and that really crushed me. I wanted to go so badly that I developed a fever over it, and I was in bed for three days. I remember when I was so sick my dad came in and said to me, "If you get better," and I thought he was going to say, "you can go to the prom," but he said "If you get better, I'll take you out and buy you a whole outfit—purse, shoes, dress, the whole thing." And of course that is not what I wanted to hear. No, he didn't give in.

I was afraid to think of going against his wishes. I will tell you why I was afraid to. My cousins would sneak behind their parents' back and meet fellows on the side, and they were caught. I remember a friend of the family saw one girl with a boy and told the parents, and I always laughed, because any problem that arose with the children, it was like the "Big Five" would meet. I remember walking in and finding my father, my mother, my uncle, and my two aunts sitting in the living room and my cousin standing in the center of the living room. It was like the Inquisition: "What were you doing? Where were you? Where did you meet him? Why did you go behind our backs?" They were all so involved in this discipline, and I think that so frightened me that I did not dare go against their wishes.

Joanna Dorio was the first female in her family to go to college; Joseph Fastuca had decided that his daughter would go to college. He also decided where she would go to college and what she would study.

My father wanted all of us to have a college education. He was very impressed with the fact that a person had a college education, and I suppose that was because he did not have one, so that from when we were children, he would say, "When you go to college, when you go to college." So I grew up knowing I was going to go to college. However, when it came to deciding on a profession, yes, there was a difference. He was delighted when he heard I wanted to be a teacher, but when he heard that I was minoring in sociology, and that might involve being a social worker, he did not approve at all. No daughter of his was going into the slums and into homes where people don't live right!

I was the first girl and the only girl of all the cousins that went to college. I remember my aunt didn't really approve, and, you know, in those days if you went to college, you were drinking, you were smoking, carousing, and everything else. That was their interpretation of girls that went to college. But my mother and father overlooked all this because they wanted me to have that education.

At that point I wanted to go to a coeducational college, but my dad said, "If you want to go to college, you have to go to Mount Mercy College." I had no choice. It had to be an all-girls school and had to be close to home. I had to commute—I was not permitted to board—and I wanted it so badly that I accepted. I got a fine liberal arts education at Mount Mercy, but it was a disappointment to me. At the time I was thinking in terms of Maryland University or one of the Big Ten universities, but that was out.

My brothers were going to Carnegie Tech at that time, and they took me to one of their fraternity picnics, and at the picnic two of their fraternity brothers asked me to attend a fraternity dance with them. So I went over to my brothers and I said, "I have just been asked by so-and-so to go to the dinner dance," and my brothers said, "Do you want to go?" I said, "I would love to go"; I could hardly imagine going to a fraternity dance! They said, "Okay, then, you're going with Charlie. I said, "Well, how do you know I want to go with Charlie?" They decided: "You go with Charlie." I said, "I don't know why we're even discussing it. I won't be allowed to go anyway." My oldest brother said, "Let me handle it."

I remember that when we got home, my brother said, "You go to your room and I'll talk to Dad." I heard loud voices in the living room and my dad saying, "No, she will not go," and my brothers saying, "Well, we're going to be there." My brother was dating steadily at the time the girl he finally married. Finally my dad said I could go if my brother and his girlfriend drove me to the dance, and I would meet the boy at the dance, and my brother and his girlfriend would have to bring me back home. The boy was not permitted to pick me up or drive me back. And I said, "No. Under those circumstances I am not going to go." And my brothers said, "Now you are silly, you know. If he doesn't mind doing it this way, why should you? Let me explain to the fellow." For some reason, the fellow agreed to do it that way. Of course, I never saw him again. That was my first date.

Her father's domination affected not only Joanna's behavior and personality but also her mother and the relationship between Joanna and her mother.

You see, my mother was born in this country and had gone to high school here in this country, so that her outlook on life was much different than my father's. But my mother had to go along with my dad. She also came from a family where her father was the dominant figure, so she was used to this kind of life. Although she secretly objected to some of the things he wanted us to do, she would not outwardly defy him.

Many times I would say to my mother, "I'm going to do it anyway." And she would say, "Never do anything behind your father's back, and I'll always tell your father what you are going to do because, heaven forbid, if you should be in an accident . . ." In college I was permitted to go to the Newman Club [Catholic social club] dances with the girls, and I met someone there who invited me to the ROTC Military Ball at Duquesne University. I asked my mother and she asked my dad. I never went directly to my dad; I always went through my mother. She would talk to my dad and then come back with the answer. That time he said it would be all right, but there was a heavy snowstorm and the dance was postponed. When the snow was cleared a few days later, the boy asked me to go to a movie with him and I was allowed to go. When he came to the house, my mother opened the door and she came into my room laughing hysterically. She thought he was the funniest looking thing she had ever seen, and she so disillusioned me that I went to the movie with him, but when he called to tell me the dance was rescheduled, I made up a feeble excuse, and I never went to the Military Ball.

In 1953 and 1954, Dorio taught elementary grades in a Catholic school. She then taught in a public junior high school for two years. Her third job was at Peters Township High School, where she taught for thirteen years and headed the Modern Language Department. She used vacation time for advanced study and foreign travel. Although her father disapproved of her traveling alone, he never refused, because the purpose of the trip—education—was one he greatly admired and encouraged. Her father continued to dominate her personal life. She lived at home according to his rules, and she came close to marriage with a man much like her father.

I was still restricted at home. Again, anything I did, I did with girlfriends. I did date, but I felt he always disapproved when I dated and it made me terribly uncomfortable. He would always say to me, even though I was a teacher, "If you go out, drink ginger ale all night, and if you want a highball, you bring the boy in after your date and I'll serve you a highball." And he did. We were always allowed to have wine or a highball at home. He did not want me to drink when I was out on a date, and, you know, again, if I was told not to do something, I didn't do it. I would drink ginger ale, come home, and both my mother and father would be waiting up for me. I had to be in by twelve o'clock. I got an extension to one o'clock when I was twenty-five years old, so you can imagine [laughter]!

I was not allowed to travel with my girlfriends; that was strictly out. Any vacationing had to be with family. I heard about the Fulbright scholarship in Spain. It meant being an exchange teacher for a year in Spain, and I applied for it. I did receive the Fulbright. When I got the letter I was so happy, and my father turned to my mother and said, "I wish she would get married." I must have been twenty-five or twenty-six at the time. I went to Spain, and once I was over there I decided I didn't want to take the whole year, so I transferred to a three-month Fulbright program and then I came back. That was the beginning of my graduate work. I was so fascinated with what I had learned in Spain that I decided to go on to get a master's degree in Spanish.

My work was fine. I became head of the Modern Language Department after about four years at Peters Township. Then I did both teaching and administration. I taught six classes a day, plus one free period to be chairman of the department. Eventually RCA [Radio Corporation of America] set up a pilot language lab at the school. This meant I had to play hostess to faculty from other schools who would come to our school to see how the language lab worked. I went to Colgate University on another scholarship to study new methods of teaching language. I also went to Northwestern University to further my knowledge of teaching languages, and then I became RCA's authority on language labs. At their request, I wrote an article which they distributed throughout the country. Then suddenly RCA went out of the language lab business, and that ended that.

My mother and father were more concerned about my getting married than I was, but, you see, their idea of getting married was that someone was going to knock on the door and say, "I want to marry your daughter." My dad didn't understand that here in the United States, you date and eventually something happens. He felt that after the second date, if the fellow wasn't talking about marriage I shouldn't be going out with him anymore. As a result, I picked up that kind of a pattern. I would date someone two or three times and drop him and that was the end. I always said I would never marry before I was twenty-five. Of course, I married at thirty-five. I overshot it a little bit, but I'm not sorry.

I dropped my master's program because I was going to get engaged to an Italian boy who didn't want me to go on with my master's degree. Luckily, I realized that he was too domineering, so we broke our engagement. Some of my credits had expired and I had to start my master's program over again.

Joanna Fastuca married Robert Dorio in 1966, ten years after their first meeting. She recalled their courtship and marriage. To the very day of the wedding, her father played a central role.

Actually, I met my husband when I was twenty-five, and I dated him for three months. I remember him saying he never dated a girl for more than three months, and I thought, "No one was going to talk to me like that." So I was just not going to date him anymore, and when he called the next time, I refused him. We met through the University Catholic Club, a club for college graduates. We were on a picnic and he asked me to dance. During this ten-year interval, occasionally we would meet at one of the university club dances or parties. He would call and ask me to go out, and I would always refuse.

Eventually, ten years later, my husband and I got back together. We started to date again, and that was it. My husband is a mechanical engineer, and he is twelve years older than I am. He is Italian, but that was an accident! I always said that I wasn't going to marry an Italian, because I assumed that all Italian men were as strict as my father, jealous as my father, and possessive as my father, and I wasn't going to get involved with that. But when I met Bob, he was completely different. Actually, he doesn't have much of the Italian culture, because his parents wanted to move away from that. He really isn't as Italian as I am. He is a very easygoing, great guy and is completely different.

When Bob called, my dad said, "I hope you're not going to date him again." Then we started to date, and my dad really liked him and was afraid I was not going to accept his proposal, because Bob had proposed a couple of times and I had said no. When I was at a conference in Washington, D.C., Bob came to my parents and told them that he was interested in getting married but that I wasn't accepting his proposals, so he was planning to surprise me with a ring at Eastertime. My father didn't say anything to me, but he really liked Bob, and when Bob came, my father, who was always there when a boy came to pick me up for a date, took off. He knew that Bob was bringing me a ring, and he did not want to be around. There was still that little bit of jealousy that his daughter, even at the age of thirty-five, might get married!

I said, "I am thirty-five, and I think I should have a small wedding." They said, "No way." I was their only daughter, and this was going to be a big wedding, and it was a big wedding. I was married at St. Bernard's Church. We had over two hundred people at the wedding, and the reception was at the South Hills Country Club. My father said I was to get anything I wanted for this wedding.

The night of the rehearsal, he said, "Are you sure that you have everything you want for this wedding, because I want it to be a perfect day for you." I said, "No, there's one thing I don't have." He said, "What's that?" I said, "Well, I want you to receive Communion on my wedding day." He said, "Now you are really going too far, expecting me to go to Communion." And my mother turned to him and said, "You told her she could have anything she wanted for her wedding day." So he kind of shrugged his shoulders and said, "All right." He went into the confessional and was out in three minutes, and I couldn't understand it, and we said, "How did you do it?" "I just went in and I said, 'Ok, what do you want to know?' And the priest said, 'And how long has it been since your last confession?' And I said, 'Thirty years.' And the priest said, 'Bless you.'" That was the end of the confession [laughter]!

Joanna and Bob Dorio wanted to have children immediately. The first year they were married, Joanna taught school in the daytime and completed her work for her master's degree in the evenings. The pregnancy that the newlywed couple antici-pated did not happen, and they faced the possibility of a childless marriage. Doctors found no medical explanation for their infertility, and treatment for such unexplained problems was very limited in the 1960s.

I wanted children very badly. My two children are adopted children. When nothing was happening and nothing was happening, I was terribly upset. I was older; I didn't have time to wait. I had done everything I wanted to do before I was married, so it wasn't the same thing as a young kid getting married and still having things she wanted to do. I went to the doctor, and he could not see any reason, but he was not encouraging me, because I was thirty-five. They made it sound as if maybe it was better I didn't have children. They started to put the fear of God in me, saying, "Do you realize what can happen when you have children at the age of thirty-five?" I said, "Well, let's start adoption proceedings, because I can't take the chance of waiting at our age."

I was determined that I was going to have children, because I can't see a marriage without children. To me a house is empty without children. Even when I called the adoption agency, they said to me, "Well, you are thirty-five." I said to them, "God doesn't even make that decision. Change of life doesn't happen until after forty-five, so obviously God would want you to have children up to forty-five if you wanted them, so I don't know how an agency can make that decision." Well, on the basis of that argument and my pursuing it, the director of the agency said, "You know, you have some good arguments, and I think we will give you a child."

Dorio was a busy professional-turned-homemaker. In spite of strong ties to tradition and dedication to family and home, she acknowledged the desire and need to do something on her own. She channeled her talents and energies into the triple role of wife, mother, and community volunteer.

I enjoyed running a household, but I am not the type even now to stay home. I can't stay home. You know, I want to be home when the children are home; I make a point of that. However, I have become active in many volunteer activities. I am a volunteer at St. Clair Hospital. Last year I chaired the Medallion Ball, and I'm active in St. Lucy's Auxiliary. I did volunteer work at Western State Psychiatric Hospital for a while. I always say that because I taught for thirteen years and have been active so long, I just can't settle down. However, I enjoy taking care of the house. I love taking care of the children and my husband. I love cooking.

My life is different now because I was never a club woman before. I was busy with my profession, and everything I did was around my career. Now I join organizations that have a base of voluntary service. For example, St. Clair Hospital: I've been chairman of the candy stripers; I used to work in the volunteer office, and now I am one of the vice-presidents of the auxiliary. St. Lucy's sponsors the Greater Pittsburgh Guild for the Blind, and that is a worthy cause, so now I'm first vice-president of St. Lucy's. I don't really enjoy playing bridge and that sort of thing.

My mother lives five minutes away from me, and she is marvelous as a baby-sitter. And I feel that as long as a child is with the grandmother, she is with the family. So I don't feel bad about leaving the children with my mother. She is my baby-sitter and she loves it, so that I am free to do things. I do try to time my activities for when the children are in school. Lisa goes to school Monday, Wednesday, and Friday afternoon; Brian goes to school every afternoon.

Dorio spoke about her marriage, about religion, and about her attitude toward the women's movement. She contrasted her hopes and expectations for her daughter with those her parents had for her.

We do have a very nice marriage. Although we don't have the same interests, we share each other's interests. We go to the Pittsburgh Symphony and the Civic Light Opera and the musicals in Mount Lebanon which I'm interested in. I share in his interests, in that we go away weekends. Every other weekend we have to go somewhere. I love taking the children places, particularly in the summer. I always make it a point of taking them on the *Good Ship Lollipop*. I take them to the zoo; I take them to the museum. I don't like to pressure them intellectually, but I do like them to see things and be aware of things. The weekend trips are family trips and that is what we want.

My husband is a very religious person. He and I and the children go to church together. Bob has always made it very clear that we are a family and we go together, so that even when they were babies, I used to carry them to church with me. Now the children go to Bible nursery school while we attend Mass. We pick them up after Mass.

I know I think differently about Lisa than my parents did about me. When Brian [six] and Lisa [four] are playing and Brian says to her, "You have to be the nurse because you're the girl and I'm the doctor because I'm the boy," I find myself saying to him, "She can be a doctor if she wants to be a doctor." And I fully approve of it. If she wants to be a doctor, why not?

I don't want Lisa to miss out on marriage with the right person—having a husband you love and children you love and want to take care of—so that I don't want her to mix her priorities. I want her to have a fine education; I want her to have a profession. She should pursue it before she is married; in the interval while she is raising children, she should put that aside; she should pick it up again when the children are old enough, or, heaven forbid, if her husband should die, she has that profession to pursue.

Their Italian heritage was always a treasured part of the Dorios' family life. The extended family continued to gather for holidays, as well as for birthdays and other life-cycle events. Dorio's description of holiday traditions emphasized the significance of food as an integral part of maintaining ethnicity.

When we were first married, all this was so new to Bob, and he really loves it now. Birthdays were always a big thing in our house, and they were always celebrated, so we make it a big thing for my children. I invite both families, and we have a big buffet dinner and the birthday cake. We have about twenty people for dinner—my brothers and their wives and their children, and Bob's sisters and their families. I think it's important for children to feel that their relatives are interested in them. You know, I want to keep family ties. I think that's very important. Christmas Eve and Christmas Day we are at my mother's, and then in the evening of Christmas Day we go over to Bob's family, and I think it's great, and it's good for the children to know that you have to respect both families, and that you know that the holidays are for the family. New Year's Eve we spend with the family. Neither my husband nor I believe in going out

New Year's Eve without the children. We go over to my parents', and my brothers come with their families, and we hang up balloons and we break balloons at midnight, and so on. And at Easter we give the baskets and we exchange gifts, primarily for the children.

We eat Italian food, and my mother always makes the Italian sausage. She makes it herself, and we have shrimp that's traditional. On Christmas Day she always makes lamb, and with that she'll have her lasagna or the soup she makes, with eggplant Parmesan. Then for New Year's Eve, she always has pizza and again sausage. We always buy the Italian rum cake. These are traditional things we have always done. For Easter we always buy the Italian cannoli, or we make them. We made them ourselves this year. We maintain the customs that way, and we enjoy them and my parents enjoy them.

I only hope that I can do for my children as much as my parents have done for me. Sure, they made their mistakes and I'm going to make my mistakes, but I hope I can give my children the warmth and the love and understanding that my parents gave me. I always felt that I was truly wanted and that I was the center of their life. And I hope I can make my children feel the same way.

December 22, 1988, Interview

Joanna Dorio discussed events of the thirteen years since the first interviews; major developments involved work and a changing mother-daughter relationship that preceded her mother's death in October 1988. In 1983, Dorio broke with Italian tradition and accepted a full-time, paid position as volunteer director of St. Clair Memorial Hospital. The change in her relationship with her mother began in 1978, when Dorio's father died. Her mother became more dependent on her, and roles of mother/daughter gradually reversed as Dorio increasingly took responsibility for her mother's well-being. Criticism from her brothers added an ethnic component to this essentially generational issue. Dorio's daughter was seventeen at the time of the 1988 interview; a degree of culture conflict continued between the third and fourth generations.

When the director of volunteers at St. Clair Hospital announced her resignation, I told Bob, "I'd love to have that job." Bob said, "Why don't you take it?" The children [Brian, sixteen, and Lisa, fourteen] were all for it. They kept saying, "Great! Go to work. We're going to be perfectly fine."

I had the most objection from my brothers. My two oldest brothers thought it was terrible that I was going to work when I didn't, quote,

44

"need it": "Why would you do this?" "Why would you leave your children?" "You'll live to regret it." It affected me. My husband didn't feel that way. So I set out to prove that I could work and my children were going to be fine. I did feel guilty. It took me a good year and a half to get used to the idea.

My mother resented my going back to work because work was taking me away from her. My children didn't need me, but after my dad died, my mother was starting to lean on me more and more and more. My main goal was to make her independent. My brothers thought it was terrible—the things I was asking my mother to do. I was teaching her how to use the bus. They thought I was supposed to drive her. I was trying to get her to join organizations. "Well, why do that?" My brothers were fighting me on one hand, and I felt it was extremely important for her to make a life for herself. She wasn't going to lean on my brothers; she was going to lean on me. My mother never had women friends. Then, when I went back to work, her crutch wasn't there any longer.

She started to go to a senior citizen center. She tried taking the bus. Inside, I really felt guilty. In the Italian family, the children took care of parents. But I knew I had to do this. I talked to her three or four times a day. I saw her about twice a week. Every Saturday I was available to take her shopping or whatever she wanted to do.

She moved into a condominium about five minutes from our home. She had decided that she would not live with any of her children. After two and a half years, she moved into an "assisted living" residential facility. She was very happy there as long as she was well.

Still, I felt guilty going on vacations and leaving my mother behind. I needed that time with the family, but I felt guilty. Then she became ill, and it became more difficult. Bob said, "You're trying too hard to make her happy, and you're knocking yourself out." I wanted to see that smile on her face, and I wasn't seeing it. She wasn't the confidante anymore. I couldn't tell her my personal problems. She had reached the point where I don't think she would have understood.

Dorio indicated that the women's movement influenced her thinking and her decision to work.

I think that the women's movement made a difference in my life. When I was raising my children, so many of my daughter's friends' mothers were working. I was torn between the two. I was feeling guilty because I didn't want people to think I was lazy and living off my husband, and then, on the other hand, my brothers were saying, "You can't go to work. You have kids to raise." So I was pulled both ways. I kind of liked the feeling of having something for myself, and when the children got older I really needed something for myself. So I say the women's movement kind of won over in that respect.

Dorio had a difficult time freeing herself from traditional Italian ideas about parenting. She was reminded of this during Lisa's senior year in high school.

Lisa was a senior in high school this year and wanted to go to the after-prom party after the homecoming dance. I said, "All right." I was a total wreck. I did not get any sleep. She came home at six o'clock in the morning and all I kept thinking was, "What would my father think?" I allowed this child to stay out all night! He would be just horrified!

Vincent and Michelena Profeta with children Josephine and Joseph, ca. 1911.

Joseph and Josephine Fastuca with their children. *Left to right:* Joanna, Michael, Emilio, and Vincent, 1949.

Anna Casatelli before emigrating from Italy, 1921.

Wedding photo of Anna Casatelli and Harry C. Yorio with Yorio's brother, the best man, Pittsburgh, 1921.

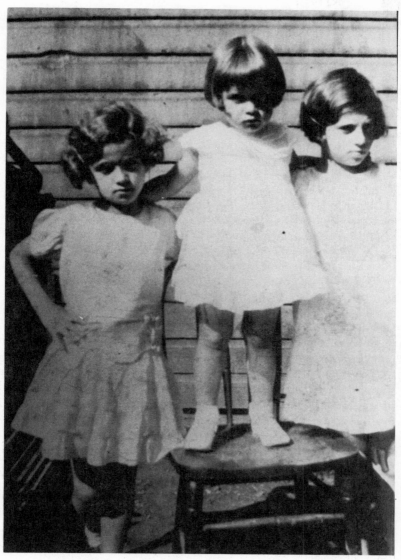

The Yorio sisters: Lydia, 7; Dorothy, 2; and Alice, 12, outside their house on Paulson Avenue in East Liberty, Pittsburgh, 1931.

THREE

Anna Casatelli Yorio Pizzuto, Lydia Pofi, and Judith Flack

The oral histories of Anna Casatelli Yorio Pizzuto, Lydia Pofi, and Judith Flack remind us that not all families of the same ethnic background are alike. The women of this small family endured both emotional and economic hardship. Marriage was the central relationship in the lives of all three generations. Sisters, settlement house, church, neighborhood, and ethnic associations provided important supports for the first and second generations.

Pizzuto was born in Italy in 1902, immigrated in 1920, and came to Pittsburgh in 1921. Her oral history tells of immigration as a single woman, work, marriage, widowhood, and a happy second marriage. In her last years, she moved back to her old neighborhood, East Liberty.

Pizzuto's second child, Lydia, was born in Pittsburgh in 1924. She spoke about her father, whose deafness was a fact her mother never mentioned. Lydia married Hugo Pofi during World War II, and the young family had a difficult time after the war; Pofi's is the only oral history to speak openly about mental illness. In recent years, the Pofis have enjoyed satisfying activities in organizations with Italian-American friends.

The Pofi's eldest daughter, Judy, was born in 1944. She married, had four children, divorced, and later married Ronald Flack. She gave up religion and, except for a few Italian foods, relinquished her childhood ethnic identity.

Anna Casatelli Yorio Pizzuto,
1902–1988

October 18, 1976, Interview

I was born in Italy on June 4, 1902. I lived in a small town near Naples with my mother, my father, and my sister and my two brothers. My father was an electrician; my mother was a housewife; and I helped in the house. I only went four years to school. One older brother was a tailor, and one was young and stayed home. One sister came to the United States, and one sister was at home. The one at home later became a nun in Rome.

For holidays the family got together to eat and drink and play and sing. The neighbors played instruments, and everybody sang together. Aunts, uncles, and cousins lived there; we saw them almost every day. Our town was small. We knew each other. Most of the people had small farms. Some sewed; some crocheted. My mother never sewed. She raised the family, and she crocheted some. I started to crochet when I was eleven or twelve. I had girlfriends. We played outside. We went to church every Sunday night when they had Novena. In a little town, everybody goes to church.

I had a boyfriend. I don't know what, but something went wrong. His mother was a little against me. She didn't want her son to marry me. They had a lot of money, and he was in college. She wanted her son to marry one with a lot of money. I said to him, "You stay with your mother. I'm going to America."

I had a cousin over here and a sister here. I decided to come to this country, and a friend of mine was going to Utica, New York. I had a cousin there, so I went to Utica. My mother and my father didn't want me to come here. My brother gave me the money to come. I stayed in Utica with my cousin for eleven months. While I was there, my mother died, and then about seven months later, my father died.

In the Italian tradition, Pizzuto's relatives secured jobs for her, first in Utica and then in Pittsburgh.

I was seventeen years old. I came in January 1921, and in June I was eighteen years old. I worked at the Mohawk factory, where they made sheets. I worked with the machine. My cousin was a boss, and he gave me the job right away. I never worked before in my life. It was hard for me. Get up at six o'clock in the morning and go to work. It was a hard job. My

God—fast! I never saw a sewing machine before. I used to get about thirty dollars a week, but I didn't like the factory. It was too dirty—all that cotton and stuff all over your hair.

I lived with my cousin and his wife—they were first cousins to each other. They had three children. I paid them fifteen dollars a month. That's all I had to pay them for room and board.

Then after eleven months, I came to Pittsburgh. My brother-in-law came to Utica for Christmas and he said, "Do you want to come and see your sister?" I said, "Sure." When I came here, they didn't want to send me back. So I stayed in East Liberty in Pittsburgh. I liked it better here. I got paid better in Utica, but here I had my sister. My brother-in-law got me a job in the Liberty Bakery, and I liked it better because it wasn't dirty, like the factory. I used to work for forty-five cents an hour at the bakery. It wasn't far from my sister's house. I used to get the streetcar sometimes, and sometimes walk.

I met my husband over at Liberty Baking. I used to work in the pie shop and the cake shop. We [women] just put them in a box. Men—only men—did all the baking. The man that I married was the boss up there. I went with him about three or four months. That's all. I got married right away. I was eighteen years old when I met him, nineteen when I married him. He was about eight years older than I was. He was born in Italy and came when he was fourteen.

I liked his curly hair. He was good-looking. He used to like me. My God, he was crazy about me. I was young then, you know—not like today.

When I got married, I lived in Homewood in a house on the second floor. My husband's brother and his wife and kids lived on the first floor. I had three rooms and a separate kitchen. I stayed home then. When I got married, my husband didn't want me to work. I didn't do anything. I just cleaned the house. Cooked. That's all. When he came home, we'd go out, maybe go to a show. We had no car—nobody had a car at that time. I liked the streetcar better than the bus. We got the streetcar to visit my sister. Sometimes we took a taxi.

I had my children right away. Eleven months after I was married, I had Alice. I was too young then. I didn't know very much, but I did know that when I stopped menstruating I was pregnant. I went to a doctor after a couple of months. All three babies were born at home. That first delivery was terrible. They didn't give me anything. It was just natural. Nothing. The doctor was there and some ladies, my friends. After she came out, everything was okay. I felt good after. When I saw the last one, I didn't want it, because she made three girls and I wanted a boy. My husband said, "You're crazy. She's so pretty." And Dorothy was so pretty. Even the doctor said, "You're not supposed to feel like that." I was crying. I didn't want her. There was nothing I could do about it. My husband and my brother-in-law kept saying, "It's okay," and, "She's so pretty."

I took care of all the children. We had a nurse for the first one for ten days. We had insurance, a medical policy with Metropolitan Life, and because we had the insurance a nurse came for ten days. She taught me how to take care of the baby. She used to make my bed, wash me up real nice, bathe the baby. Then my husband helped when he was home, but he used to work every day, seven days. He started work one or two o'clock in the morning and came home early afternoon.

Sundays my husband worked. Every Sunday, I went to church all the time, and my children too. After Mass we used to come home and have breakfast. I made pancakes and coffee. I didn't bake too much, a little bit. My husband used to bake. He would bring home cakes, pies, any kind.

Kingsley House Settlement sponsored the Lillian Taylor Home in the country for mothers and their children, as well as recreation and social services in the neighborhood. The settlement played an important role in the lives of Pizzuto and her children.

One time I went to Lillian Home with the three girls. We paid six or seven dollars each for ten days. It was nice. They had a swimming pool. They had shows at night. They used to hide things in the woods and find them in the night, in the dark. I enjoyed it very much. I didn't have to take care of the children. They had teachers who did that. They slept separately too. Only the baby slept with me. She was about three years old, and she slept in a crib beside my bed. But the older two slept in beds with a whole lot of kids.

When we came home we found a sheet cake this big [Pizzuto demonstrated with her hands], with a bouquet of flowers and a note from my husband, "Welcome home, gang."

I liked him and he liked me. We never had one fight. Nothing. He was real good with the children, with me, and with everything.

I started to go over to Kingsley House when I had all three of my kids. I used to go to Wednesday Mothers' Club. We had a party and a dance in the night. My husband used to make me go out. I used to go to the Mothers' Club dances and he used to watch the kids. He never went to Kingsley House. At Mothers' Club, all the women danced with other women. No men were there.

I had three small children. I couldn't go out with three small kids and go to a party and things like that. Not like today—we didn't get baby-sitters. Kingsley House was nice. They had parties, sometimes a banquet. And things for the kids to do—not at the same time.

When the kids were small, I had everybody at my house. I'd have forty or fifty people for Christmas at our house. They'd cook everything under the sun. We made lasagna and ravioli and the traditional Christmas Eve fish—everything. Everybody came in to eat and drink. Santa Claus came for the kids, all dressed up.

When we were at home, my husband wanted me to talk Italian to the kids. He used to say, "When they go to school, they'll learn this language." When my first daughter went to the hospital to take her tonsils out, she didn't know how to talk one word in American. Nothing at all. And she was five years old. She learned English when she went to school. My second daughter knew how to talk. My husband used to speak English then. He knew how to read and write. He never went to school in this country; he taught himself.

Yorio's sudden death permanently changed the lives of Pizzuto and her children.

And then he died. That was in 1938, depression time. He was only forty-two years old, and I was thirty-six. I had to go to work to take care of my three children. It was hard. I got along, though. It would have been different for the kids if he lived. Because he wanted my kids to go to school. He wanted them in the house, their homework done, in bed at nine o'clock. Oh, he was strict for school.

He died very fast. We ate. I washed the dishes. He said, "I'm going to sit on the back porch." We had a back porch inside the house. I said, "I'm going to sit on the front porch." It started to rain, and I said to my daughter, "Go upstairs and close the windows. My windows are open." She came running downstairs crying, "Oh, Ma, Daddy's lying on the bed. He looks so funny. He looks like he was laughing." "Oh," I said, "Get out of here. You're always playing with your father." They were always jumping around and everything. He used to go on the floor, put the kids on his back. Go around the house. Play with the kids. When he would get off the streetcar, all three used to run. One over here, one over there, another over here. Then I thought, "I'll go upstairs." I said to my friend Helen, "I want to get a sweater for Dorothy." She was little. I went upstairs and he was dead on the bed. He was already dead. I screamed. We called the doctor. "He's gone," the doctor said. Just in five minutes. Just like that.

I felt terrible for so many years. I had to go to work. Everybody was broke at that time. I had a little bit of insurance. I paid for the funeral and had a little bit left over. I got along all right. I raised my three kids. Alice was going to be sixteen in September when he died August fourth. Lydia was fourteen and Dorothy was about eight years old. I went to work about six months later. By that time I felt a little bit better, so I went to work. They gave me a job right away because my husband worked there all his life. When I went back to the bakery, I worked on the pie machine making pies. And doing packing. All the bakers were still men. Everything was the same.

According to her daughter, Pizzuto was refused relief after her husband's death because of the small insurance policy that paid for Yorio's funeral. The family was completely on its own. Pizzuto spoke of her second marriage.

I wanted them to finish school. Alice went to eleventh grade, and then she quit. The other one went to eighth grade, and at sixteen she was married already. It would have been different if my husband lived; he wanted the kids to finish school. The girls had boyfriends. Their friends came to the house all the time. I worked, and at home I cleaned the house and washed clothes. I saw my sister all the time. Sundays we'd sit down and talk. The girls quit school and went to work. Then they got married. I worked ten years and then I got tired of working. I went to live with Lydia.

The kids lived pretty close. Only Alice lived in Mount Washington; that was a little far. They all married nice men, but I didn't want Dorothy to marry so young.

Then a lady friend of mine brought my second husband to my house. His wife was dead. His children were all married. My girls were all married. I used to say, "When my kids are all married, then I'll find somebody that I like." I didn't want a man in the house with my kids. I went with my second husband for thirteen months. I didn't know what I wanted. I wanted to get married; I didn't want to get married. I couldn't make up my mind. I didn't know. I thought, "What's the use of getting married?"

He was real nice. He never called me by name. He always called me "Honey, Honey." All the time. When I was sick, he called, "Honey, how do you feel?" He was always afraid something would happen to me. If I was sick, he would cry. I said, "What are you crying for?" He answered, "Oh, if something happens to you, they better bury me too."

Both my husbands were nice. They were both Italian. My second husband worked in the mill. I was married to him for twenty years. He died the twenty-third of November 1974, almost two years ago. He built me a new home in North Versailles [about a half-hour's drive east of East Liberty]. I had a good life with him. I stayed in the house and cleaned my place and cooked for my husband. We used to go out all the time. We'd come to see my kids and to see his sons. He had three sons and a daughter. All married. All had homes. He took me to Cleveland and to Niagara Falls. I went to New York. We took little trips—not too far. We liked to go out to restaurants. I enjoy that still. We used to go to the drive-in movies all the time. And we used to garden. He planted tomatoes, figs, plums. We had cherries in the backyard. He used to like to have the house nice, with grass around, flowers in the summertime. It was beautiful. He took care of everything. Then, in the last year, he didn't feel so good. I had the boy next door cut my grass and trim my trees.

Pizzuto moved back to East Liberty. She talked about the meaning of neighborhood in her life.

When he died I had to sell the house, because my kids were living in East Liberty and I didn't know how to drive. They wanted me near them in case anything happened to me.

Now I stay home and watch television a lot. I have my hair done once a week. I go every Saturday to the beauty parlor on Moga Street. I don't go to clubs or places like that. I go to my daughter's house. I like to go for lunch when my daughters take me. I'm afraid to walk now. I do like to go out—I like to go and see my friends. We're all scattered now. Now one moved over here; one's over there. I used to have a lot of friends in East Liberty. Now everybody is far away. I don't drive a car; I have to depend on Lydia. My girlfriend Helen came here last week. She said, "My daughter moved so far in a new house." Helen lives with her daughter [in a suburb], and she says, "They don't have a bus, no streetlight, and I don't have friends over there. I have a beautiful home. What's a beautiful home do for me? I'm by myself. Over here I used to get the bus to come and see you, or see another friend. To pass a little time." When you're old, where are you going to go?

East Liberty was my home from when I came here in 1921. When I moved in my house in North Versailles, I didn't like it over there. They were all strange people. Then I made friends. I got used to the place. When you like your house, you get used to the place. I used to come to East Liberty once a week, though. It was my home, because I lived here so many years. A long time.

Now I cook for myself, and sometimes I invite people. My sister wants me to come to her every Sunday. They want me here; they want me over there. Christmas isn't the same, but we still make lasagna and ravioli, and the fish for Christmas Eve. The [daughters'] husbands buy it, and they make me fry all the fish.

I talk Italian to my sister, and we go to Our Lady Help of Christians Church. That's Italian. In North Versailles our church wasn't Italian. I don't know Italy any more; I'd like to see what it looks like now after so many years. I wanted to go this year, to tell the truth. But I couldn't go, because I was sick in the hospital for two months. I still feel close to Italians. And all three daughters married Italians. But all born in this country, and their parents too. Lydia's husband's mother and Dorothy's husband's mother were born over here. Lydia's husband knows how to talk Italian. Alice, my oldest one, used to talk Italian and she knew how to write it too. But now she's forgotten. My grandchildren did not marry Italian. None of the grandsons married Italian girls. Ronnie's wife is German; Frankie's wife isn't Italian.

At Kingsley House when we used to go, everybody in our club was Italian. It was a nice place. They had weddings and dances, but they closed it down. The neighborhood changed, and most of the people who went to Kingsley House moved away.

Now I'm busy seeing three doctors. I had an operation and still go to the doctor. I have high blood pressure and go to a doctor for that, and I go to a doctor for my eyes. When I'm by myself, I cry all the time. I feel good when I see my kids. That's all.

For my granddaughters, I want them to live nice and have a nice life, a nice husband and a nice family. That's all. A husband who comes home happy and is nice and doesn't yell. She should take care of her kids, and the husband is supposed to work. I was most happy when I was married. My [first] husband worked all the time, and we didn't have too much, but they were good years. And I had a happy life with my second husband. He was nice.

What I want now is to feel good. That's the best I want. If I'm going to die, I say, "God, take me right away." I don't want to lay, you know, and bother my family.

Anna Pizzuto died December 2, 1988, at age eighty-six.

Lydia Pofi,
b. 1924
October 26, 1976, and April 24, 1989, Interviews

We lived in East Liberty all our lives. I was born in 1924 and I grew up with my mother and dad and two sisters. We had a second-floor apartment. I remember two different places, both second-floor apartments.

I remember that I was very close to my father, closer to him than to my mother. Dad was totally deaf; he couldn't hear a word, and for some reason or another, he could read my lips better than anybody else's. Anytime he went shopping, he would take me with him. If he had any business of importance, I would go along with him, and if he couldn't understand the people, I could talk to him and he could read my lips perfectly. He always called me his "ears." I was with him all the time.

He was not always deaf. I can remember when he could still hear. We had to get real close to his left ear and talk into it, because he was losing his hearing very slowly. From what I understand, he was in the service and they removed his tonsils, and right after that he began having trouble with his ears. All of a sudden he was stone-deaf. But he worked every day. He was a baker. They kept a pad and pencil beside him all the time, and if they had anything to say, they would write it down.

He came here when he was fourteen. Our name was really Iorio. When he came to this country and became a citizen, he had his name changed to Yorio because he wanted it spelled the American way. He loved this country; he really did. He was proud to be American. He educated himself. He spoke English fluently. He never wrote a letter without the dictionary right next to him, to make sure he was using the right words and spelling them right. He always said he wanted us to have a high school and a college education, because he believed in that. He never lived to see it. I was twelve when he died.

Mother was a housewife. That's all. My dad played with us kids, and he was a real good companion. He wasn't like those strict Italian fathers that would eat and drink and then go to bed. He was really different. Some of them were like my husband's father. He was a real strict Italian. He drank a lot and ruled with an iron hand, and he was the type, if anything went wrong, he would hit before he would ask you if you did it. My dad wasn't like that. Not him. He would spend time with his family, and he was a very good father. He never raised his voice. He didn't drink. He was just a good man. He just wanted us to be good people. He said that a lot.

We did things together. We went to Highland Park for picnics. We didn't have a car, so we were limited. Our Sundays we always spent together. We'd go to Mass in the morning. Dad wouldn't go. He'd have breakfast ready for us when we got home, and the relations and Italian people would all come in after Mass and have a cup of coffee, and cake. We would have dinner in the afternoon. Dad had a brother. We'd go visit them, or they would come down and visit us. It was a day of visiting.

My mother's sister was here. She had seven children, and my dad's brother had four. He had a lot of friends, an awful lot of friends. We went to each other's houses. We would go shopping together in East Liberty.

East Liberty was beautiful. In the summertime, people were always out and on their porches—it seemed that on the street that we lived, it was one big family. They were almost all Italian people, and we all knew each other. It wasn't just going to one person's house all the time. We would go to each other's houses; we didn't have money to do anything else.

My parents had a wonderful relationship. I never heard them raise their voices to each other, I can honestly say. Decision making was between the two of them. If we did anything that wasn't right during the day, Dad had to know about it when he came home. That was the way it was supposed to be, and we would get punished. Our punishment was that week we weren't allowed to go to the movie, or we would have to go to bed an hour earlier, but we never got paddled. He did not believe in that.

Growing up, he wanted us to be in bed at nine o'clock. We went to a Catholic school, and most of the time we had to be there for eight o'clock Mass. The school was part of Help of Christians Church, an Italian church, right up the street.

We all had chores to do. Dad believed that we should help mother. During the school week we had to do the dishes. Mother wasn't allowed to touch the dishes at all. When she was done cooking, that was it. So my sisters and I would clean up the kitchen. On Saturdays it was like a ritual. One had to take the refrigerator apart, and one had to take the stove apart, and the floor had to be scrubbed. That kitchen had to be clean. That was one area of the house that we really had to take care of. We didn't have to do walls, but doing the stove and refrigerator was a ritual. We did that on Saturday mornings; then we had the rest of the day off.

Pofi recalled holidays and traditional Italian festivities.

I remember Christmas especially. None of the decorations went up before Christmas Eve. We'd go to bed at nine o'clock as usual, and when we got up in the morning, the tree was up and the house was decorated. I know Dad used to stay up all night and do it, because he loved it. We never saw the tree until Christmas morning. The stockings would be stuffed, and then would start the parade of relatives coming in. I don't remember much about New Year's. I think we were allowed to stay up until twelve o'clock to celebrate the New Year coming in. Thanksgiving was a big thing. We usually had family in, and Easter was the same way. It is a very religious holiday. Our holidays meant a lot to us.

The church kept up some of the Italian saints' days. They had parades up Larimer Avenue; they had a band there and concession stands. This would go on for Saturday and Sunday, for two days, and after the big parade, at night the band would play and we would all congregate. On feast days we were all dressed up in our Communion dresses and our white veils, and we thought that was a big deal. We were in the procession all through East Liberty with the statue of St. Robert, St. Anthony, or the Blessed Mother. These were the three big holidays that we celebrated. In the evening the band would be up at the "club yard," as we called it, and the concession stands sold different things. Those were big times for us! We belonged to the Society of the Blessed Mother at the church. We had church activities like meetings and spaghetti dinners.

I belonged to Kingsley House. It was beautiful then. The man who ran Kingsley House, Mr. P., was a wonderful man, a big man. He must have weighed three hundred pounds and must have been six foot five inches tall. He was enormous, and he ran that place with an iron hand. He would open the house every morning, and the younger children loved it. The gym was opened to us, and they had it sectioned off like little playhouses with toy furniture and dolls and dishes. We would spend two or three hours there playing, and then we had pottery classes and sewing classes. We had use of the swimming pool, and as we got older, we played volleyball and basketball down there in the gym.

In the summertime, they would block off the whole block and they would have a shower right out in the middle of the street, and we were under the showers for hours, because it was real hot. They had the Lillian Taylor Camp then, and Mother took us there one year. I didn't care for it, because I was away from my father and wanted to get home. I spent a lot of time at Kingsley House.

We would go there after school, and then as we got older, we had dances every Saturday night. I met my husband at one of the dances there. They had the crowning of the May queen and the May king, and did a dance around the maypole with flowers. Everyone that we went to school with was down there, because we were all from the neighborhood. They were all Italian.

Sundays we went to church, and in the summer we usually went to Highland Park to swim. Saturdays my mother, sister, and I used to walk through the farmers' market in East Liberty, and then to the five-and-ten to shop around. In the evenings we'd spend time with Mom. When we started to date, we went to the Flamingo, where they had skating and bands.

Pofi recalled discrimination against Italians when she was in high school in the 1930s and early 1940s. At that time minorities seldom fought back. Her parents taught their daughters to avoid trouble.

In high school, people who were not Italian discriminated against us. We were in a Catholic elementary school, and we were all Italian. In public high school, the Italian kids were looked down upon. They said we were "hunkies off the banana boat." We didn't fight over it. We weren't allowed to fight. We wouldn't dare fight. We were taught that you don't fight with anybody.

The death of Harry C. Yorio left the family without a breadwinner in the midst of the depression.

I was devastated when my dad died, believe me. I was the one that found him on the bed, dead. It was just like a big part cut out of my life. Everything was so hollow. It was horrible, just horrible. I remember the day of the funeral. That night his brother wanted us to go stay with him for a couple of weeks and my mother said if I ever left the house not to come back, so we stayed at home. I remember my two sisters and my mother and myself all sleeping in the same bed, and we wouldn't get out of it because we were so scared. Not scared because he was dead but scared because we were alone. For the longest time, we all slept in the same bed. We just didn't want to be separated. It took a long time until we learned to live with it and accept it. It was hard at three in the afternoon, the time that he used to come home. He died in August and we were on school vacation yet, and the loneliness in that house was just horrible. When we went back to school it made it a little easier on us because we had something to do, but it was hard on Mom because she was left at home.

Things were really rough. My sister quit school first, and she went to work for the Penn-Ross Supply Company. She was making up the routes for the linens and clothes deliveries. Not long after that, I quit school. I was in the eleventh grade. I went to work for Pittsburgh Hospital. I worked first for the dietitian—that was a disaster. I think I got only fourteen dollars every two weeks. I quit there and went to work at National Biscuit Company. That was even worse. I was making a little bit more money there, but it was awful work for me. First of all, I was very small. I only weighed seventy-eight pounds when I got married. When I went to National Biscuit, the girls were a lot older than I was and most of them were married and had really been around. They used to call me "the virgin." They used to make me so mad because they shoved all the dirty work on me. I hated it.

They used to make long pound cakes and ice them and put nuts on top. They would put me on the end belt to pack them in trays, and then I put these trays on a dolly. I couldn't raise the trays, because I was so tiny, and I couldn't get them up. Every time I tried to put one up on the top shelf, I'd surely drop one on my head and have icing all over me. The boss had been on me something terrible, and I kept telling her I couldn't reach those top shelves, and she would tell me it was my job to do it. I'll never forget one day I was doing it and two men from the union walked in. Just as they walked in, I was raising a tray over my head and it fell. I didn't know they were coming. He called [my boss] down for it something terrible. He said, "When they're that small, they are not to do that kind of work. They can really hurt themselves." After that she really got after me. She made my life so miserable that I had to quit.

I left there and went to work at Penn Overall Company. I worked in the stockroom. I liked it there; there was no trouble there at all. The pay wasn't too great. I think it was seventeen dollars a week take-home pay for five and a half days. That was all week and a half-day on Saturday.

We would turn our money in to our mother, and the doctor bills got paid. If we could afford it, we'd buy a pair of stockings or a new dress, and if we couldn't, we did without it. My sister and I were almost the same size, so if she had to go someplace, she would buy a new dress, and if I had to go for something, they would hem the dress for me and I'd wear it. That was the only way we could do it.

I worked from eight to five every day. We would all get home at the same time, and by the time we washed our nylons and did our hair, it was time to go to bed. On the weekends we dated, never during the week. It was just too hard. I did an awful lot at home. I used to do the washing and ironing too, even after I was working.

I started to date when I was sixteen. I knew my husband, but I had several other boyfriends. In our neighborhood there were more boys than girls. They'd come over to the house and ask if we'd like to go to a dance that night, and if Mother approved, we'd go. We'd have maybe the first, middle, and last dance with him, but the rest was with everybody else. Everybody danced with everybody else's girlfriend or date.

Our mother wanted us all to get married and have good husbands and have good lives. She just wanted us to be happy. Our dad used to say he was looking forward to the day when he would walk us down the aisle and they would get grandchildren. And that's what I wanted. I did want to get married and did want to have a family.

Pofi's teenage romance and subsequent marriage to Hugo Pofi were typical of their time. During World War II, Pofi left home and family for the first time. Her marriage, pregnancy, separation, and childbirth experiences were shaped by the war.

I was about fifteen when I first met my husband. A whole crowd of girls went on a steamer excursion on the river. I was standing near the rail when he came up to me and said, "I'm going to marry you." I said, "You'd better get out of here." I told my girlfriend I thought he was crazy and I didn't like him. I was about fifteen and he was seventeen. Then one night my sister arranged a date with him. . . . We went out that night and we had a really great time. I said no a few more times when he asked me, and then I started going out with him to the dances at the Kingsley House. When he graduated, he asked me to the prom, and I went with him, and that's when it really started to get serious.

He was Italian and Catholic. His father was born in Rome and his mother was born in this country. His father was a marble man and his mother was a schoolteacher. She taught us at Our Lady Help of Christians. Before he went in the service, he worked and he went to Robert Morris Business College. He was a good dancer and a very sociable man. He's very athletic.

Then the war broke out, and he enlisted in the air corps. He made second lieutenant, and he was a pilot. When he left in October of 1942, we had already talked about getting married. Then in June of 1943, he won three hundred fifty dollars in a crap game. He wired it to me and said, "Come on down and we'll get married."

My mother didn't want me to go, and his family didn't approve of it; they wanted us to stay here and get married here. But he knew he wasn't coming home, and the training was rough. So I went to Montgomery, Alabama, and we were married there on July 17, 1943.

My husband told me everything about sex. In school they showed us some things and told us some things, but not the way they do today. It was actually a scary experience getting married. But I have a good husband who is very tolerant, and he was well educated, believe me!

Pofi followed her husband from camp to camp. One time, for lack of a bed, she slept in a jail cell. She was often hungry and uncomfortable, and she was pregnant.

I came home in May of 1944, and he was sent overseas. I had Judy on the nineteenth of June. I got pregnant when I was married two months, and I was happy because I wanted a baby very much. I never dreamed that he would be overseas. He didn't see Judy until she was a year old. I had a beautiful pregnancy, regardless of how little I ate and all the moving. I didn't get very big. No one knew I was pregnant until my ninth month. I started to wear maternity clothes in my eighth month. Judy was very little. I had a hard and horrible delivery. They put me in a room and left me. I labored for eleven hours in hard labor. It was during the war and the night I delivered Judy, Dr. Barone—everybody went to him—had delivered twenty-seven babies in twenty-four hours. At least I wasn't alone. My mother, mother-in-law, his aunt, and my sisters were all there. All I said when it was all over was, "Thank God."

Then I was awfully sick. The stitches were infected, my breasts were infected, and I was in the hospital for two weeks. I swore I would never have another one.

I took an apartment in his mother's house. I wondered if he would come back. He flew thirty missions over Germany. He was a pilot, and he was hit seven times. I didn't go anywhere; I just took care of the baby and the house. My mother was working at the time, but she used to come over after work, and then I'd see her on the weekends. My sister Alice was married and living in Corpus Christi, Texas, with her husband, who was in the service. My younger sister was married and had a baby. We'd get together during the day, but we had no car, so we didn't go out at night. The baby went to bed at six-thirty.

The Pofis faced and overcame serious problems after Hugo Pofi's discharge from the air corps.

My husband came back after a year for a month's leave. It was a nice month; my sister-in-law watched the baby a lot. We went out with friends to eat and to the movies. Then he was gone again. After another leave, they put him in the hospital because his nerves were bad; after six months, they gave him a medical discharge and he came home. When he came home he was a total stranger to me. He had moods, and I imagine it was depression. He had nightmares and would wake up screaming. For the first year it was really hard. I went to talk to a doctor. He wouldn't go. He had been in a hospital and had psychiatric counseling, and they told him it just takes time to get over it, and eventually . . . but he doesn't talk about it. He will not talk about the war.

It was very hard for him, because he couldn't get a job. He tried to get a job with the commercial airlines, but he would have had to put in another thousand hours of flying time to qualify for commercial flying. We already had one child and another on the way, and he said he couldn't go back to school. I tried to talk him into it. I said, "We struggled before; we can struggle again." But he wouldn't do it. Then he went into construction. In the summer months he made good money, but the winter months were very slow.

In 1949 we bought this house. It wasn't beautiful like it is now. The plumbing was shot. The furnace only heated the first floor. The wiring was shot, and there was barely any plaster on these walls. We bought it out of desperation. We got enough money together to plaster the first floor, but we had to move in with all the rest of the house just as it was. We all slept in one bedroom and we rented the rooms on the second floor. We really struggled for the first six or seven years.

Judy was a year old when he came home. I had three girls. He enjoyed the second and third ones especially, because he never had that baby time with Judy. My youngest one was seven and my oldest was thirteen when my son, Michael, was born. Everyone was thrilled. It was like having a new toy in this house. They really did everything together. My husband taught him how to swim and took him fishing and joined Little League with him.

Pofi discussed her health problems, including mental illness and drug dependency.

I'm healthy now, but I've had major surgery, I don't know how many times. I had two nervous breakdowns. The first one was in 1966, right after my hysterectomy. I think I put my family through a living hell. I just went into a shell and wouldn't talk to anybody. After the second breakdown—two years later—I had a psychiatrist who believed in pills, and I got hooked on pills. One day my youngest daughter saw me ready to take a handful of them and said, "You're no better than a junkie." She ran into her room crying, and I got on the phone and called the psychiatric hospital and told them I needed help. The next morning my husband and I were there. A psychologist and a psychiatrist saw us. I was in therapy there for eight of the most horrible months of my life. I begged for pills and the doctor told me to talk. It was cold turkey. The psychologist worked with me in individual therapy. I really don't know what I talked about, but whatever it was, it worked. I've been fine, but I do have trouble remembering things that happened during that time that I was sick. There are things that I don't remember at all.

Since her recovery, Pofi has led a satisfying life. She expressed her hopes for her children, concern about her aging mother, and rather traditional ideas about women and work.

Now our children are grown. My two younger daughters live in New Mexico, and my son is thinking of going to school there. The youngest daughter works at the university in the biology department. She's a teacher, and she's working on her master's degree. My second daughter is a beautician, and she sews and makes quilts. Judy, my oldest, has a good marriage now, and she's raising her four children.

We joined the ISDA [Italian Sons and Daughters of America], and we joined a group called the Fifty-Plus Club. We're almost all Italians. A whole crowd of friends belongs. The women have been friends since we were in high school, and we belonged to a sewing club for almost twenty years. As the girls started to move out to the suburbs, we broke up the club, but we've always been in touch. We just have a ball, and the husbands enjoy it too. We made new friends too. We go on minitrips, and now we're planning a trip to the Caribbean. When we have a meeting, everybody brings something and it ends up to be a banquet.

At home I clean, and now we're remodeling our basement. My husband was in construction, and he knows how to do the work. We go to flea markets, and I have Sunday dinner here.

I worry about my mother's condition. I had my mother here three days last week and went to her house one day. I take her shopping and to her doctor appointments, and she has dinner here at least four times a week. We tried to talk her into coming here to live, but she said no. She wants her own place and her own things. She does get lonesome and sometimes she does complain about it, but the minute we mention selling the furniture and moving in with us, she says no.

I see my sister Dorothy at least once a week, and my sister Alice about twice a month because she lives farther out. She'll be here tomorrow because she is picking up Mother to go out to the lake.

I don't approve of mothers of young children working, because they are missing the best years of their lives. I worked once when Michael was still in grade school. I worked for six months at Penn-Ross Supply Company, where I worked before I was married. At the time, my husband was working for his brother, so he was home at lunchtime. Michael left for school about eight-fifteen, and I'd leave at eight-thirty; I was back by three o'clock, before he came home. But he was home for lunch and my husband was home for lunch. One day Michael looked at me and said, "Mother, I don't like this." I said, "What do you mean?" And he said, "I don't like you working." I said, "But, honey, you're not home alone. Daddy's here for lunch." And he said, "It's not the same. I want you there." I talked it over with my husband and quit the job. It wasn't that we had hardship and money was necessary; if we definitely depended on that money, I would have talked to him and explained it to him. But I was doing it just because I wanted to do it. I said to my husband, "It isn't worth it. I didn't do it with the girls, and I don't think I should do it to him." I quit the job and never went back. The only job I have is once a year working at the polls on election day.

I do believe in education and a career. I can see now that I should have stayed in school, because if anything happens to my husband, I have nothing to fall back on. An education means everything. As far as high positions, if women are not married, it's perfectly all right. If they're in a high position, and their husband's position is not as high as theirs, they are going to have trouble. A man doesn't like to be belittled by a wife making more money than him. I don't think any man does.

For my daughters I want good health and to be comfortable. I want my son to get a good education and a good job, and if he does decide to get married I hope that he won't have any hardships. That's where marriages end up in divorce courts. A husband and wife together make a good marriage.

I'm happy now. Ever since I got over that thing with the pills, I'm closer to my husband and my children. I just want to be comfortable and have good health.

In 1989 the Pofis continued their activities with friends in ISDA and the Fifty-Plus Club. Their four children were married, and the Pofis had nine grandchildren and two great-grandchildren.

Judith Flack,

b. 1944

December 20, 1976, and June 21, 1989, Interviews

I was born on June 19, 1944, in East Liberty in a neighborhood that was mostly Italian. I lived with my mom, grandma, and grandpa, and my dad was in the service. World War II was going on.

My grandparents [paternal] were super people. They spoiled me rotten. They spoke Italian with my mom and my dad. I wish I could have spoken the language; Grandfather tried to teach me, but I never learned. I only know the bad words. He used to listen to the Italian stations on the radio, the Italian hour on Sundays.

I was closest to my dad. He came home for good when I was two, and I remember especially how he played with me and took us to the park.

When my dad first started to work, he was in the memorial business and engraved tombstones. At home he liked to remodel the house. He used to put models together. He would knock out walls and put in new ones and new windows. He'd make a cupboard, lower ceilings, plaster, and all kinds of work. I remember him doing that when I was five and we moved on Moga Street.

Moga Street was one little street with about eleven houses on it. They were mostly all Italians—in fact, they were all Italians—and there were lots of children. We children played on the hillside. We used to build shacks and grottos to the Blessed Mother, and we'd light candles. Someone called the police to stop us once, and we had to get off the hill. We used to play baseball and football and ride our bikes. Everybody was pretty friendly on the street. I lived there until I was nineteen years old. My parents still live there.

We followed a lot of Italian customs when the grandparents were with us, but as we got older and the grandparents passed on, it sort of slacked off. We belonged to Our Lady Help of Christians, which was Italian, and we went to church every Sunday. When my grandparents were living, they used to go to church on holy days and go to all the festivities that were held at the church. The church used to have socials, like Valentine's Day dances, Easter parties for the children, and Christmas parties.

We always celebrated Christmas holidays. All my dad's side of the family used to get together at somebody's house, and all the kids used to get together, and Santa Claus would come and pass out presents. Everybody would exchange gifts, and drink and eat. We had the Christmas dinner with fish and all that traditional Italian food.

On one of the saint's days the Italian women used to make pizza and homemade bread, and they used to sell it at a place they called the "club yard." There was an Italian band, and everybody used to dance and sing.

I have two sisters and a brother, and I was the firstborn. I was my daddy's pride and joy. I was, and he did treat me a little extra special. My two sisters came along, but when my brother came along, I didn't like that. Because he was a boy, and I thought, "Oh, oh." I was in high school, in ninth or tenth grade, at the time.

I was embarrassed because my mother was pregnant. You don't think your mother and father do things when . . . but children do think that. I was so embarrassed I wouldn't even tell my friends, and I was praying that it was a little girl. When we found out it was a boy, Daddy was elated. He was painting the house and was just so excited. I was with Aunt Theresa, and they called and told us it was a little boy, and I was mad. I told Aunt Theresa that I didn't want to go home. I was jealous because there were three girls and he always wanted a boy. The third girl he thought so surely would be a boy that even though her name is Rose Ann, he called her Mike. Then my brother came along, and his name is Michael. I was very, very jealous and wouldn't go near him at first. Then I got used to him and loved him to death, of course. I think my tenth-grade jealousy over a little baby was mostly embarrassment.

My daddy made the decisions in our house. Mommy and Daddy talked it over, and Daddy made the final decision. If we wanted anything, we were told to ask. We were told if we ever wanted to smoke to come to him and ask him.

I think I was fifteen and I asked him if I could smoke (which I already did), and he said, "No, not until you're sixteen. Do you smoke now?" I said, "Yes." "Don't ever let me catch you," he said. "You have one more year." So when I was sixteen he gave his permission. He said he would rather have us smoke at home instead of at Bolan's [ice-cream parlor], where we used to go after school. . . . I remember we used our own judgment on dating and coming in. We weren't allowed to date until we were about sixteen, but he never set a time. He left everything up to us, and we respected him. I know I was always in by eleven or twelve o'clock. If it was a party and we were going to be late, all we had to do was call and tell them where we were. We never took advantage. . . . We wouldn't stay out until four or five o'clock in the morning.

When I was in high school, I went to school all day and then I would come home and do chores that I had to do, like straightening up the room and hanging clothes up and bringing dirty things downstairs. Friends used to come over to the house and we used to sit on the porch. There was a school yard up the street from us, and we used to go up there and sit and talk with the boys or play baseball. Weekends it was dates and parties. We loved to go roller skating on Saturday. We took lessons and just thought we were all the cat's meow with our short little dresses and covers on our skates! That was a really big thing. We really enjoyed that.

My dad was very important at that time in my life. I'd go to my dad with a problem and ask him what he would do if he were in my position, and he would say, "Well, if I were you, I'd do it this way. How would you do it?" I'd say, "I'd do it this way," and he'd say, "You do what you feel." I'd do it and it would always be wrong. Then I'd go back to him and say, "Why didn't I listen to you?" I'd always go to him, and he'd tell me which was the right way, and I thought I was all big and was going to do it my way, and it would blow up in my face.

My parents didn't have any special goal for me. My mother expected me to finish school and get a job. But she never said I was going to be a doctor or nurse. As for my dad, whatever we wanted to do, that was it. I wanted to work and make a lot of money. I did work, but I didn't make a lot of money!

Flack talked about menstruation, sex education, marriage, and medicine. Many oral histories recorded shock and fright at the first menstrual experience.

I learned about menstruation from my mother. She never said anything to me until I got it, and I was scared and mine was very heavy. That was what frightened me, because I thought I was going to die and bleed to death. I think I was thirteen years old when I got my period.

I learned about intercourse in the street, in school, and from friends. We had a course in school in hygiene, where I learned about reproduction and having babies.

I thought marriage was all a bed of roses. I really believed that. You know, get married and have children and live happily ever after. But I found out it's different.

My dad hated doctors. He changed because of the grandchildren, but he was an optimist, and he always thought everything was going to be all right. I'll give you an example. My little boy lost an eye in an accident. My dad said he was going to be all right and would be able to see, and that was the way he was. He gets very upset when he has to go into hospitals. But Mom sort of feels safe when she's in the hospital. She feels they know what they're doing and it's okay. But my dad has really changed since then.

Flack was one of the few single women of the third generation who contributed to family income.

After high school I worked at Chatham College. I did everything. I would sort mail and work in the post office. I would mimeograph and addressograph, photostat, and mail. I was also Bell trained and worked on the switchboard. Every day I went to work, went home, and collapsed. I was constantly moving—that job was never boring. I liked working at Chatham because I was doing something different all the time. I didn't have to sit behind a typewriter or a switchboard for eight hours. I loved it. I really did.

I was happy, but I was very sensitive. I didn't care for my boss. She was the boss, and I guess it was her position to say, "Do this and that," but I was the type that didn't like to be told what to do, because I knew what I had to do.

I would contribute to the family pay. I had to pay board. I had to take care of my own clothing and buy my own personal things. At home I had to do my own clothes. Mom would wash them, but I would have to iron them. I had to keep my room. Saturday was the day that everything got cleaned up, or else! I used to work and come home and get things ready for the next day. I very seldom went out during the week, but the weekends I'd date or go out with the girls and sneak into a bar. I did that, and then when I was twenty-one [legal age in Pennsylvania] I didn't want to go to bars anymore.

I didn't take life seriously. I should have. I just thought it was a big bowl of cherries. I could see my parents struggling a little bit. But everybody sees that, although I was the only one that did give money when I worked. I used to be offended when people said that nothing ever bothered me. I never express my feelings, but I'd be hurt inside. I can't explain it.

Flack described her first marriage, her divorce, and her children's health problems.

I knew my first husband when I was about fifteen. We used to go roller skating together. He was a typical Italian: the spaghetti twice a week and the pasta. His parents were like my grandmother and grandfather. They went to all the festivities and the churches. His grandparents and his mother and father were born in Italy and came here.

He's a year or two older than I am. He was nice looking. He was nice and kind and loving and giving, but that all changed. I was nineteen when I married him. We lived in Morningside [a section of East End] about ten blocks from my family. I stayed home and he worked. I used to visit girlfriends or go shopping or talk with his sister, who lived upstairs in the same house. I saw my family often.

He really changed when we got married. He started to run around when the first child was born, and it continued and continued, and I tried and tried. We talked it over and he would say he wouldn't do it anymore. . . . My duty was to try to keep it together, and I did. Then the same thing happened again, and stupid me just kept having children. And it went on and on until the last baby. When I was pregnant with her, I told him he had to leave, because I couldn't take any more of it. I said, "The children don't have a father." They used to go to my dad. It was a very bad experience. I block it out of my mind. I didn't tell my parents until he was gone. I got the divorce right after the baby was born.

The emotional stress was terrible. During the course of all this, my second boy lost an eye. He ran over the hill to get a football and tripped and fell. A stick went into the corner of his eye and severed his optic nerve. He was five years old. Then I almost lost the baby. My oldest boy is an asthmatic and almost lived in Children's Hospital. He was seeing a psychiatrist because of the feuding in the house. The second little girl had eczema very badly on her arms. The baby is asthmatic and allergic, but not as severely as the older three.

I was happy the first time I was pregnant. I was excited when the baby was born. He was cute. They're adorable and little. I loved taking care of him. My mother helped. My kids have been raised entirely differently than I was, but the way things were at our house, I had the attitude "Let the kids do anything they want." They didn't have to clean up their rooms or pick up their toys. They were very spoiled by their grandparents that lived right around the corner from them. Their father didn't pay the slightest bit of attention to them, and they would always go to my dad. In fact, they called him Dad instead of Grandpa sometimes. They were sick kids. My oldest one was always in the hospital, and he went regularly for therapy until I remarried. They told me that he grabbed onto another father image, and that was what he needed, and they released him. He had somebody that he could really call Dad.

A second marriage brought joy to Flack and security to her children.

I knew Ronnie when I was young, too. He lived a couple of blocks away. We were really little, and it was like puppy love. Ronnie's Irish. We were in high school when he asked me out. He was Peabody High School's big letter man in football. All the girls would say, "Oh, you got a date with Ron!" That was fantastic because he was a big football star. I dated him a couple of times, and he was very good-looking. He is altogether different from the other one. He is exactly the way he was before. There is nothing different. He's straight-arrow with you. When Ronnie went into the service, I dated my first husband and we got married.

While my husband and I were separated, one day I walked over to my mother's house, and there was Ronnie sitting in my mother's kitchen. I hadn't seen him in fifteen years. It was so long. We started talking. "I hear you have four beautiful kids," he said. Even though she knew there was trouble, my mother told him how happy I was. About two weeks later I got a phone call from Ron; he asked why my mother and I had lied to him. He said, "Judy, I have been following your life for the past twelve years. . . . I liked you from the first time we knew each other." You know, I got all tongue-tied on the phone and I said I would be straight with him. He said, "Judy, you don't have to tell me anything I don't already know." He knew everything. After that I didn't hear from him for a long time.

Then one Christmas time I was with a group of girls at the pub at the mall. The waitress brought over drinks and said, "Compliments of the gentleman over there." There he was. He came over and we started talking. He knew the situation with the children. We started seeing each other, and we got married.

It was like something out of a fairy-tale book. I really did like him . . . maybe because he was such a big star at school. I did like him and heard from him when he was in service. He's a super guy. He really is. What is love? I loved my first husband, but I also hated him. There is a thin line between love and hate.

With Ronnie, it's different. He accepted the four children. It was rough and he bit off more than he could chew—that I know. It's rough to raise somebody else's children.

He tried too hard at first. You could see the kids maybe taking advantage, and I said, "Ron, you're doing it the wrong way. You had better start cracking down." He would feel bad if he had to give one of them a crack on the rear end, or punish one of them. I said, "Don't feel bad, because that is what these children need, because I never gave it to them. I wasn't a consistent person. Their father used to whack them because they were in the way, but you're giving them what they need."

Ron is really super with the kids, and the kids go to him before they come to me. They get along great. Don't get me wrong. We do have moments with them and he gets sort of discouraged, but he never gives up. They call him Daddy. They never once ask about their real daddy.

Our life is hard now because of Ronnie's work. He's a road man. He drives a truck and goes out of state. He can get called out at four in the morning, like this morning. He goes to work and the children go to school. If I have the car I'll go shopping or something. I always hurry to come back here, knowing that he might be home, and if he's sleeping, I'm very quiet. I don't like to leave, because I don't want the phone to wake him up. It's tough to be married to a truck driver. Ronnie and I haven't had much of a marriage, because of the fact that he's a truck driver. I'm always in the house. The only time that I go out without feeling that I have to rush back is when I know he's going to be gone a couple of days. It's hectic, because when he comes back, he's beat from driving twelve hours, and he comes in and stays up with the kids, goes to bed, gets a couple of hours' sleep, and then back to work again. I'm a wreck because if he comes in at eleven in the morning and the kids come home at three, I have to be sure they are quiet. Sometimes he is gone for three or four days, and then I go out and do what I have to do. I always come home thinking that he will call. We really haven't been alone, except for a couple of days when we were first married.

My week gets very boring. I pick up my crocheting or needlepoint, and I get disgusted and throw it in the bag. When Ronnie's here I can lick the house and the world, but when he's away, I feel so bad and don't feel like doing anything. I make the beds, run the sweeper, dust, and make dinner for the children. I wonder if Ronnie's okay or getting his sleep. I worry terribly about him. When he's here, I'll go outside and wash the windows and do this or that, and he says, "Judy, what are you doing? I never see you when I'm home." I say, "When you're here I feel safe, but when you're gone, I feel like you took my two arms with you." It's really like that.

After Flack remarried, she faced new problems—infertility and (unexplained) conflict with her parents.

I feel very fortunate that I have somebody that married me with four children. Ronnie never had children, and after I had the last baby I had my tubes ligated, and that meant no more children. I wanted to have it reversed and I had surgery. I know two girls that had it done and got pregnant four months after their surgery. It's been six months since my surgery. But my husband is hardly home. What are you going to do? I take a fertility pill, and I have to be checked for cysts that the pill might cause.

There's a little conflict between Ronnie and my parents that's causing conflict here in this house. Ronnie told my parents that they are welcome to come into the house anytime, but he does not want the children in their house, because my children were so dependent on my mother and father because of my first marriage. My children used to play on their street and would go to my mother's to go to the bathroom and to have lunch. Ronnie knew this, and he thought they had done enough, and that the atmosphere down there might only remind the children of their life before. He wanted them to have a whole new life. Ronnie talked to my folks and told them they were welcome to come to the house whenever they liked, which they did. They were always here and everything, but something changed. When I was in the hospital my dad never came to see me, and my grandmother was one floor below. My mother came to my room a couple of times. Now she says she's uneasy coming here. Every time Ronnie and I talk about my folks we get into an argument. This has been very upsetting.

Flack and her family have given up Italian tradition and Catholicism.

Being Italian is much less a part of my life than when I was a child. Then, I was Italian and everything I did and all my friends were Italian; I went to an Italian church and school. Now, outside of making Italian dishes for Ronnie, I can't think of anything. Ronnie loves Italian food, and I enjoy cooking it.

None of our neighbors are Italian, and none of them are Catholic. Ronnie isn't Catholic. I don't belong to any Italian groups, and I don't go to a Catholic church, and the children go to public school. I went twelve years to Catholic school and I vowed that I would never send my children to a Catholic school. I didn't like praying in the classroom, and I didn't believe in confession.

My husband's uncle is a minister in Arizona, and when we were out there, I was baptized in the Holy Spirit. Now my children go to Bible school in the church near here. They sing and praise the Lord and read from the Bible. I go too and read my Bible and I love it.

Flack expressed her hopes for the future for herself and for her children.

I want my children to grow up and be happy. I want them to respect people. I want them to amount to something. I don't want them to be doctors and lawyers, but I want the girls to meet a nice man who will treat them decently and have a nice home. I want the boys to do whatever they want. That's what Ron and I want for them. It would satisfy me to know that all my children would be happy.

I want the boys to treat their wives like Ronnie treats me. I want them to have a happy marriage, if they do get married. I want them to respect people and to respect things, because before they didn't.

For me, I hope to enjoy my husband more once the children grow up and are gone. I've only had two beaus in my life, and they are the two I married. Outside of my dad and my family, no one has ever treated me the way this guy does. He's just—Ronnie.

Judith Flack's life changed a great deal since she recorded her oral history in 1976. The Flacks had moved to Tucson, Arizona, hoping for a better climate for the child with asthma. Although they liked Arizona, Ron Flack was unable to get steady work as a trucker, and after two years the family returned to the Pittsburgh area. They bought a house in a town twenty miles east of the city.

When I spoke to Judith Flack on June 21, 1989, she had been working for five years as assistant activities director at the Beverly Manor Nursing Home in Monroeville, Pennsylvania. She started to work on July 25, 1984.

She reported that her children [adults] had left home and that she had three grandchildren. She no longer attended any church, and ethnicity had not been part of her life for a long time. At the time of the interview, she was estranged from her parents.

Jewish Families

FOUR

Sylvia Sacks Glosser, Naomi Cohen, and Cathy Droz

The oral histories of Sylvia Sacks Glosser, Naomi Cohen, and Cathy Droz trace geographic mobility, family ties, and religion through three generations.

Sylvia Sacks Glosser was born in Burlington, Vermont, in 1896, the seventh child of Russian immigrant parents. She has left us an insightful account of family life and traditional gender roles in a rabbi's home in a small New England city. She married David Glosser in Johnstown, Pennsylvania, which is an iron- and steel-manufacturing town located seventy miles northeast of Pittsburgh. The Glossers raised five children in Johnstown.

Naomi Cohen, one of twin girls born to the Glossers, tells of growing up wealthy and Jewish in a gentile community. She married Jesse Cohen, and together they raised a family in Pittsburgh, where they participated actively in Jewish community life.

The Cohens' second daughter, Cathy, was born in 1947 and became politically and socially active at college in the 1960s. She married Dan Droz in 1981 and since that time has successfully combined a career in television with the responsibilities of marriage and raising children.

Sylvia Sacks Glosser,
1896–1980

June 16, 1976, Interview

I was born in Burlington, Vermont. My father was the first rabbi in Burlington, and he was rabbi of the synagogue there for more than thirty years. He and my mother came from Russia to this country in the 1890s. They came with seven children—five girls and two boys. Two children were born in this country—one son and myself. I was born in 1896; my brother was the youngest, and I was next to the youngest.

It was nice growing up in a big family. We didn't have any cars. I remember it was such a big occasion when we got a telephone. It was announced in the newspaper, "Rabbi Sacks was the first one that we gave a telephone to." Then we had electric lights, which was really a big event. We enjoyed everything in a natural way.

We had a big garden, and we grew plenty of vegetables from our garden to sustain the family. We all took care of the garden. We had chickens; we had a cow. We had a horse that we used to ride. We enjoyed our childhood and that was it. We didn't have luxuries, but we didn't know luxuries. The luxury was getting on a horse without a saddle and riding. Or my brother used to go and milk the cow and bring a bucket of milk in. We had a big icehouse. In February, when Lake Champlain would freeze over, we'd fill the icehouse with ice. Then we would have ice for all summer. The boys used to cut the ice into portions and put the tubs in the icehouse. We didn't have refrigerators. The boys' job was to take care of the icehouse and the cow and the horse.

We used to have a cellar that was partly sand. That's where we stored our vegetables for the winter. My father used to take carrots, onions, red beets, potatoes and dig them into the soil. Then we'd go and pick them, just like fresh grown. I remember that's the way we lived.

The girls used to do things around the house. I had a lovely flower garden. I was always interested in flowers and plants. I used to go out in the woods and pick arbutus or jack-in-the-pulpit and put it in the garden. I cherished that little garden of my own.

We didn't have a furnace. We had stoves that you used to put coal in—hard coal. We would keep them going in the very cold weather. It got very cold in Vermont—we used to have temperatures twenty below zero. The windows were so frosted that we couldn't look through them. We children used to take pennies and put them in the frost on the window to make the design of the Indian head. The object was to make the most perfect penny.

We didn't have a car; we had a horse-and-buggy. I remember the first family in Burlington to have a car. They owned a store on Church Street, which was the main street. They used to drive through town and everybody came to look at the car. It was quite an event if they gave us a ride in their car.

School was at least a mile and a half from our house, and we used to walk in the stormiest of weather. We took our lunch with us. On very stormy days, we had what was called a solid session: we would go to school until one o'clock and then go home and not go back for the afternoon. After school we played in the snow. Even in the winter, we used to go into the woods and collect the sap from the maple trees. We would take big chunks of snow and pour the maple syrup on the snow and make suckers. We looked forward to that. And we had sleigh rides. We would heat up bricks days ahead in the oven, and then put them in the sleigh to keep our feet warm while we had sleigh rides. Most nights we stayed home and did our homework. The nights were very cold; we all stayed around the fire.

I'll tell you another thing we liked to do: we'd gather in homes and make feather beds, our own feather beds. We used to take the feathers and pick them and then we used to make pillows with them. They'd kill a lot of geese and we'd have all those feathers, and we'd sit around and listen to the phonograph. We'd put on the phonograph and we'd all flick the feathers and make feather beds.

My father being rabbi, we had a very religious home, not fanatic, but a very lovely home life. We had a big family; we had a big house. We were content and happy and got along very nicely with my gentile friends—there were very few Jewish families in Burlington at the time. We had a synagogue, and there was another little congregation that they called a minyan where the very, very religious Jews used to meet. The synagogue had a lovely Hebrew school that had a lot of pupils, a good rabbi—my father—and good assistants. Social life and religious life was centered in that one synagogue; it was really the community center.

Country people—peddlers, storekeepers, dairy farmers—from all around used to come to Burlington for the High Holidays, and naturally they would stay at our house. During the High Holidays we had as many as forty and fifty people in the house. They slept on the floor, on the porches, wherever we could put them. Each one of them brought great big baskets of food. They brought roasted chickens, roasted turkeys, *challah*, which were loaves of traditional egg bread for the Sabbath and for the Holidays. Those Jewish people who lived in the countryside came to Vermont to work, or because they knew someone who went there before them. The same way my parents got there. All the Jewish people in town knew one another, because the community was small. They lived scattered all over the city, but mostly there was one center on First Street. Naturally, it wasn't far from the shul [synagogue], so that we could walk to shul without riding. Some of the Jewish people in Burlington had stores. I remember secondhand stores, soda fountains that sold pop, and a fish man who used to go around to the homes and sell fish. Years ago, that's how we got all our food. They used to go fishing and men used to come with big strings of fish. Then, we children got together and shopped. Across the street from our house there was a little grocery store that a Jewish man had. We used to go in and buy a quarter of a pound of butter . . . didn't have any freezers like you have today. So you bought supplies for a day. There was a big bakery next door. We used to bring in our fresh bread.

Sylvia Glosser spoke of Sabbath observance and gave an account of the foods that were an important part of traditional Jewish life.

On Friday night we used to put the *cholent* in the bakery, and Saturday morning a gentile girl used to bring the *cholent* to our house. *Cholent* is a mixture of meat and barley and vegetables in a certain pot. You put it in an oven overnight, and the next day it's done. We didn't work or cook on Sabbath, so someone not Jewish took it out for us on Saturday morning. The pot of tea was on the stove all the time on Sabbath, and a small electric light was burning all night and day.

Sabbath was very lovely. My father used to take a bath and cut his beard. He never shaved but did cut his beard. He used to wear a Prince Albert. He went to shul for Sabbath Eve service [Friday evening] with a four- or five-cornered velvet hat. After shul he came home; he made kiddush [blessings for the Sabbath, for wine, and for bread], and we all used to sit around and enjoy a real Sabbath dinner. It consisted of gefilte fish [chopped cooked fish balls], chicken soup, chicken *tsimmis,* dessert of something that they baked pareve, that contained neither milk nor meat products. We girls loved to go to Friday-night concerts. We were never allowed to go until after kiddush, which Father read at sundown, and after our dinner was over. These were public concerts that were held in the park. It was a big event. There we would meet other boys and girls and we'd have fun.

Saturday we went to shul in the morning and came home. Of course, we always walked. We'd have lunch at home, and people would come in for a treat in the afternoon, to drink tea and discuss the Talmud and the affairs of the week.

Glosser described the separate spheres in which men and women practiced Judaism, as she recalled traditional Sabbath afternoons.

The women sat in a different room, because the men spoke of things that didn't interest the women as much. They discussed Talmud and higher education. But the women were interested in their daily affairs and so forth. The women had very little to do with religion outside of the home. Outside of going to shul, that was it. There was no Sisterhood or the kinds of activities that go on today. No Sisterhood and no meetings. The men took care of that part. The women were merely hausfraus, women that watched their home and children. That's it! The men went back to the synagogue for the afternoon service. After that, Father would come home and make habdalah—the service ending the Sabbath—at the dining room table.

Of course, the men of the town respected my father very much. When they had a serious argument and a grudge against each other, they would come to our house and each tell his side of the argument. Then the rabbi—my father—would tell them how to settle the argument and make peace between them. The men would take a white handkerchief; each held one end of the handkerchief and they would shake it. That meant they were at peace again.

We got a Jewish paper every day, the *Tageblatt,* and another that came once a week. My mother used to follow the stories in that paper. They were continued Jewish stories, like soap operas, and on Friday that paper came and we children used to ask, "Mother, what happened now? Did Rachel get married? Did she have her baby yet?" Everything interested us.

My mother was an only child. She went to Hebrew school in Europe and was very well versed in Hebrew. She spoke Polish and Jewish [Yiddish]. As we grew up, we children taught our mother to write English, and she wrote a little English. First she wrote her name. Her name was Rachel, and she was very proud that she wrote her name in English, Rachel Sacks. Then she began to read easy books that she could understand, and we children used to help her. At home we spoke Yiddish, but we children all spoke English because my brother and I were born here and all of us grew up here.

In the following description of Jewish education, Glosser again referred to sexual distinctions.

I learned Hebrew at Hebrew school. My father taught us. I went to Hebrew school after school from four until six o'clock, and so did all my brothers and sisters. Mostly boys went to Hebrew school, and a few girls who were interested. But we didn't learn as much as the boys did. Of course, the boys were more important.

Adults used to go to night school at the YMCA to learn English. Even at the religious school, the Talmud Torah, they had classes in English, Hebrew, dancing, even cooking Jewish food. A woman volunteer teacher came and gave her time, so young people would know how Jewish people used to live—what they ate and how they lived with their families.

My father used to study the Talmud [rabbinical scholarship]. He knew all the branches of the Talmud. Boys came from all over Vermont to learn Talmud with my father. One of them became a famous rabbi in New York.

Sometimes it was not easy to be a rabbi's daughter. During high school we used to go to proms and affairs. My older sister used to sew for me, and I always worried if I would get the right kind of dress. It was a little difficult, because the whole town watched what the rabbi's daughters did. If there was an affair going on in town, other mothers would call my mother and ask, "Mrs. Sacks, are your children going to this party?" I remember once it was a candlelight dance, and my mother said, "Yes, I trust my girls to go." And then they would all send their girls. If we didn't go, they wouldn't let their children go.

Paid work played little part in Sylvia Glosser's life. When she was sixteen, she took a business course, and at seventeen went to work at the only paid job she ever held. She earned five dollars a week, "enough spending money to buy silk stockings and go to the movies." She dated and enjoyed a happy social life. When she was eighteen years old, she left Burlington to live with her sister.

I had a sister who lived in Boswell, Pennsylvania, a little mining town not far from Johnstown which was famous for its iron and steel industries. A cousin that we knew in Europe somehow settled in Boswell. When he got there he heard that Rabbi Sacks from the same town in Russia had gone to Burlington. And he heard that the rabbi had several daughters. He came to Burlington and married one of my sisters. He was a very fine man. He had a little department store in Boswell. I went to visit her, and then she came home to Burlington for the High Holidays. She was very, very lonesome. She told my parents, "I will not go back to Boswell unless Sylvia comes to live with me." That's how I came to the Johnstown area. It was terrible at first. It was lonesome; I didn't have any friends.

Then I began to go into Johnstown. My brother-in-law hired a hack; he used to take me with him to buy kosher meat. Then we went to the synagogue in Johnstown for the High Holidays, and that is where I met Jewish boys and girls.

I began to go to the Jewish affairs. I sang at a party one evening. It was a summer evening and all the windows were open. A bunch of boys walked by outside, and one of them came up and said, "We want to know who was singing." And they brought him over to me and introduced me to him. His name was David Glosser. Immediately he asked if he could take me home and I said, "I'm sorry but I came with another date, but I'll meet you after my date." So I met him after our date and from then on we began to go steady.

He was a perfect gentleman, and he came from a very nice family. I must tell you of this incident, because it is very, very important. We used to go to the Jewish butcher shop to buy all our meat. I came with my sister to shop there one day, and it was raining real, real hard. There was another woman there who was also shopping. It was pouring and I said to her—I didn't even know her name—"I'll take you to the car line because I have an umbrella." I took her to the car, put her on the trolley, and she went home. I never saw her after that. When I started to go with Dave, he said, "Do you know, Sylvia, I think you should come and meet my parents." When he took me home to meet his parents, who do you think came to the door? It was the woman that I took to the car!

Dave told me that his mother told him, "I met a wonderful little Jewish girl. Her father's a rabbi. She came from Burlington and I'd love for you to meet her." But you know how boys are. They never want to meet the girls their mother wants them to meet.

Dave and I met in October and we were married in June. Around Christmastime I began to go into his store to help out because they were busy. I was a pretty good saleslady. I used to be in the millinery department. At that time, women wore hats. I had a pretty good head for a hat and I'd put a hat on. Every hat I put on fit me. Customers would buy it because it looked good on me. And I used to have the highest sales in the department.

I was puzzled, because Glosser had said earlier that she never worked except for a very short period in a lawyer's office. I asked, "When did you go to work at Glosser Brothers?"

Oh, I never worked there! I just came to help them out. There was a time they wanted to pay me, but I said no. So when Dave went to New York, he went shopping. He came home with a beautiful outfit for me—a pussy-willow taffeta dress with a jacket—and I was so proud. Then he asked me to marry him, and I said, "I'll have to have my parents meet you before I say yes." My parents came in May. They were satisfied and we all agreed, "Let's get married." We became engaged on May fourteenth, and my mother and father stayed in Johnstown until the wedding. We were married at the Crystal Hotel in Johnstown on June first, 1916. All my brothers and sisters came to the wedding.

Glosser talked about her marriage. Her baby's death was the first tragedy of her life.

It was very hard to get an apartment when we were married. It was during World War I. We lived in the Crystal Hotel until we found a three-room apartment on Stoney Creek Street. I was pregnant right away; I only had one period after I was married. She was a seven-month baby, very tiny. She was born eight months after I was married. They didn't have incubators then. I took her home and I took a basket and lined it with pockets, and I took six hot-water bottles that I kept going all the time to keep her warm. She only weighed four pounds when she was born. She grew healthy and strong . . . until she got the flu.

I lost my first baby during the flu epidemic of 1918. Mr. Glosser and I and the baby all had the flu very bad. My baby took convulsions, and I ran to the store to get a doctor. When the doctor came, he said, "How about you and Mr. Glosser—are you well?" I said, "Fine," but he took our temperatures and we had over a hundred and four, so he took all three of us to the hospital. My baby died. The baby was twenty-two months old. After my baby died, I never went back to that apartment. My in-laws made me come and live in their house until we found a house of our own. Then I was pregnant again and my oldest daughter, Ruth, was born.

Glosser recalled good years as her family and the business grew and as members of her family moved from Burlington to Johnstown to share the family prosperity.

When I had only one baby, I used to go down to the store almost every day. When they were busy I would help out. I had a young girl who came after school, and she took care of the baby for me while I went to the store. I went to the store often all through the years. It was a pleasure for me to come to the store and see it grow from babyhood to manhood. Another floor was added; another store was added; another building bought. That's the way it was.

Dave and I had a very nice life. We had friends, and we had our congregation. We used to get together with friends and play Five Hundred. We played bridge a lot; we held picnics. The whole little congregation would get together. We would go for the whole day to have a picnic and would auction off food. It was done simply—it was small-scale. We didn't bother about clothes; whatever we had, we wore. One lady liked to entertain the young people, so she used to have a *latke* party at her house. That was the party: eating *latkes*. You know what a *latke* is—a potato pancake made from raw potatoes.

And my five children were born. There were Ruth and Betty and then the twins, Naomi and Doris. Paul was born six years later. We were so happy to have a boy, but we made up our mind we were not going to spoil Paul; he was going to be just like other boys. They were all born in a private hospital. I didn't get up until ten days after the baby was born. I had a little girl helping me at home, and when I had the twins I had a niece come from Burlington to help me. She was my older brother's daughter, and we brought her and her husband to Johnstown. He worked in the store, and she stayed at the house while I was in the hospital and then helped me with the children. I brought my two brothers and their wives to Johnstown, too, and they both worked in our store. They were very successful buyers for several years. Then they opened their own stores. One went to Cumberland and the other to Boston.

After we were married, we saw my parents in Burlington in the summers. One time we went on the train in the winter. The train was so covered with ice that they couldn't open it and we couldn't get out of the train. We stayed on the train and went back to Johnstown. After that, we bought a little cottage on Mallet's Bay in Burlington and spent a few summers there. A few years later, when my father was ill, I brought my parents to Johnstown. My father died, and my mother lived with me for fourteen years.

Glosser described holiday celebrations at her sister's home in Boswell and at her own home. Her daughter Naomi discussed the same topic from a child's perspective. Both were very much aware of the different economic circumstances of the two families.

My sister in Boswell was the only sister I had here. We saw each other often. I used to pack all the five kids in our big Cadillac car and bring the whole Sabbath dinner or the whole Pesach [Passover foods] to their house. We used to have our seder [Passover ceremonial meal] at their place in Boswell, and then we'd go home at night. Now, for the High Holidays in the fall, they used to come to Johnstown. All their children came. By then, we had a big house in Westmount, a big dining room, and we had help. We had lovely holidays. We all went to shul and then would come back to celebrate very nicely.

Glosser recalled busy times managing the household in Westmount. She laughed as she described shopping, cooking, and entertaining for family and friends who filled the house.

I used to drive a car, of course. I'd always drive to town while the children were in school. And I always tried to be home when they came back from school. When they came home, the first thing they did was call, "Mother!" If I was home, it was good. I did my shopping, came home, took care of the evening meal—I always had help. Two sisters were with us for thirteen years, so they knew how to do everything I could do. Our family evening meal was always an event; that was the only meal where we all sat down and talked things over. We had a big breakfast room, and we all sat together and enjoyed a lovely dinner with a white tablecloth on the table. After dinner the kids would go to a movie or do homework.

When my husband came home, he left everything in the store. It was a new life all over again. He lived with his family and wife when he came home at night; he didn't bring his worries home with him. He spent time with my mother, too. She lived with me for fourteen years after my father died. Dave used to read to her; she enjoyed that very much. She lived to be eighty-six years old. I'll tell you one thing we used to do. Once a week, we and all our five children used to get together with a Bible and we all used to read certain paragraphs of the Bible. Ten minutes, fifteen minutes, but we tried to do that once a week.

The children came home at four o'clock. I had a private rabbi who used to teach a little Hebrew and a little Yiddish. He taught all the children. By the way, this rabbi was Mr. Glosser's sister's husband. He was really a teacher rather than a rabbi, but a learned man. The children looked forward to Fridays. I always used to make *gribbenes* [crispy fried snacks] from chicken fat, and I'd have a big plate on the kitchen table when they came home after school. And homemade bread—we'd always have homemade bread. Our house was open to all the children. I remember on weekends we would bake three great big chocolate cakes. We would put them on the windows to cool. We'd come back and find only one—the kids would steal the chocolate cakes. We had a big home and we had a lovely basement. It was fixed as a big den. The children named it Dave's Dive.

Judaism mandated giving to charity.

Our family was always very charitable. We had a Sisterhood at the synagogue and used to give affairs to raise money. Mr. Glosser and I were both brought up to give to charity. When Mr. Glosser's mother died, we found a big pillow slip full of receipts for charity that she had given. Besides all the good causes here, his family used to keep up a little town in Europe.

And we were always interested in Israel, long before it was Israel. We were there in 1934, when hardly anybody traveled to Israel. It was all swamps—there was nothing there. Then we went about six years later, and there was such a difference. Tel Aviv, Haifa, Jerusalem were all flourishing cities. Altogether, we were there seven times. I haven't been back since my husband died in 1964.

Glosser gave up keeping a kosher house during the war years. Kosher food became important in the family once again when granddaughter Nancy became a religious Jew. Nancy and her husband became part of the Lubavitcher movement of Hassidic Judaism; her commitment to religious orthodoxy affected the entire family.

My granddaughter Nancy and her husband are Lubavitchers. They are very religious, which I am not a hundred percent with. I'm sorry because they have to miss so many lovely things in life on account of their being so religious. Nancy's mother had a thirtieth anniversary; they couldn't stay for the dinner because they couldn't eat unkosher food. And little Esther can't stay with me or her grandmother—I hate to see her miss so much enjoyment. It's hard for me to understand how people can be so possessed with religion.

For myself, I like to be more modern, like we are, like her parents are, like her husband's parents are. His parents are modern people who live in Israel. I believe that you should enjoy your religion, not punish yourself with your religion. I have a very rich, happy life. I enjoy being a Jew, and I enjoy the comforts of a good life.

The final question I asked Sylvia Glosser was what was the greatest source of pleasure in her life. She answered with eyes glowing.

My greatest pleasure is to see my children happy. When I go to their homes and I see the family life that they lead, the way they conduct themselves with their parents, the respect they give their parents, and being respected themselves—that's my best pleasure. Another thing that made me very happy is that all the children married and no intermarriages, and all are living a good life, respected by the whole community. That is the biggest pleasure of my life.

Sylvia Glosser died in October 1980. She was eighty-four.

Naomi Cohen,

b. 1924

April 9, 1976, and December 1, 1988, Interviews

Our home was in Westmount, the residential section on top of the hill, where it was very residential and white middle class. Very few Jewish people lived there—maybe five families. Living at home with us was my grandmother [from Vermont], five children, and my mother and dad. Mother was born in Vermont. Daddy came over from Russia at the age of twelve and settled in Johnstown because that's where his father came earlier and started a small store and then sent for Daddy and his brothers.

We were fortunate that Daddy was successful, and so we were always able to afford a big car. Our biggest treat was for Daddy to take the five children on Sundays to go exploring. The children absolutely revered my father. Anything Daddy said, that was the law. We always said that if Daddy said it was snowing outside in the middle of summer, we would have said, "Of course it is, Daddy, because you said so." Mom was the type of woman who was always dressed in a clean housedress when Daddy came home, and all the kids would be waiting at the door for Daddy to come home. On nice days we would walk to the incline to meet him. He always walked to the incline and would take the incline to the bottom of the hill into town. We walked to meet him and jumped all over him to welcome him home every day. My father had two brothers and a sister living in Johnstown. My mother had one sister who lived in Boswell, Pennsylvania. Going there was a big treat.

On Sundays we would drive to Boswell and take all the family, or else the Boswell cousins would come to visit us. Boswell was a very small mining town. My aunt did not have very much money, and they lived upstairs above a theater and a store. It was a big treat for us to go there, because we used to bring water from the well and it was quite a few blocks. It was our big deal to carry the water. They had water in the house, but evidently it wasn't drinking water. That they got from a well. And they had a coal stove. The backyard was all dirt, and we used to play marbles out there and shoot baskets. Then, we could hear the movies playing. Rin Tin Tin was [featured in] the movie and we heard the dog barking in the theater. We always wanted to sneak in, but we never did.

We'd go there for the Passover seders. And with all the nine kids—they had four children and we had five—plus Grandma, my aunt and uncle, and Mother and Daddy, it was supergreat! Just unbelievable—it was like a whole other world. We lived very differently from this family.

In the 1936 flood, our store was flooded up to the second floor and the town was a mess. We heard rumors that the dam was breaking, and we were terrified when Daddy said he had to go into town to the store. Our house was safe—we lived high on the hill in Westmount. Our cousins from Boswell had moved into Johnstown by then, and they had to leave their house in town. They moved into our house with all their kids, and another family with five children moved in. There must have been thirty people staying at our house. They were sleeping everywhere. I remember the cooking and the food and candlelight, because the electricity was off and the phones weren't working. I remember playing Monopoly by candlelight, and the Monopoly money was covered with candle wax. We kids thought it was exciting, because there were so many kids at our house and people in and out all the time. And mother was busy in the house and busy thumbing a ride to try to buy bread. She worried about feeding this group at our house. Of course, our grocery department at our store was totally washed out. After the flood was over, they sold cans for a penny a can. You took your chances on them, but for a penny, people did buy them. After the flood, we went down into town and the smell was horrible. There's a certain thing about a flood smell that stays with you, and it was awful. It was heartbreaking for the whole town and for my daddy and the family, because they worked so hard.

We belonged to the Orthodox synagogue. I remember that it was small; there were only nine in my confirmation class. From the time we were little, we went to services for all the holidays—Purim, Succoth, Rosh Hashanah, Yom Kippur. On Simchas Torah [last day of the Succoth, the harvest festival], we would pray with the Torahs and get apples. And Purim we would have noisemakers to clap. We always walked to the shul on the High Holidays. We would walk to the incline, go down the incline, and then walk from there to the synagogue. Mother would dress us all up and we'd always have new clothes. We all went together except my grandmother. She had a broken hip and walked with a cane, so she had trouble walking. She died when I was about ten or twelve.

Naomi Cohen's grandmother was an unusual woman for her time. Cohen was embarrassed because her grandmother spoke Yiddish and critical because she was not a soft, home-oriented "grandma."

My grandmother spoke Yiddish, which was a bone of contention on our side. We resented her terribly for speaking Yiddish in front of our non-Jewish friends. I really didn't like her. She was tough. Mother and I have talked about it, and Mother told me that she was unusual for her time. Women in that era were mostly housewives, mothers, fantastic cooks—did nothing but cook and bake, like my mother did. My grand-mother wasn't like that. She was a very bright woman, and my mother remembered that when her father, the rabbi, would bring men over to learn and discuss the Talmud, Bobba would always sit with the men because she wanted to learn. Mother recalls that the girls [Sylvia Glosser and her sisters] took care of the house because my grandmother did other things. Bobba wasn't the greatest homemaker. She would rather be learning with the men. She liked to talk business. Evidently we missed that softness in her that we found in our mother. It is interesting that our mother had it and her mother didn't.

Mother was strictly a mom. Her days were mostly spent—she would go downtown and market and bring home the big orders, planning the meals. I guess with a family of five children and running a house that was big, she was busy all the time. We had lots of company for dinners. She was the kind of mother who was home with the children and just wonderful.

Daddy made the decisions. No question about it. There was sibling rivalry, especially between Betty and Ruth; that was part of our growing up. My sister Ruth always seemed to aggravate Mother. Doris and I, as the twins, never got into too much trouble. We—and I think our whole family in those days—did whatever Daddy said. There were no two ways about it. It was with an iron hand, but always in a kind way. I don't remember any specific expectations or rules. We seemed to know before-hand what we could do and what we couldn't do. We were really very well behaved.

The Glossers' concern that their children eventually choose Jewish spouses was shared by many Jewish parents who raised families in a non-Jewish environment. They made a special effort to see that their children socialized with other Jews.

I think the biggest worry that Mother and Daddy had was that we would marry out of our faith, because of our relationship with the non-Jewish children in the neighborhood. None of us dated Jewish boys. Consequently, when Betty and Ruth were juniors and seniors in high school, they went away to a girls school. [Our parents] did not send Doris and me away. But summers we spent six weeks in Atlantic City, from the time we were two until we were sixteen. There we would meet other Jewish families from the Philadelphia area. We all drove up together in a big, seven-passenger car. We'd pack a lunch and picnic on the way. Our biggest treat was to be able to go out in back of Convention Hall in Atlantic City and buy hot dogs at a stand. We could never do that in Johnstown, because there were no kosher hot dogs there. I envied the kids at our school when they had hot-dog sales, 'cause we couldn't eat them. As soon as we'd pile out of the car, we couldn't wait. Daddy would say, "Okay, we're going to get hot dogs."

There were certain things about being Jewish that we minded a lot, living in Johnstown. From when we were in grade school through eighth grade, all of us took Hebrew lessons. An uncle of ours used to come to the house and teach Doris and me together. He taught Ruth and Betty together, then Doris and me together, and as Paul got older, he taught my brother, Paul. We resented being called in from play for Hebrew lessons. Also, there was a country club in Westmoreland County where there were no Jewish members and they asked my father to join. But Daddy didn't want to be the so-called token Jew, and he said, "Until it's open to all Jews, I'm not interested." I used to envy our friends because they could go swimming there in the summer.

Cohen talked about her teenage years and learning about sex.

At sixteen and until we were married, Doris and I were totally together. We dressed alike until the day I got married, which sounds ridiculous. At the age of twenty-two, on the way to my wedding, we were dressed alike! We look at it now and we just laugh. In those days it was not like now, when people think twins should be separated. Mother didn't know any better, nor did we, and we enjoyed it.

In a lot of ways we were still babies at sixteen. In Johnstown we dated our non-Jewish friends. We went to basketball games. They would have parties called "gym-jams" after the games. As I look back on it, compared to our children at sixteen, we were like twelve. Here's an example. At sixteen we were still going to Atlantic City, and we met the same girls there year after year. They were city kids and they were much more worldly. We were small-town kids. Sixteen-year-old boys in Atlantic City dated, but they never asked us, because we seemed much too young. We were very naive—even stupid.

We learned about sexual intercourse from my friend Carlin. She had a brother who was getting married, and his girl, Dorothy, told Carlin everything. The three of us—Doris and I and Carlin—used to sit on the church steps and discuss sex, whatever Dorothy would tell her. So we were finding out right . . . what it was really all about, because we really didn't know. We still laugh when we talk about Dorothy today. I once said to her, "Boy, Dorothy, if it wasn't for you, we wouldn't have known anything!" Dorothy never told us. She told Carlin, then Carlin would tell us. We didn't know about childbirth. We learned during the war when we worked as nurse's aides in the hospitals.

At home Daddy fixed a game room in the basement. We named it Dave's Dive. Our house was the meeting place for all the kids. I think we had the first record player where the records used to flip like a jukebox. It was just automatic that the kids came to our house. And when Betty and Ruth came home, there were always parties with their friends. Mother always had chocolate cakes baked and cookies, and the kids all knew it, and everybody would come and help themselves. At the Glossers', everybody was welcome.

Mother had help, and her help baked too. And Mother was a fabulous cook. She made all the Jewish dishes—the *tsimmis* [carrot, sweet potato, and honey mixture] and potato *kugels* [a pudding of grated raw potatoes].

The family's participation in the Christmas festivities of a gentlemen's caroling group was related to David Glosser's position among the town's business elite.

Interestingly, on Christmas Eve as far back as I can remember, a group came around singing Christmas carols. The group was called the Gwents. I think the men who belonged were part of the Masons. Every year on Christmas Eve they dressed up in green and red and sang Christmas carols. Fabulous male voices! And they would go to different houses in the Westmount area. And when they came to our house, it was standard procedure that Daddy would have liquor and cold cuts and sandwiches. They would carol at our house for at least an hour. We loved it. We would wait for them every Christmas Eve. Now the interesting thing is that ours was the only Jewish house they caroled at and the only watering hole they had. We got to know them all, and they knew all of us as children. Our gentile friends would come to our house to hear the Gwents sing. Then Mother and Dad let us go to Midnight Mass with our friends. It was very special. By that time we knew very well that we were Jewish.

Cohen recalled that the family gradually gave up the practice of kashruth, or keeping a kosher home.

When we were sixteen, Grandma had already died and Ruth and Betty were away at school. I could see our house becoming less Orthodox. When Betty and Ruth went away, of course they were eating meat out. Our store for many years had a supermarket and sold meats. But my mother continued to buy meat at the kosher butcher shop. Daddy would say, "Sylvia, as long as the two older girls are away at school eating *traife* [nonkosher food] anyway, let's not be so particular at home." In other words, Daddy didn't care. He said, "It's not so important." So Mother agreed it would be easier for her to order through the store and let the store's truck deliver it. So, very quietly Mother got away from a kosher house.

Cohen spoke of the impact of World War II on her life and that of her twin sister.

We had graduated from high school in 1941 and we were at National Park Junior College in Washington, D.C., when war broke out in December. Of course, being in Washington, we were very conscious of the war. We had blackouts every night. The day of December 7 we had been touring Washington, and we passed the Japanese Embassy about two hours before war was declared. When the broadcast came announcing that the Japanese had bombed Pearl Harbor, we were scared to death. We didn't even know what we were afraid of. We were frightened, and we were still homesick even though we had each other.

Immediately after we entered the war, National Park School organized a first-aid course, an in-depth first-aid training program planned in case of bombing. One time we had an air-raid drill, and certain of the girls were picked to be victims and others were chosen to be the nurse's aides. Doris was chosen to be the victim. So they carried her down on a stretcher. She was covered with fake blood, with bandages, and I was terrified. When I saw Doris bandaged up with blood, I got hysterical, as if it was really happening. It remains so vivid in my mind, because we were doing it under warlike circumstances, in a blackout, and trying to see how we would organize if we were bombed at this small girls school of four hundred students. They handled it well, and we learned. Everybody at school was involved.

That summer we took a course in Johnstown at Memorial Hospital and became nurse's aides. We were at the hospital almost every day. The course was pretty extensive, and we were "capped" at the end of it. We learned all kinds of things—nothing too professional, but we learned how to bathe patients and things like that. They always put Doris and me together. Originally, they put us in the men's ward, but we did not like it at all and we asked to be transferred out of the men's ward.

We were transferred to the nursery, and it was quite an experience. It was pleasant, but we also saw sickness and death. I wandered into a back room and saw a little deformed baby left to die. I'll never forget that, but I never questioned what was done.

We asked to be allowed to watch a delivery, but at that time nurse's aides weren't allowed. We knew about childbirth by then. We had no fears about it. Never did. I looked at it as something beautiful and something special, to have children. I always felt that way and looked forward to that.

Then we found out that we couldn't go back to National Park Junior College. That summer, Walter Reid Hospital took over the school. Carlin, our best friend, also went to National Park. That summer the three of us met every day, saying, "Well what do you think we're going to do?" Actually, Daddy said, "Go to Penn State; it's close to Johnstown." We didn't want to go there, but of course we did. Most of our male Johnstown friends went into the service, and we watched the death notices in the paper every day. We lost quite a few of our friends. At Penn State in 1942, our first year there, the boys were still there; by 1943, there were no men anywhere.

We kept doing nurse's aide work all through the war. We continued knitting. We were collecting whatever we collected in those days. We had almost a devil-may-care attitude toward school. I don't know if it was because of the war years, but we never knew who was going to be shipped out tomorrow or where they were going—and they were being shipped out so fast. We didn't want to take things too seriously. We were too concerned about where our friends were and the box numbers and "Where do you think he is?" and all the APOs [Army Post Offices], all the mail.

By the beginning of 1944, Penn State was completely service oriented. We didn't want to be there anymore, and by that time Mother and Daddy had bought a home in Florida for the winters. We transferred to the University of Miami and lived at home.

Cohen met her future husband in 1942. Her romantic and idealized approach to marriage was not unusual among her generation.

I met Jesse the summer of 1942 in Atlantic City. He was a junior at Penn State and I had finished my freshman year at college. We thought Jesse was very handsome, and I only hoped I would ever have a date with him! Anyway, that September when Daddy took us to start Penn State, we walked into a restaurant on campus, and Jesse happened to be sitting there with a bunch of his fraternity brothers. Now, we had known his parents for years, and when he saw Daddy, he came over to say hello. Daddy said, "Well, the twins are going to Penn State, and Jesse, I'd certainly appreciate it if you'd look after them." Well, Doris and I had only been at small schools; we had been very sheltered, and we were scared by the size of Penn State. There were only six thousand students in those days, but it was tremendous compared to National Park.

Jesse invited me out; I started to date him in September, and he gave me his fraternity pin in February. I went with him for three years. He left Penn State in July of '43 to enter West Point. I never really went with anybody else. That was it. I think he was the second Jewish boy I ever dated. There were ups and downs those three years. We had many fights, and many times I sent back everything he gave me. He'd say, "I'm sorry. OK?" We were supposed to be engaged, and he said, "I don't think I'm ready." I would always ask Daddy's advice. Daddy said, "Tell him you're not ready either." In the meantime, Daddy was very fond of Jesse, and he wanted it to work out.

Jesse was handsome and he was strong too, and I knew I needed a strong guy. He was nice—not as sweet as Daddy, but nice. He graduated from West Point on June 6, and we were married on June 9. I never made any plans before we were married. All I thought was that I was getting married and was going to marry the man I loved, and that's all I cared about.

The war was over and housing was at a premium. Jesse had a bad back, a ruptured disk, so he needed surgery. First we had a two-month honeymoon in Florida. He was practically crippled from his bad back, and he had surgery at Johns Hopkins in Baltimore the following September. It was hard for me after, because I had to help him and practically dress him, and I worried about his getting better. The good part was that he didn't go to work until November, and I had him with me every day. After the operation we moved to Canonsburg, Pennsylvania, and lived with his folks. They had a furniture store there, and Jesse had decided that he was going into the business. My father asked him to come to his business, but Jesse very strongly felt an obligation to his father. So he went into his father's business on November 1, 1946. Then I was alone with nothing to do. I got along very well with my in-laws. But I realized that this was no way for newly married couples to live, in their parents' house.

Marriage meant separation from her twin, which was difficult for both sisters. And marriage brought problems as well as joys.

After we moved into our apartment, Doris kept visiting all the time, because we both hated the separation. In fact, when we were on our honeymoon in Florida, Doris called me and said, "Hey, Naomi, I'm coming down." I said, "Doris, you better not. I don't think it's the right thing to do." Well, she was crushed. She cried through the whole wedding. The last picture in our wedding book shows Doris absolutely in tears. I said, "No, you can't come." As it was, I was calling Jesse "Doris" for the first year! We were so close. It was really difficult. She visited us an awful lot because I wanted her to be near, close by. Doris was married in September of 1948, two years after we were married. Then she lived in Pittsburgh, so it was great.

I had Nancy in July of 1947, and I always knew I would have three children by the time I was thirty. Our marriage was good, but we were both spoiled. I thought Jesse was more spoiled than I was. I felt that I was more giving than he was. I never told anybody about it. We had a couple of big fights during my pregnancy. Yet even when I'd become angry, I would say to myself, "How can I be fighting with him when I love him so?" We were from two sheltered backgrounds. We had both had everything we really wanted. We were learning to live and share with someone else. I don't think that's easy. I was twenty-three when I got pregnant. I felt incredible. I thought nobody could be as lucky as I was. The pregnancy was the greatest. Going to the hospital was the greatest. Looking forward to labor pains was the greatest. Having that baby was the greatest. It was all super. I flipped from that child! When I knew I was pregnant, I told everybody. I called the whole family right away.

I learned by hit or miss. I learned most from my wonderful pediatrician. And I had a young nurse from the Pittsburgh Home for Babies come and help me. When Nancy was eight months old, I found out I was pregnant. Shocked! I went to the doctor's crying, "I'm pregnant." He looked at me and said, "You can afford it. Thank God, you're well. You have a healthy baby. Please God, you'll have another healthy baby. You should see women who come in here and can't conceive. Consider yourself lucky." At first I wasn't so sure about that. Then I did get excited. She was another little girl and she was gorgeous. They were seventeen months apart. I had lots of help. But the girls were awfully close and there was tremendous rivalry. Nancy was very headstrong. And poor little Cathy, I think, got the short end of the deal because Nancy used to physically beat her up all the time.

Cohen recounted the years of raising children and doing volunteer work.

Jesse in those days was working five or six nights a week. Friday-night dinners we didn't have anymore because Jesse worked Friday nights. He was so involved trying to build a business. Now he says, "I really blew it." When the children were very little, we spent all our vacations at Mom's house in Florida with the kids. Other than that, very little time with the children. I started doing volunteer work. I was one of the organizers of the Pittsburgh chapter of ORT [Organization for Rehabilitation through Training]. ORT supported vocational schools for displaced and unemployed Jewish youth in Israel and other countries. I was on their board and was membership chairman and a vice-president. I worked for ORT three or four days a week, always leaving the children with help. During one of my pregnancies we had the ORT bus. I used to go on the bus and sell second hand clothing. I spent a lot of time away from the kids. In retrospect, I left my children under outside help too much. No question about it.

It was much different from when I was raised. I knew the relationship we had with Daddy at our dinner table, when the children did the talking and Daddy was the listener. In our house, when the kids started to talk, Jesse wanted to talk about business or about how his day was. Consequently, our mealtimes were not exactly pleasant. The children came to me with all their problems. Much different from my childhood. We were running to do volunteer work—totally different than our mother was with us.

I had Timmy four years after Cathy was born, and that was good. Timmy was a little rascal and adorable, and we were delighted to have a son. We moved into Squirrel Hill, and I continued to do volunteer work. We went to Rodef Shalom Temple on Rosh Hashanah and Yom Kippur, and the girls went to Sunday school. All three went to Wightman School and then to Linden School. Nancy went to public high school. She was very outgoing and popular. Cathy asked to go to private school. She did not want to be involved socially like her sister. She became more of a loner. Meanwhile, Nancy was into everything.

Nancy joined the Lubavitcher movement in 1973; it was difficult for Naomi and Jesse Cohen to adjust to their daughter's religious life.

Nancy is living a good Jewish life. That first year they were married, Nancy taught in a little Jewish school for girls. Yitzhok [Nancy's husband] studied, studied, studied. The rebbe [chief rabbi of the Lubavitcher movement] says that after a year of studying it is time to support a wife. They had a choice. Yitzhok could have gone to Israel to join his father's business, gone to Detroit to work for the movement, or come to Pittsburgh to join Jesse. In the Lubavitcher movement, you ask the rebbe before making important decisions. The rebbe said, "Go to Pittsburgh to your father-in-law." [Yitzhok] came into Jesse's business. Religion comes first with them. He can always work in Jesse's business, but he'll never give it the time that we're used to having managers give. . . .

I worry about Nancy. Her baby's only seven weeks old, and she's nursing and she's cleaning her house from top to bottom and changing her whole kitchen for Passover. In the summer we'll go to Nantucket. Nancy said, "Mother, I guess you're going again this summer, aren't you." I said, "You'd like to go, wouldn't you, Nancy?" She said, "Of course I would." I said, "Well, I don't see how you could, since it's not a kosher home. And what could you do there? You don't put a bathing suit on because you're not allowed to bathe in mixed company." Now we have a granddaughter, and she won't be able to come with us either. Nancy says that she will have strong beliefs because of the way she is being raised in her home. But how will our relationship be with this child? I don't know.

December 1988, Interview

Cohen's desire to remain close to Nancy and her family (Nancy and Yitzhok had six children by 1988) has led to many accommodations. The Cohens celebrated a special anniversary by taking all of their children and grandchildren to a resort hotel that observes Jewish law. Cohen spoke about her life in 1988.

It makes me feel good that all the children are married and have good families. I feel good if I can help Nancy and make things easier for her and her six adorable children. I feel good when I have lunch with my daughter Cathy; I feel good that she's married and has children. I feel good when Timmy calls on the phone and tells me all the good things about him and his family.

But the best part—Jesse and I were just talking about it. It's when the two of us are together, especially when we go to our apartment in Florida. I can't tell you how exciting it is when the plane lands there, to know that all we have to worry about is each other. It's beautiful. To make dinner down there with just the two of us, without the responsibilities of a big house, just with an apartment. Knowing that the only thing we have to worry about is where to play golf or whether to go to the beach. I love the time we have together.

Cathy Droz,

b. 1949

November 1, 1988, Interview

I was eighteen months younger than my sister Nancy. My brother, Timmy, was born four years after I was. For a few years we lived in Mount Lebanon [a suburb of Pittsburgh]. I went to kindergarten there, but my memories are very vague. Nancy and I were very close in age, so we did spend a lot of time together, and we spent a lot of time with my mom's family.

We often went to Johnstown to visit my mother's family. My grandparents lived in a large house, and it was an old house, in contrast to our relatively new house. There was a big dining room table and I remember that my grandfather sat at the head of the table. There was a great card room where the men played cards and smoked cigars; the room always smelled a little musty. We [children] sat at that table, and we played cards in there. All through my childhood, we would all pile in the car and go to Johnstown. We went for various reasons. My grandma lived there—my grandfather died when I was only four—and two of my mother's siblings. My Uncle Paul—my mother's brother—always entertained us. We would go shopping at Glosser Brothers [the family-owned department store] and spend time with my grandmother. That was the gathering place. It was really everybody's favorite place to go. My grandmother usually stayed in the background; mostly it was her house as a place, rather than her as a person. She surrounded us with this perfect place and just let us go at it.

We also went to Florida once a year. Grandma had a house in Florida, and she spent her winters there. She had done this ever since my mother was in college. She lived next door to my Aunt Ruth and her husband and three children; they lived in Florida all year long. We would go down for vacation for two or three weeks, sometimes more. Sometimes my parents would put us in school there. That was sort of a fatherless environment, because my father and my Uncle Lenny [Aunt Doris's husband] did not come to stay; they came for weekends or at the end of our stay. It was a very maternal group, which was my mother, my grandmother, Aunt Doris, Aunt Betty, and Aunt Ruth next door. Her husband was not that much involved. At Grandma's house, the boys would have a room and all the girls would have a room.

My grandmother was very much in charge of that household. She gave us this house that was filled with joy and pleasure. I was never aware that my grandmother had a separate life outside of the family. When I picture that house, my grandma was always in the kitchen, even for breakfast. And she had help. She cooked and she supervised help.

We would go to school in the morning. Then a bus would pick us up and take us to the hotel. We ate in the coffee shop, and we went swimming and played all afternoon. It was the greatest life for a kid in the whole world. There were eleven of us. Two were a little older, so most of the time we traveled as a troop of nine. The boys were Jimmy, Timmy, Billy. The girls were myself, Nancy, Jodie, Winnie, and Penny—and Wendy, who was the baby of the group. We did this from the time I was in kindergarten until my cousin Penny died of cancer when she was thirteen. I was twelve at the time. We still went down, but when Penny died, that changed the tone for everybody. There was a lot of togetherness; it was a real group. It was a kid-oriented society, and it was very much fun.

I can remember the Passover seder at my grandmother's Florida home. It was in a long Florida room that extended the whole length of the house. We set up one huge table. That's when my father and Uncle Lenny came down, and it was just very special. That was the first time I was allowed to drink wine! And we kids sat with the grown-ups, not at a separate table. Passover didn't always coincide with our Florida vacation, but when it did, it was special. When we had to have a seder in Pittsburgh, we resented it; I wanted to be in Florida—it was much more fun. In Pittsburgh we went to my father's family, and it was much more serious. My grandmother Cohen was more strict about religion. And I didn't have ten cousins here. There were no girls my age.

Cathy Droz talked about high school, her relationship with her sister, and her first experience of discrimination.

I went to grade school at public school. High school, I went to Winchester-Thurston [a private school for girls]. I was very involved in a lot of activities at school. I was on the newspaper and the yearbook and the student council: the whole gamut. I was yearbook editor my senior year, and I liked that a lot.

Winchester was a new environment for me. There were not very many Jewish kids at the school in those days. I wanted to go there because I felt intimidated about going to Allderdice [a large public high school]. It seemed much too big. I was very, very little; I was not developed at all. Our parents saw Allderdice as a very wild and woolly place, and I saw it as such too. I thought Nancy was pretty wild, and that was one of the reasons that I saw the school that way. I was very different from Nancy. She was much more extroverted, much more rebellious, much more independent. I was much quieter, much more reserved, much more cautious. Nancy was impulsive; I was careful, always checking things out. I was more timid, and more intimidated. I was more serious. Nancy and I were never really great playmates. She was stronger; she was rougher. It was not a good sibling relationship. In fact, it didn't get good until Nancy left for college. Nancy intimidated me a lot. Nancy always had many friends; I had one or two friends. We shared a room, and that was never comfortable. She was bossy, and I was distrustful of her. We fought all the time, and Nancy always won.

I liked Winchester. I felt safe there, and one reason was that Nancy was not there. Also, I felt safer in the small environment. I was always good in school, so schoolwork was not an issue. At Winchester I remember working, and I remember wanting to do well.

I felt I had to do well. After I had started there, I found a letter to my parents saying that I was not admitted. They had never told me about the letter. Evidently [they] had used some influence to get me admitted. I was sensitive to that, and a part of me felt that I had to do extra well because of that. My parents never knew until years later that I found that letter.

Teachers liked having me in their classes. I do remember that everyone told me that I was smart. My father gave me the sense that I was capable. Schooling was my father's domain. From a very early age, that was the only area where it was clear that my father was involved with our everyday lives. He was involved with schooling and education; he corrected papers or went to talk to our teachers. He was in retailing and we hardly ever saw him. He was never home for dinner. We would leave our papers on his nightstand, and he would correct them. My mother would correct the English, and my father would correct the math. There was that male-female breakdown!

The traditional aspirations that Droz described were widespread among women of her age-group, most of whom were raised by traditional parents. Feminist awareness developed in the late 1960s or the 1970s.

As for the future, I knew that I was going to go to college, and I also assumed that I would work. I thought I would work when I finished school, but not in an important or serious way. I never thought about being a doctor or a professional. Advertising looked like fun. I thought I would get married and have children. I would pretty much do what my mother did, but she did not finish college and I figured that I would finish college. My mother did not like being a student. I did not particularly like it either, but it was something that I was relatively good at.

My father had been a student, and I was a student. He liked that, because he had gone to college and to West Point. I was often compared to his sister, my Aunt Sylvia, who went to college and was a very good student. He wanted me to do what Sylvia did—go to college and be successful and then get married. I had no ambitions for myself. I did encourage my brother, Timmy. I put a lot of my fantasies about what I would have liked to do into him. I was ambitious for him. It did not matter what I did, but I wanted Timmy to think about being someone on his own.

I graduated in 1967. It was still a time when most women went to school and then got married and had children. It was a funny time, because the women's movement had barely begun. What was happening was the beginning of the countercultural revolution. But I was not rebellious, not in high school. In Pittsburgh in the sixties there were stirrings, but protest had not taken a strong hold. Winchester was anything but a hotbed of political activity. Things changed when I went to college. I went to Northwestern. I felt safe about it because it was a relatively small school, and my Aunt Sylvia had gone there.

Northwestern University had changed since Aunt Sylvia's time. Droz discussed her college experience from 1967 to 1971.

I was very undecided when I went to college. I had no idea what to major in, and I had no great interest, because I did not have a lot of pressure making me take school seriously. I got in on my own. I did not have the fear that I might be kicked out. Deep down, I always hated Winchester because they made me feel that I did not deserve to be there. I held this inside me all through high school; I kept most things inside me while I was growing up.

I still never thought about what I would be; I never pictured myself as looking for a job or a career. To the day I graduated I didn't know what I was going to do. I chose a major my junior year—radio and television film. That was fun. I was not much of a student in college. By this point I was on the fringes of political involvement. This was 1967 to 1971. The Vietnam War was going on, and that was a big issue. It's almost embarrassing to talk about it now, but we wanted "relevancy" on campus. We shut down the university and we marched and protested against the war and the draft. We spent a lot of time discussing what we would do. It was much more of an issue for the boys. I was politically involved, but I was never really committed to anything. There were a lot of things going on. This was a time of protest.

There was racial conflict going on at Northwestern. There was a small black community, and the black students protested and took over a building. I worked in the cafeteria, and I became friendly with a lot of the black kids who also worked there. This was the first of the black power stuff. I was in a group of blacks and whites, and we took over a building and protested for equal treatment. We took over the dean's office, and at night we slept outside the office and nobody could get in. We did this for three days, and then the school officials met with the black students. That was my freshman year.

We were involved in drugs. We all used marijuana and hashish, but nothing else. My core group of friends were not committed to drugs, but we were involved. The theater school was a very way-out school, and my best friend in college was in theater first and then transferred into film. So she brought me into the theater group, and they were pretty wild and crazy and some were drugged out. They were not involved politically, but they were involved in drugs.

Religion was also of interest to me. I had taken a lot of religion courses and considered changing my major to religion. My roommate was Catholic. She was from Minnesota and had never met a Jewish person before in her whole life. We stayed together all four years, first as roommates, then in the same apartment shared with other friends. She was involved in much straighter political issues. Her fiancé at the time was a social worker in Chicago working with poor blacks, so he was involved from a government position.

A summer in Israel was an important new experience for Droz.

Chicago was a hotbed for all the protests. I missed the major protests in the summer of 1968 because I was out of the country. I wanted to be in Chicago for the [Democratic national] convention, but I spent that summer in Israel, first with the family and then on a kibbutz with Nancy. At that time we never saw a drug in Israel. When I went back in 1973, it was altogether different.

I liked the summer in Israel. First of all, Nancy and I were on our own and we were for the first time beginning to confide in one another. For the first time we lived kind of parallel lives. She started to go with a guy from the kibbutz, and I had a boyfriend and my own friends and my own life. We felt comfortable on the kibbutz. We lived together, but we were each on our own. We had an older relative who lived on the kibbutz, and he was wonderful to us.

That experience had an influence on me. That summer I came to like Israel very much. I saw this idealized life, and it was very appealing to me. I saw it as connected to the political things that I was doing at Northwestern. "Kibbutz" meant to me this beautiful socialist life. There was equality and communal living, and I thought it was just perfect. It did nothing religiously for me; I loved the pioneering aspect. I liked farming, and I liked the whole communal ideal. I didn't want to live in Israel. I would have liked to be on a kibbutz in America. That was my attitude coming back. I started to talk about communes, and in college at that time people were living in communal houses. The majority of my friends were Jewish, but some of them were not, so whether the commune was Jewish did not matter to me. I felt strongly that I did not want to isolate myself into a Jewish-only arrangement. I had lots of Jewish friends, but I never wanted to be in a totally Jewish environment.

Then I was back at Northwestern. Panic set in when I was about to graduate. Believe it or not, I still had no expectations. It is embarrassing but true that I had no better idea what I was going to do when I finished than I did when I started. I had no skills. We spent half of my senior year closing down the school. I didn't even graduate, because I boycotted an exam. Our protest changed from emphasis on Vietnam to this counter-culture. We wanted "relevancy." We believed we should have classes not about history, not about film, but about what was "relevant." That year it was the black experience. That's when Afro-American studies were started. The business school, which had been Northwestern's strongest school and is again today, didn't have one student. The women's movement hadn't started on campus, but we were very concerned with racial equality and with "relevancy." We protested against the university telling us what to do; we didn't want them serving as our parents.

Anyway, I did not have any idea what to do, but I had done a lot of photography, film, radio, and TV, so that is what I knew and I figured I would do something with that. The first thing I did was to travel for a while, and just floundered, and saw people that I knew. I worked, just doing anything, all kinds of jobs. I cooked doughnuts. I was not quite a hippie, because I was not comfortable with being uninhibited.

In school I worked in the cafeteria for two years; I worked doing interviews for a psychologist; I worked in the library for six months. I got jobs through the university. I worked for my father one summer. I went camping in Maine one summer with my friend Debbie. After I graduated from college, I applied to VISTA [Volunteers in Service to America, a government program to aid people in distressed areas of the United States]. I wanted to go to an agricultural area. I didn't get into VISTA, because they were looking for people with skills. I decided to go to Israel, and I lived there for a year.

It was a very positive experience. I studied Hebrew in an Ulpan [intensive language-training school]. I worked at a kibbutz next to the one I had stayed at before. In the beginning I picked pears. Then I worked in the dairy. I was in charge of the baby cows from birth to a few weeks old. We took the babies from the mothers, because there was too much danger of them being hurt. We bottle-fed them. I was the only one working with the calves. It was the closest I'll ever come to being a veterinarian, which was one of my childhood dreams. The dairy workers were considered the hardest-working people on the kibbutz. I liked being with them.

I was in Israel from December of 1972 to after the Yom Kippur War of 1973. The war changed my thinking about my family. The grief of parents whose children died in the war overwhelmed me. I decided I was going back to Pittsburgh.

Droz entered a new stage of life in Pittsburgh in 1974.

When I decided to go back to Pittsburgh, I applied for a job at WQED-TV [Pittsburgh's public television station], and I received a positive response from them. Also, my sister was getting married in New York, and I came home for the wedding. I spent a week in New York with Nancy before her wedding. Then I came home to Pittsburgh and started work for WQED. It was a great opportunity for me. I worked in local programming for a couple of years. I had no experience and I was close to twenty-five. I worked with a great group of people, professionals who had been working there since college, and I learned a lot about television.

Droz left WQED to do independent film work and in 1979 returned to the station. She joined Family Communications, the production company operated by Fred Rogers of "Mister Rogers' Neighborhood." She worked full-time until she had children and, at the time of her interview, was working part-time for the same organization. She talked about her marriage to Dan Droz and her adjustment to instant motherhood.

I have been married seven years. We married in November 1981; I was thirty-one. Dan had been married before, and he has a daughter, Lani. When I met Dan, Lani was five, and he had been divorced for three years. He had always been the custodial parent, and that was something that I saw as both positive and negative. The positive was that it made me like Dan more; the negative was that I did not want to be a mother that fast. Lani started kindergarten at Winchester-Thurston School. Her mother had moved away from Pittsburgh a year earlier.

Marriage was a very complicated thing. I was very scared; there were so many issues for all of us, including Lani. She seemed glad to have somebody to call Mommy. At that time Dan and I both worked full-time, and we took Lani to Winchester. She went to school all day, and after school she went to day-care. I picked her up there. She had been in day-care since she was two years old.

The first year of our marriage was tough. It was no honeymoon. My identity changed completely. I used to spend all my time at the TV station and with the group there. Now I was leaving the office at five every day to pick up Lani, go home, and make dinner. It was a shock to my system. The adjustment was less for Dan, because his life did not change as much. After a while, things did get better. Lani often stayed with Dan's parents. Dan's father was very involved with his grandchildren, and he took them at least one day a week.

Interestingly, what really made our life more balanced was having David. We tried to have a child for about a year and a half before I became pregnant. My pregnancy was fabulous and very easy. I quit smoking and I was really happy. David was born April 24, 1985. My whole family was in town when the baby was born. Lani immediately loved having a brother. I think it really made her feel secure. I was scared at first, but in a very short period of time I felt very confident about being a mother. After four months I went back to work part-time. My job was basically the same but much more flexible. I had a baby-sitter, and David was a very easy baby. Then Ben was born, May 4, 1987. I did not have any trouble getting pregnant, but I had two miscarriages, so I was worried again. I wanted another baby from the minute that I had David.

Droz concluded her interview with comments about her parents, her sister, and her family-oriented hopes for the future.

I see my mom and dad a lot. My father is in a new stage of life since he closed his business, so I hope I'll see him more. My parents are away for the winters, but I see them a lot when they are here; we live around the corner from each other. Before I got married, my mother and I took some trips together, which was fun. I see Nancy about once a week. The children are not very close, because Nancy is so religious and their lives are very different. One of the problems with true believers is that they think that everybody should believe as they do. It is not my nature and never will be to embrace something wholeheartedly, and Nancy's nature has always been the opposite.

Right now my hopes rest a lot with my children. I hope that they will be happy and that they will have a positive influence on the world around them.

The family of Rachel Leah Sacks and Rabbi William Harris Sacks in Burlington, Vermont, ca. 1913. Sylvia Sacks Glosser stands at far left. Photo by Jonas Photography, Pittsburgh.

The children of Sylvia and David Glosser in Johnstown, Pennsylvania, 1932. *Left to right:* Doris, Naomi, Betty, Paul, and Ruth.

Eva Dizenfeld and daughter Belle, Pittsburgh, 1918.

Ruth Zober, Belle Stock, and Jordanna Zober: granddaughter, daughter, and great-granddaughter of Eva Dizenfeld, Chicago, 1988.

FIVE

Eva Rubenstein Dizenfeld, Belle Stock, and Ruth Zober

The overriding theme of the oral histories of Eva Dizenfeld, Belle Stock, and Ruth Zober is one of close intergenerational bonds. Despite wide differences in experience and formal education, each expresses respect and intimacy and strengthened relationships over the years.

Eva Rubenstein Dizenfeld came to Pittsburgh as an immigrant child of eight. She was working in a tobacco sweatshop at nine, and at age sixteen she married Sam Dizenfeld. She worked for fifty years in several mom-and-pop stores with her husband. Yet in her oral history she never mentioned that she worked after her marriage; the single focus in her life was her children.

The Dizenfelds' daughter, Belle, grew up in Ambridge, Pennsylvania. Her oral history tells of the life of a working-class Jewish family in a mill town; of traditional Jewish values; of marriage to Aaron Stock, a research scientist/physician; and of her children, who were the focus of her life and that of her mother.

Ruth Zober is the youngest child and only daughter born to the Stocks. She was active in the causes of the sixties and early seventies. Her oral history focuses on a Jewish identity that was very strong and on a quintessential feminist issue of the last quarter of the twentieth century: women, work, and family.

Eva Rubenstein Dizenfeld,
1893–1986
January 27, 1976, Interview

I was born in Russia in a little town called Pliscov. We had no mother—I was two years old when my mother died. Our stepmother raised us. She was a very nice person. I had two sisters and a brother and myself when my father remarried. Then my stepmother had children. My father, Lazar Rubenstein, left her behind when he came to America, because a child was to be born. He was away only six months before we came here. Then, in this country, my stepmother had three more boys.

My father couldn't see any future for his children in Russia, and he came to the land where there is opportunity for everybody. He went because he heard that America was a wonderful land and he decided that's where he was going to raise his family. There was no schooling there—although most of us didn't have schooling here either, because we came here and went to work right away. I never went to school in Russia, and my brothers didn't either. I guess I wasn't a very smart kid.

In Russia we lived in a little town that was all Jewish. Most houses had straw roofs, but we had a tin roof. We had a very nice house because my father was the president of the shul. My mother's sisters, my mother's brother, and my father and his four sisters and three brothers—we sort of all lived together. We never met any Russian people. We never met anybody but our own family, and do you know what? It was almost the same thing here in America. We all lived together down on the Hill District and never really mingled with others, because my father, as I said, had four sisters and three brothers. Everybody had a big family.

I remember coming to America. We came by train and by boat. We came here in December in 1902. People were very nice to my stepmother. She couldn't talk to people; she would point to the clock or something. We came to Pittsburgh, to Pennsylvania Station. My father thought we would come with the B & O Railroad, so he went to the B & O station. And we walked from Pennsylvania Station. I can see us as clearly as if I'd walk on Murray Avenue [in Squirrel Hill] just now. From the Pennsylvania station she walked with us, with four children and a baby in her arms and a lot of packages, to what was called Tukston Street in the Hill District. She had a piece of paper and she showed that piece of paper to different people on the street. And we came to the house with that address. It wasn't easy! I was eight; I was going to be nine in March. Esther was five, and Rae was three. And it was very cold.

And we came to this house. Well, the woman knew my father went to the B & O station, and when she heard him coming into the alley, she told us to hide. When he came in, he was very much disappointed that we didn't come. He didn't know what happened. And we all came out! Right away, [the woman] gave us all something to eat! My father already had a place for us on Twenty-fourth Street at Fifth Avenue. We lived there for a little while. My father used to go down to Logan Street to do the shopping, and then he would come back and we would have breakfast. Then he would go to work. But it was too far for him to go every morning from Twenty-fourth Street to Thirteenth Street or Eleventh Street or Logan Street, so we moved down to the Lower Hill between Townsend and Fulton. We lived there for a little while, and then we moved to 1609 Webster Avenue.

My father was a carpenter, and already when we came my stepmother brought four children here with her, and my father, my older brother, and my sister came six months before. All my father made was one dollar and a quarter a day, and after a year and a half he was able to buy a house—1609 Webster Avenue. I suppose we moved there in 1903. I lived there six years; then I got married.

My father bought a big, beautiful house because he didn't want to rent with a bunch of kids. He knew he couldn't afford to live in that house, so he rented out the second and third floors, and we lived on the first floor. We had one bathroom, but I don't remember ever taking a bath. My brother told me, "You didn't. You used to go to Center Avenue for five cents to the settlement house, and that's where you would take a bath."

I told you my father was a carpenter. So from the basement he made some rooms. First he rented them out, and then the children started to grow up, so we took the basement also. Then we had the basement three rooms and three rooms on the first floor, and we had a boarder there with all the children, so you ask me about recreation! It was a lot of work in the house.

We were the first of our relatives to come here. After my father bought the house at 1609 Webster, then everybody came to our house. My father first sent for my sister. She came with her husband and with a child. You heard of the big Dr. Rubenstein? He was my sister's child. Then my father's sisters and brothers and their children came, and the children grew up, and they lived around us. A family with no children lived on the second floor, and my sister lived on the third floor and she had three children. She had two rooms and she had two boarders.

Eva Dizenfeld described her first years in the Hill District before she married. The organizations she spoke of were landsmenshaften, *societies of people from the town of Pliscov.*

My stepmother washed, cooked, patched, sewed. She did plenty. She didn't have an automatic washer and drier. She did nothing for fun. She raised a family. She did everything. I never did anything around the house. My father organized the Pliskover [society of people from one Russian town]; he bought the cemetery and built the Miller Street shul, and he made the free-loan organization. That's all. We never heard of B'nai B'rith or Council [service organizations of Jewish women]!

In the house we spoke Yiddish, and we got the *Forward* [Yiddish newspaper]. I never went to Hebrew school. All I went to school was the third grade and all I knew was work. I started to work right away. I worked in a tobacco factory, although I wasn't allowed. You know, there must have been a law then, but my sister was eleven and she worked. So when she went to work, she took me with her. I still don't know what my job was, and I'm going to be eighty-three years old. They called it a "stripper." Tobacco comes in leaves, and you sort of pull the stem out. Then I pressed it on a block, and I made five cents a day. I gave the money to my father.

Then I had to go to school. Everybody went to school, so I went. My sister [who was] eleven years old never went to school. I started at Franklin School, and I only went as far as third grade. That's how smart I was! I must have been thirteen . . . but a depression came then, and I dropped out of school. I went back to the tobacco factory, and I worked till I was not even sixteen. Times were bad. The man didn't need me anymore, so I got married.

Dizenfeld was married at sixteen in 1909.

My husband worked for the railroad. He was a tinner. That's how he started out. My father, on his carpenter's pay, supported nine children— I won't say ten, because my sister was already married. My brother learned to be a plumber; then he left home when he was about seventeen. My sister Mrs. Calig wasn't even sixteen when she got married.

I met Sam Dizenfeld at my sister-in-law's house. He was kind of related through marriage. His brother was married to my brother-in-law's sister. It was sort of a *shidich* [arranged match]. He came because we were all *machatonam* [extended family through marriage]. We didn't have dates. He would come to the house. We used to sit with the family. He was only in this country three years, so he didn't know very much either.

My father said, "Get married," so I got married [laughter]. My husband [paid for] a big wedding. My father didn't have the money. So my husband bought my wedding dress, and he paid for the wedding. No honeymoon. We went to New York a year later.

Dizenfeld spoke about the early years of her marriage and about her hard-working husband. She did not mention that she worked at his side in one little store after another for more than fifty years.

We had two rooms when we got married. We had it fixed up—in fact, we still almost have the same furniture! I didn't know anything about marriage. I knew about periods, because my cousin started to menstruate before me and she told me. I didn't find out about sex. I had five children, and I don't think I know sex yet [laughter]. The same cousin that started to menstruate before me got married before me. She told me that it hurts a little bit, and stuff like that, and that's all. Really, I didn't know anything. All I knew was I was married, and I didn't have a child right away, and I was very much upset. Why didn't I have a child? Then I had a child.

My husband didn't know anything about sex either—I don't think he knows yet! There are a lot of things he didn't understand when the kids were growing up. You know, he came to America because his brother sent for him, and he started to work, and that's all he knew until twenty years ago. In 1955 he had an accident and he stopped work. When he worked for the railroad it was hard. He was a peddler and he worked hard. Then we had a fruit market, and he worked hard. He never knew about—there were a lot of things he doesn't know to this day yet.

After I got married I didn't work. I went back and forth to my father's house. I did my little bit of work, cooked my one meal for my supper, really nothing, and visited my family. As I said, we had a big family, very large family. I sat outside with the elderly people. Really very dull.

What did I expect? Nothing. I didn't know what I wanted. I married a very nice husband. I had a very good life. I called it good because I didn't expect anything. I didn't want; to this day I don't want. I raised a nice family, and that's all I was interested in.

I knew how to keep house, because my sister was a very good house-keeper. What did I cook? I took a piece of meat and put it in a pot with a few beans and a little bit of water, and they told me I had to cook it so much, and put a carrot in, and that's what I cooked. You think I made steaks and made roasts and roasted chickens?

My husband thought he was a big salaried man. He was making twenty-eight cents an hour because he was a mechanic. I knew I bought whatever I needed. I had to go to the butcher every day because every day you go to the butcher and every day you cooked almost the same thing. The butcher was around the corner on Webster Avenue. I knew you couldn't throw money away. We saved a thousand dollars. I don't know how, but we saved it. As I said, I was not a gourmet cook. I didn't go to parties. Nobody ever gave me a penny, but we saved it.

We bought a house on Mercer Street together with my sister and brother-in-law. My sister lived downstairs with four children. I lived on the second floor with one child and had three rooms, and a cousin lived on the third floor with two children, so how many more people did I have to know? How many more do you need then? So did you need a Council or a Sisterhood, and an ORT or Hadassah [service societies of Jewish women] and everything else?

I was only married five years when we started to move around to different places, and I met people because we moved around. I never met any strangers outside the family while I lived in Pittsburgh.

I was married, but I didn't become pregnant. I went to a doctor and he gave me treatments. I knew what he was doing like the man-in-the-moon does, but anyway, I was married May 9, 1909, and my first child was born August 1911. It seemed a very long time. So then after I had a baby—so I was busy with the baby. And the baby only lived fourteen months and died. He had the measles, and then something else set in and he choked. It was very hard, very hard. I had him in the crib and I had a teakettle boiling where I could see him. Anyway, I lost him, and then ten months later Belle was born, in 1913. Belle was born on Cliff Street on the Hill. Then we were living in Ambridge, and in 1917 I had a stillborn baby.

My mother died in childbirth, so every time I was going to have a baby, I was worried. I was afraid. I was scared. I didn't read much, but I heard that there were babies born with maybe a split lip or six fingers. Belle must have been two years old and I was still counting her fingers. I'm telling you, I wasn't a very smart kid [laughter].

I had my fifty-seven-year-old boy (he lives in California) in 1918. Then in 1920 I had my youngest, and I was twenty-seven years old, and I didn't have any more children.

Dizenfeld described an old-world custom carried over to America. She sought the best in medicine for her children but resorted to old-world practices as well.

My boy who is in California was sick when he was a child. He used to have convulsions. I had lost two babies; it seemed like I couldn't raise two children at one time. Now this is what my father did. Mrs. Pittler had seven healthy sons. So my father sold my little boy to Mrs. Pittler because she had a big healthy family and in her healthy family he should grow up and be healthy. My father believed in such *narishkiten* [foolishness]. My father sold my child to the Pittlers for a nickel. It was a superstition; he's supposed to have a long life because of this.

Dizenfeld explained that the family left Pittsburgh because her husband was fired for union activities. They lived for many years in Ambridge, Pennsylvania, a mill town twenty-two miles northwest of Pittsburgh. Moving from one town to another in search of a steady living was a frequent pattern among immigrants.

In 1913 the railroad was on strike, and they didn't take the strikers back and my husband was out of work. With another fellow that was also a striker that worked for the railroad, he opened up a hardware store and tin shop in Charleroi and we moved there. That didn't work out, so we came back to Pittsburgh. Mister [her husband] was out of work again, and that was already 1915. I had a cousin living in Ambridge—I bet we had a hundred cousins. Farber, my cousin, worked in Ambridge, and they needed somebody with citizenship so they could get licensed to peddle. Mister was out of work and Farber said, "Look, we need somebody with citizenship papers, so you come to Ambridge. You don't have to know the trade—we know the trade, all we need is you." So that's how we came to Ambridge in 1915, and we stayed there until 1972, but in between we were in Sharon and we lived in Beaver Falls too. We had produce stores. And we went to Rochester, Pennsylvania, and we opened up a grocery store there. That wasn't a good place, and we went back to Ambridge. That was a lot of years of moving around, but I got to be at home in Ambridge.

I raised my children there. I took good care of my children. I was too careful. I never allowed Belle to jump rope. My kids never rode a bike. I was afraid. Oh, believe me, I took good care of them.

Dizenfeld's heartfelt expression of love for her children and grandchildren was almost eloquent.

They [her children and grandchildren] meant everything in the world to me, everything in the world. When my brother's daughter says to me, "Aunt Eva, you shouldn't do" this or that, "you raised your family; let them raise theirs," I said, "What would you do if your kids were in need? Would you take them in? Would you help?" She said, "Yes, my kids I would, but not my great-grandchildren." I said, "My great-grandchildren mean to me as much as my children did, because Belle's children are my children, and if they are Belle's children's children, they are my children." I don't feel any different towards them, only that I know more today than I knew then. But I took good care of my children. They meant the world and all to me.

I raised those children. My husband didn't do anything at home. He worked. He was the provider. If we didn't agree, we had a fight [laughter]! Really, he's not much of a critic. He's a very nice man, and he left it all to me. It was my responsibility. All the responsibility he had was to work, and he worked mighty hard, mighty hard.

When Belle came from work—she was a secretary, and she worked at a school and she came home for lunch—she would say that Mamie or Susie had such a beautiful blouse on today. She went back to work. I didn't wash the dishes or anything. I went up Merchant Street. Everything was together, the butcher, the baker, the post office, the drugstore—and I got a piece of material maybe for fifty cents, and when Belle came back, already I had a blouse put together. I learned to sew in the Hill District. I had a good neighbor when I was first married. She showed me.

Dizenfeld expressed feelings of inadequacy many times in her oral history. She was superstitious and was afraid to hope for too much for her children.

I didn't know anything about getting married. Are you going to ask me did I know to tell Belle? I didn't. She read books and she had girlfriends who read books. And she never asked questions.

I was a dumb kid. Yet I raised a beautiful family. Honest, I did. I never wanted anything special for my kids. Maybe I was afraid. I didn't know who Belle was going to marry. I just never wanted her to work hard when she was young, for fear she would have to work hard when she was married. Maybe she would marry a butcher or a grocery man. I never built air castles.

For my sons, I didn't think anything special. They got their education and . . . we thought the older one would be a lawyer. So war broke out, he went into the army, he met this beautiful girl, he married her, and that was the end of the law.

The relationship with her daughter was always very close. Dizenfeld thought only of her children in good times and bad.

We didn't have serious problems. My children never gave me that much trouble. I sat up at night till Belle would come home and had her tell me all the things she did and where she went. I told a lot of people: if I was to live life over again, I'd want it the same.

There was only one bad time. When World War II started, when my son had to go in the army, when my son-in-law went into the army, when my other boy went into the army, and when my daughter had to come and live with me and raise a child, and when her husband left her she was pregnant, and she had a baby when she was with us—those were the hard years.

Belle went with her husband for two years; then three years he was overseas. She took David—he was fourteen months old then—to Texas and came home from there when [her husband] went overseas. She came back home with one child. Naturally, I was waiting already to see her, and when she started up the steps, she said—this is the first thing she said to me—"Ma, I'm going to have a baby." "*Oy vey is mir,*" I said; "a war is going on and you are going to have a baby?" It hit me so hard. After I slept on it, the next morning I thought, "That's the way it had to be."

And now that baby is a doctor. That baby saved our lives. We were so busy with him; we were so busy. Belle wrote to her husband every evening, every evening. Maybe two o'clock in the morning, Mister would stand in the window watching while we went up to the corner to mail the letter. We were so busy with the two children.

I worried about all the boys. So before my son—the one who was sick, that my father sold to the Pittlers—went to the army, I said, "You have to go see your other mother." And I made him go—our whole family went—to Mrs. Pittler to ask for her blessing. So when we got near Dinwiddie Street near Fifth Avenue High School, there were five or seven stars in the window. I was ashamed. I said, "How can we go in?" We all decided, all five of us—Mister, myself, and the three children—that we had to go in. The stars meant she had that many children in the war. I was afraid I was bothering her, but she said, "Eva, Eva, come in. You have to believe in God."

And they all came back well. We raised Belle's little boy until he was almost three. When Aaron [Aaron Stock, Belle's husband] came back, they moved downstairs in our house. Aaron didn't want to commute. He was a doctor and he worked at Presbyterian Hospital. He bought a little piece of land in Stanton Heights in East End. They built a little house there.

I used to come twice a week. I came to help her a little bit and to kill time. It was very, very lonesome after she moved out. I kind of wanted to help raise them. Then, after Aaron came back from the war, Belle had another child. Not a war baby. The war baby was her doctor. . . . She had Ruthie after the war.

I like music, and I understand a little bit music, and I love it. Before Aaron died, I used to sing even to myself. When I would scrub the floor I would sing. They would say, "Eva is singing already." I wasn't a singer, but I'd sing. But when they came to Ambridge and told me that Aaron died—and here I was supposed to come into Pittsburgh in the morning because Belle's children were coming in from Cincinnati and . . . and from Michigan. I did the cooking and I was going to bring it in. (Belle isn't great for cooking; she would rather work.) And here they came. I was in the bathtub when they came to tell me that Aaron dropped dead. I screamed, and since then my voice has never been the same and I have never been the same person, because Belle, my children, were my whole life.

Dizenfeld cared about her children to the exclusion of almost everything else. The only anti-Semitic incidents that she recalled concerned two of her grandchildren.

I loved Ambridge. I was only twenty-two when I went there, and I was seventy-eight when we moved back to Pittsburgh. I lived in one house forty-two years. I got to love Ambridge. I never knew gentile people before I lived in Ambridge, and only a couple of times did I have a bad experience with gentiles.

It happened when Belle lived with us and Aaron was in the service. We lived downtown, and most of the Jewish people had already moved up on the hill. A little girl came outside, and David was standing on this side of the fence and the little girl on the other side. She said to him, "I'm not allowed to play with you anymore." He said, "Why?" and she said, "Because you killed Jesus." That was all that David had to hear. He was three years old, and he came running upstairs, and he said, "My father is a doctor, and he is helping, and she tells me that the Jews killed Jesus," and he screamed and he cried. Well, if she had cut my throat, I would not have felt it that bad. I ran down and said, "What did you tell David?" "Nothing, nothing," she said. Her parents apologized. I was going to go to the priest, but I cooled down. I didn't go.

OK. Then came Ruthie, a few years later. Ruthie was playing over the same fence, and Ruthie was crying: "Allison said she's not allowed to play with me because I'm a Jew." Wow! Down again I went. I was ready to go to the priest again. I didn't go. The first little girl was one sister's child; the second was the other sister's child. Now, they call me on the telephone and they come to visit.

In 1971 the Dizenfelds moved from Ambridge to a modest apartment in Squirrel Hill. Being closer to Belle, aging, and health problems motivated the move. The move was very difficult.

We came to Pittsburgh to Squirrel Hill when I was seventy-eight years old. It was fifteen years too late. We came here because of Belle, and we have to live here in these three rooms. This was the best thing we could get when we came here, and I thought, "When the lease runs out, we'll move." We are going to sign the lease again; we are getting too old to move. I think this is going to be the end of my story.

At eighty-three, Dizenfeld was still helping her daughter and her grandchildren. She recorded her oral history during a period of stress in the family. Dizenfeld's musician-grandson was unemployed; he, his wife, and their three children were living at his mother's house. Dizenfeld expressed a confidence in her grandson that proved to be well founded: David Stock has earned international renown as a composer and conductor of contemporary music.

I go a little bit to the Anathan House [center for senior citizens] and to the Pliskover Ladies [Society]. I'm happy when I'm busy, but now I'm too busy. Belle teaches English to the Russian immigrants. Belle's son, David, and his wife and three children all live at Belle's house. He writes music. He's a composer. He has been out of work because his university had some trouble. They live in her little house with three children. I know he will do well. He's an all-around man. He is a great musician. So now Ruthie came back with a child, so you can imagine what's going on at Belle's house!

Dizenfeld spoke of her unhappiness at growing old away from the town that was home for so many years.

Belle thinks I should be happy here. She tells me, "Ma, you should be ashamed to say you're not satisfied here. There are so many places to go here, and it doesn't cost money everyplace." But we can't go. Mister is lying in bed sick right now. So if he's not so sick, I'm sick. Yesterday I was sick. We get free transportation. A minibus picks us up, but we just can't go.

I was never as unhappy as I am since we live here. We don't go anyplace; nobody knows us. The family died out. I'm glad that at my age, not only can I take care of myself and my husband—he's ninety now— but I can still help take care of my daughter and my daughter's children. Sometimes I'm happy, but when I'm tired, I'm not happy, and then I feel like a stranger here. In Ambridge, everybody knew us. Belle said, "Ma, nobody was left there." We were the oldest in Ambridge already. There were all young people there. I don't know. I guess there are some things I don't know the answer myself.

Considering her very traditional upbringing, Dizenfeld expressed a strong degree of feminist commitment. Her total devotion to her children and grandchildren meant acceptance of their chosen life-styles. Her definition of a "better life" as one richer in Jewish knowledge and Jewish culture was echoed in several of the oral histories.

I think both a career and marriage are important. To be a maiden girl, I don't approve of it. I believe in careers for women. Today any woman that has a little bit of intelligence isn't going to stay home and wait for her neighbor to come in and have a cup of coffee. She's going to be out doing something that is interesting. So I believe a woman can do more than wash and scrub and take care of children and a husband. Do you know what? Today it is almost compulsory for a woman to work, because who can make a living today with one person? I've seen by my children.

They [women] have to finish their educations. A cousin of mine thinks Ruthie is doing the wrong thing, living here in Pittsburgh while she finishes her master's. Now Ruthie is my own grandchild. How can I be against it when my grandchild is doing it? Ruthie is married, has a child, left her husband in Boston, and she goes to school here. If it was some-body else's child, I'd say it wasn't necessary. She's married; she has a husband; she has a child. Let her take care of her child and forget about her career. Now, I won't say that, because my grandchild is doing it.

I think women should go to the top if they are capable. I don't care if she's Italian or Jewish or what. I think a woman president could be even better than a man. I think a woman can figure things out to be able to hold a position like that.

I hope my granddaughter has a life like her mother did up until she lost her steady. They were never rich. You know, Belle was never rich, but there wasn't anything they missed. She never asked for beautiful clothes, but they had the best life anybody could have. In the summer-time, Aaron would take a month off and they would travel all over the world. Belle was in Paris, in Israel, in England. When I see on television somebody wins a trip to Madrid or Rome—*oy*, what a happy feeling! Well, Belle had all that until . . .

Belle's life was richer than mine. Because her kids all know Hebrew. Her boys can go up and daven [chant the traditional Torah reading]. Belle's life was good, but her children's lives are richer in *Yiddishkeit* [Jewish learning]. Ruthie is richer than Belle because Belle doesn't read Hebrew and her daughter reads and talks Hebrew very, very fluently. Ruthie has all the privileges in the world. With education, with seeing the world . . . there isn't anything you can talk to them about that they wouldn't know how to answer. They are rich in everything. Not money.

Now I live for my children. When things go good with them, that's when I'm happy.

Sam Dizenfeld died April 13, 1977. And Eva Dizenfeld did sing again. In 1983 she was heard on National Public Radio in "The Golden Cradle," a series of programs on immigrant women. She sang Yiddish folk songs, and her voice was warm and joyous. Eva Dizenfeld died November 27, 1986, at age ninety-three.

Belle Stock,

b. 1913

February 27, 1976, and June 26, 1989, Interviews

I was born in Pittsburgh in 1913. My mother and father and two brothers—five and seven years younger—and myself lived at home. We were a very close-knit family. My mother had a stepmother and a father, and two sisters and a brother. They all lived in Pittsburgh, and we lived outside in a small town down in the valley. When I was still very small, my grandfather moved out of the Hill District. He bought a big house on Heths Street in East End, and once he moved, all the relatives moved out of the Hill to East End within a few blocks of each other. My aunt and her married daughter and family still live in my grandfather's house on Heths Street. We kept moving quite a bit, but we always came to Pittsburgh to my grandfather's house on Sundays. The family all used to gather on my grandfather's porch, and everybody talked. The only way you could be heard was to talk loud, so everybody talked loud, but my grandfather talked the loudest! Jewish holidays we spent with the immediate family. We went to shul on Rosh Hashanah, Yom Kippur. Maybe Passover we used to spend with different parts of the family, but other holidays we spent by ourselves.

Our little family lived in a lot of little towns. In Rochester my father had a little general store. We all helped around it. The store was in the front, and the kitchen was in the back, and the sleeping quarters were upstairs. The store was open long hours. We didn't do much together, but we were together quite a bit, as you can readily understand. That is how we spent our childhood. We came home from school and my mother left the front of the store and came back and served us lunch.

My father was a great fixer. When he wasn't working, he did a lot of fixing. He was handy with his hands. From Rochester we moved to Beaver Falls. When we got to that house, it didn't have a bathroom inside. It had a toilet but not a full bathroom. He put the bathroom in by himself.

Belle Stock talked about her mother's desire to make her childhood as carefree as possible.

My mother sewed. When we were real little, she read to us. I was the oldest. My mother had a very, very firm belief that although I was the oldest and I was a girl, I did not have to be responsible for my brothers. I could take them if I wanted to, but I didn't have to. She never imposed them on me. I could be the boss, but I was never allowed to hit. I did not have great responsibilities. I was a child, and that was just how it was.

My mother usually made the decisions. My father is a very quiet, sort of unobtrusive man. My mother is very wonderful but a little stronger willed than my father. He was perfectly satisfied that she took charge.

In the store we waited on customers and we emptied boxes. We did all the things that children could do to be helpful. I think we enjoyed it. We felt that it was our job, and we did it. We sold tobacco, butter, eggs, cheese. We didn't have meat or canned goods.

We lived in many places. When I was very small we moved to Ambridge; from Ambridge to Rochester; then to Beaver Falls; and then we moved back to Ambridge. We always lived in small towns. The last time we came back to Ambridge I was in the eighth grade. I suppose I was thirteen. I didn't want to move, so I finished that year of school in Beaver Falls. Every morning I took the train to Beaver Falls and came back every evening. In Ambridge we lived in a very middle class, ordinary kind of neighborhood. It was a small town and there weren't that many different kinds of neighborhoods. The more affluent people who were higher up in the steel mills lived outside of town. They lived up on the hill. We had very little slum area, unless I wasn't aware of it. Ambridge is a very mixed ethnic town. I played with the kids that I went to school with—Poles, Slavs, Italians. There weren't many Jewish people in town, but the Jewish people that were there [and were] my age, I played with them. My mother's sister and brother-in-law and their six children lived next door to us in Ambridge for a long time, so we didn't really need anybody else.

Stock developed a sense of Jewish identity when she was very young. In the small towns of western Pennsylvania, Jewish organizations provided social life and charitable activities.

My mother kept a kosher home, and we observed the Sabbath. We observed the holidays. It was just like what anybody would expect a Jewish household to be like. We had a congregation in Ambridge, but we didn't have a synagogue or a rabbi. When somebody had a *yahrzeit* [memorial anniversary of a deceased relative], they got a *minyan* [ten men, a quorum for prayer] together, and one of the people led the service. On High Holidays they either got a student from the rabbinical school or a rabbi from some other place. That was the only time that we went to services. There was a Sunday school run by the Southern District of Pennsylvania under the auspices of the Council of Jewish Women. I belonged to the Junior Council. My mother belonged to Sisterhood and was very active in the Council of Jewish Women. Everybody was; it was a small town and everybody had to be. By the time I was sixteen, I was teaching Sunday school in Ambridge. We had a Council of Jewish Women Junior, and I belonged to that.

I used to go to church with my Catholic friends. I had a lot of friends that were very, very different than we were. I always liked being Jewish. I knew what I was and I knew what it was all about. I was very, very comfortable.

English was the language most of the time, except my mother and father spoke Yiddish. When we went to Pittsburgh, they spoke only Yiddish, because my grandmother didn't speak English at all, but she understood. So we spoke English to her, and she spoke Yiddish to us. We were brought up in a Yiddish atmosphere. I never spoke it, but I can if I'm pressed to do it. I understand it perfectly.

I was always very close to my mother. She was always there when we needed her. She was very understanding. As I got older, I looked back and realized that she was much beyond her generation. She had great understanding. No matter what happened, I could always go to my mother. I don't think my parents had any expectations of me. To my mother, I was always special and she expected me to continue to be that way.

Stock remembered her first menstrual period in detail.

I started to menstruate when I was very young; I wasn't eleven yet. I really can't remember how I learned about menstruation—probably my mother told me. My mother was the kind of person that if you asked a question, if she could answer it she'd give an answer. She never went into great depth, but I'm sure that's how I learned about it. It just wasn't an open book as it is now, and I don't think we were that much interested. It was a bad experience. We were coming from Beaver Falls to visit my aunt in Ambridge. We saw an accident. We saw two little children on a sled come down off a hill into an oncoming car. We heard the car hit them, and we knew right away that they were dead. The bus that we were on kept moving. We weren't in Ambridge yet when I started to flow. As I got older and looked back, I always had the feeling that this might have brought it on.

I menstruated very, very hard. Every single month they carried me home from school or work. My mother took me to the doctor, and the doctor would always tell my mother and me, "When she has her first baby, it will be better." I always thought, "Well, it can't be worse." They wouldn't do anything in those days to help a young girl. They wouldn't touch you.

When a family's means were limited, males were favored for education. In Jewish families, sisters often worked in order to help send brothers to college.

In the depression, times were bad. We were fortunate that in Ambridge my father was in the fruit business, so we were never really hungry, and Ambridge was not hit as hard as a lot of other towns. I had an opportunity to go to school. I had been given a scholarship and a job offer—a chance to wait on tables at Indiana State Teacher's College, now Indiana State University. I could have handled it, but I was offered a job paying sixty dollars a month and I was the only one in the graduating class who got a job. It was my choice. I felt that the sixty dollars a month was needed at home.

I got a job. I helped at home. I know I should have gone to school. But in the back of my mind was the thought, "If I stay home, my brother will be able to go to school." I was afraid that if I went, he wouldn't be able to go. That may sound farfetched to the next generation, but that's how it was. Now that my friends are retiring from teaching and they are making such good salaries and have good retirement programs, my mother says to me, "Why didn't you do it?" But at the time, that's how I felt I should do it. I knew he'd need money for college.

I knew my husband from the time we were very young. Even at sixteen already, I was hoping that he'd be my husband. I didn't have too much hope, but I was still hoping. We went to dances, always connected with the Council of Jewish Women. They were at Slovak Hall or one of the other halls in town. Again, the interesting thing that my kids can't understand when I tell them is that the boys went with their mothers. My future husband—his mother was very active too in the Council—went with his mother, and he did the hatchecking in the cloakroom. And I went with my mother, and we helped with the refreshments or whatever else had to be done. All the girls hung around the cloakroom and thought, "Why doesn't everybody hurry up and get their coats checked so that the boys can ask us to dance?"

Stock described her courtship and marriage. School systems (and many businesses) did not employ married women in the 1930s.

After I graduated, I went to work as a secretary in the public high school in Ambridge. One night a week I went into Pittsburgh to a class. I had to walk almost a mile from work, and I got the train not too much later. My mother always had dinner on the table for me. I grabbed a bite to eat and got on the train. At that point I was going to the "Y" in Sewickley also one day a week. My husband was in medical school then, and I took some courses at Carnegie Tech [now Carnegie-Mellon]. Our great date was that I would finish class and he would wait for me. We would take the streetcar to the train station, and he waited with me until I got on board my train. This was our date!

He was only two years older than I. He was quite a brilliant person, and he was four years ahead of me at school. He was in college when I was in high school. As I said before, we knew each other as kids. I think his family came to Ambridge a year after we did. I knew him all those years. We were in Sunday school at the same time, but not in the same grade. I don't think he was aware of girls then. Times were different. Nobody had any money. We went to the Nixon Theater together. I bought my ticket and he bought his ticket. He came down and met me. We sat together. He went back to the hospital and I went home. That's just how it was. I was twenty-three when we got married; he was twenty-five. His father was an engineer and came from Boston for a job with Bethlehem Steel in Leetsdale, the next town. I don't think his parents were very happy about his marrying me. He was a brilliant doctor. He graduated medical school at twenty-two. His father was an engineer and my father was a huckster.

We married after he finished his internship and residency. He had a job in the laboratory at Children's Hospital. His salary was very, very low when we got married, but we made do. Our own conditions were very good, because we went home every weekend and my father filled the fruit basket. We never had any real problems then.

I had to give up my job; the school system didn't permit married women to work for them. Then we moved into Pittsburgh. We lived in Squirrel Hill on Hobart Street for five years and then moved to Covode Street, also in Squirrel Hill. I had a wonderful first year of marriage. I went to the library when I pleased, and I did all the things I wasn't able to do when I was working. If we went to a movie or theater, he was never interrupted like a doctor in private practice. Weekends we always came home to visit his parents and my parents in Ambridge. During the week I took advantage of all the things that were available in Pittsburgh. We went to a lot of movies.

I always wanted a big family. My oldest son was born in 1939, and we wanted him very, very much. My pregnancy was a good one, but I had a long, hard childbirth. It was a difficult forceps birth. My mother said I had so much medication that when she got off the elevator, she followed the smell of the medicine and it led her to my room. You were heavily sedated in those days. After I came to, I was thrilled. Except for the difference in times, I think I raised my children pretty much as I was raised.

My husband was in the army for five years—two years in this country and three years overseas. We went to Alexandria, Virginia, in the army.

Then we went to Texas. We wanted another child, and I became pregnant in Texas. My husband left in November. I came home to Mother and Father, and the baby was born in February. He was two and a half when Aaron came back. Then we had a third boy, and Ruthie was born in 1949.

My husband was exactly what I expected him to be. I knew that he was never going to go out and make a whole lot of money, because he wasn't interested in private practice. That turned out to be exactly correct. I knew he was going to be busy with his bugs [laboratory research], and that was correct. I think I knew pretty much what it was going to be, and it just turned out that was how it was. We spent a lot of time together. We had a lot of friends, but we never bothered to go with a lot of people. If we wanted to go to a movie, we just went.

He was not a great helper in the house. When he came home in the evening, then the children were his responsibility. He'd take them for a walk or something like that. When we went anywhere, we all had to go. If we were going to take the kids to the zoo, I would say, "Take them. Give me this opportunity in the house to get some housework done." He'd say, "No, no, no. You have to go too." So we all had to traipse off, which was wonderful—except the work didn't get done that I would have liked done.

I was never much of a disciplinarian. I didn't follow any rules. We look back at it now when we're all together, and [the children] say, "Mom, when you said no we just didn't challenge it, because we knew you meant no." My husband went right along with it. It was very rarely that we disagreed on how the children should be raised. We were in accord, and I think that's what makes a good marriage. We always made decisions together. I have to be a little slanted—I mean, I always made the final decision, but we made it together.

I think with Ruthie growing up, I did pretty much what my mother did with me. I never made a special point of telling any of them. If they asked a question, I gave them an answer, and I think Ruthie probably learned that way. If she asked, I told her. She was young when she started to menstruate, but not as young as I was. Then they grew up and just naturally started to leave home.

When my husband came back from the army, we came to Pittsburgh, to Stanton Heights. We had a good family life together. We were all in France for a year. My husband was on sabbatical, and he went to the Pasteur Institute in Paris, and we all went with him. That was 1960—David was twenty-one already. We all went, and it was a wonderful experience. They have all been back, and when they go back they have friends there and it's a continuation.

Stock talked about her husband's death, financial difficulties, and the making of a temporary home for her adult children and her grandchildren.

My husband died in 1967. I started to work part-time in the School of Public Health at the University of Pittsburgh when Ruthie was in high school. Then after my husband died, I went back to working full-time. I'm a secretary in the Graduate School of Public and International Affairs.

My children are in and out; they keep trickling back home. Last year I had two sons and their families in London, I had a daughter in Israel, and I had a son here. Four children, and not one knowing whether they were going to have a job next year. The only one that I really wasn't concerned about was the ophthalmologist—the middle son. My youngest son was finishing his Ph.D., and I was helping him get it typed and footnoted. My son-in-law sent his master's thesis from Israel, and I was finishing that off. It was a wild and woolly year. We came through that all right.

Now they are more than trickling back! David and his whole family and Ruthie and her baby (she's expecting another) are all here. She came from Boston to finish her master's degree at Pitt. I take care of the baby the days she goes to school. If I can give my son and his family a hand, I do. I left my job the last day in July because I'm so busy with everybody here. The month of August I went twice with my daughter and son-in-law to Boston to help them find a place. Then we went to New York to meet my son and daughter-in-law and their three kids who were in London all last year.

Stock felt responsible for her children and her parents. She appreciated her children's work and gave them her complete support.

Right now I have more responsibilities than I ever had all at once. When I face problems, I talk out loud with myself, and I usually work it out. That way I have no regret about worrying the others, my mother, especially. Last week was not a good week. They took my father to the hospital with a lung infection. I stayed with my mother almost every night, because she had never been by herself. My daughter took him home this morning. She said he looked pretty good, but he lost a lot of weight.

I would like to see my children settled, knowing at least which direction they are going. I feel that I am halfway there. My middle son is now in practice. The youngest one, who came out with his Ph.D., got a wonderful job teaching at San Diego State. He loves it. And my daughter is going to finish her master's in April, and she can go back to her husband. They will struggle through and be all right.

I am hoping that what my oldest son is trying to accomplish, he does, because it will be good, not only for him, but it is really a fantastic and very exciting project. He's trying to bring new, contemporary music to the fore. He is trying to get a group together so people have an opportunity to really hear it, and I think, in a way, to train the younger people to listen to it. It's been a struggle. It's exciting, but it's hard on the nerves.

Stock compared her own life-style with that of her daughter and her mother.

I don't think the modern woman's life is more satisfying than mine was. Mine may not have been liberated according to your standards, but it sure was liberated according to mine. I didn't have to go out to work because everybody else went. In my time, I was liberated. Once my children went away from the house or when they went back to school in the afternoon, if I wanted to walk out with them and walk back before they got in—that was my business. I had to account to no one. My husband felt that was absolutely OK.

I think life is harder for young women. I know women should have careers, but I think when children are young, the mothers miss too much if they're out all day working. I'm not even worried about how they take care of the children—they can work that out. I think they are missing a part of their life that they should not miss. They should be able to enjoy the little ones. Our life wasn't that easy. Believe me, we had problems. You know, we had many problems. Every day wasn't Sunday.

Today a woman has to go out and make a living, and I didn't have to. My problem was (and still is) to make stretch what came in. That was a problem because my husband was in a field [in which] there was a lot of money to be made and he didn't make it. We had to do things that people who were making a lot of money did. So it was always a very fine balance. We were always figuring how we were going to handle this and we handled it. And I'm still figuring. I worked full-time for seven or eight years. My husband's social security was based on a salary of forty-seven hundred dollars a year, and when inflation came, I was really stuck. It's hard to believe what professors were paid! I would have liked to have more money to work with. I would have liked to have had more help in the house. I would have liked to have a lot of things, but I got along without them.

When my mother came to visit, she used to give me a great big hand. She helped me with many things, and she would say, "Now, the big difference between your life and mine is that when my children went to bed, I could get myself cleaned up and go to bed too or do the work during the evening that I couldn't get done during the day." She said, "When your day is done, you have to get dressed very presentable and go out and start another day." She always felt that my life was harder than hers, although she worked harder. She meant because I went to a lot of meetings and I went out a lot. I was always doing something, and she felt this was a great pressure. I enjoyed it, and it was pressure. She worked harder physically, but she didn't work as hard mentally—I mean, with as many pressures.

Mine was a very, very busy household. I was the hub and I still am, and I see that everybody hears from everybody. And that's how it was. I love being able to help the kids. I teach English to a class of Russian immigrants, and I love the Russian class. I belonged to the Hadassah and the B'nai B'rith. My husband was not a meeting goer, so I went to PTA and to Boy Scouts and to Girl Scouts and the music meetings—my children are all musical. For the future I would like to stay well, continue to work a little bit, travel because I enjoy the world. Since my children are spread from coast to coast, I can do a lot of visiting. These are the bonus years, if I stay well.

June 26, 1989, Interview

I think back on that time when they were all here in the house at the same time. That was the ultimate. It was really tough. I couldn't handle work. They were all there, and none of us had any money. If we got through that we can get through anything.

Stock's relationship with her mother was always close, and after her father's death, an unusual pattern developed.

My mother and I were very, very good friends. I enjoyed her company. After my father died, for seven years I was there every single day. I ate there. I slept there. I'd go home and clean up my house and come back. I used to come and stay. There wasn't any reason why I shouldn't. I knew that my mother didn't like to be alone. I think originally I thought I'd go over for a week, and I stayed for seven and a half years. She'd make dinner for me. I'd go home to wash my clothes.

Stock's concerns continued to focus on her children.

I have four children and eleven grandchildren. They live in Pittsburgh, Chicago, and San Diego. The oldest grandchild is twenty-five; the youngest is almost a year. Right now I'm staying with my granddaughter, while her parents are away.

In 1989, Belle Stock worked part-time, continued her volunteer work, and swam regularly at the Jewish Community Center in Squirrel Hill.

Ruth Zober,

b. 1949

February 13, 1976, and June 27, 1989, Interviews

I was born in 1949 when we lived in Stanton Heights, and I remember a lot of things: playing with my brother, going to school, playing with a cousin the same age who lived across the alley. I remember visiting my grandparents in Ambridge when I was very small. I was closest with my parents and my three brothers—all older—and my grandparents. Even when I was very small, we did a lot of traveling, and when I was older we camped across the country a couple of times. As my brothers got a little older, I remember going to concerts with them.

Birthdays were special, and when one of my brothers graduated or accomplished something, we had a celebration. On Saturday mornings we always went to the library. Then we went to the old Station Street and had hot dogs. Sundays, my youngest brother and I went to Sunday school together. Then we had our little rituals for Saturdays and Sundays. We were picked up from Sunday school and whoever was in the age-group at that time would go with my grandfather to buy magazines. We used to walk in the afternoons, sometimes with my grandfather. My father's parents used to come from Ambridge every Saturday. My mother's parents also came very frequently, and we went there quite a bit.

My father was associate professor of microbiology at Pitt [University of Pittsburgh Medical School] for a living. At home he listened to records a lot. He was very musically inclined. He was an avid reader—he used to read two or three books a day. He belonged to a lot of medical groups.

My mother read, knitted, cleaned the house. She was very active in PTA and things like that. She went to a lot of meetings of that type— B'nai B'rith, Hadassah. She went out to meetings, but at home she was either knitting or sewing or reading or cleaning. When I was in high school, she worked part-time outside the house.

Zober was always aware of relationships with non-Jews and with other Jewish people.

We lived in the same house that I'm staying in right now while I finish my master's degree. There were a lot of kids around our age or a little bit older. I have a cousin who is three months older than I, and we were very close friends. We did a lot of playing together. We walked to school together. We went to Sunnyside, then later to Morningside, and later to Peabody High. There were a lot of children, and we were a pretty tight-knit group. On our street and the next street over lived either Jews or Catholics. Now we didn't have as much contact with the Catholic kids as we got older, because they started going to Catholic school. They used to play Holy Communion and things like that. I remember when they started school, they stopped talking to me because one of the nuns told them that they shouldn't associate with Jews because Jews killed Jesus. I remember that being an upsetting experience which I didn't under-stand. In high school it was a little different. I went to Peabody, which is pretty mixed ethnically. I had a group of friends—Jewish, non-Jewish, black, white: there were a few of each of us.

We all went to Hebrew school and Sunday school. I was bat mitzvah [ceremony initiating a girl into the adult religious community, tradition-ally at age thirteen], and my brothers were all bar mitzvah [similar for boys]. We had candles on Friday night. On the High Holidays we all went to services together. On Kol Nidre night, Yom Kippur Eve, we would all ride to the synagogue, B'nai Israel. My father wasn't as religious as we were at the time. We would all walk back [observant Jews do not ride on High Holidays or Sabbath], and he would bring the car back. Very often, we would go to my grandparents'. I remember the seders. Every Pass-over we had a seder either at my grandfather's or at our house, with all the traditional kinds of things going on behind that.

At home everybody spoke English. My mother spoke Yiddish with my grandparents, especially my maternal grandfather. He is ninety now. He has been here since [he was] twenty, so that's seventy years, but he still speaks Yiddish better than English. When my mother and grandmother didn't want us to know what they were talking about, they spoke in Yiddish.

From the time she was a teenager, Zober participated in Jewish organizations as member and volunteer. She recalled experiences that heightened her awareness of being Jewish.

I was in Brownies, then Girl Scouts, for many years. I was affiliated with the IKS [Irene Kaufmann Settlement had a branch in East End for about fifteen years]. At home I was expected to practice. I played the flute. I was expected to do my homework. I used to set the table. That was my official job, and I helped a little to clear the table. We were supposed to make our beds, but I don't remember doing that too often. I really didn't have a lot of responsibilities in the house until we got older. My parents took care of decisions. I think my mother had a lot of influence on decisions.

When I was eleven, my family and I went to live in Paris, France, for a year. We went because my father was doing some research there. Then I went to a French public school. There I found a big difference, because the children had never really known what a Jewish person was or seen a Jew before. As it turned out, there were other Jewish kids in my class— they just never mentioned the fact that they were Jews. The girl who became my best friend happened to be Jewish. One girl in the class said to me once, "That's funny. When you told me you were Jewish, I thought that was very funny because you don't have horns." It didn't bother me, because I was well accepted as a person after the initial "Oh, you're Jewish. What does that mean?"

In Peabody High School I was part of a large group of friends. We went together more or less as a herd—girls and boys. We did a lot together after school. I had a couple of girlfriends that I was very close to. I was in Jewish organizations—Young Judea, United Synagogue Youth, and for a while in B'nai B'rith Girls. I did a lot of volunteer work. I worked with the School for the Blind. I read for them. I used to do a lot of entertaining for groups like the Home for the Aged and things like that. I was a good student, pretty intelligent, pretty serious and cheerful.

Zober, like her mother, did not remember specific sex education but recalled her first menstrual experience clearly.

I don't remember how I learned about women's things. I guess through friends. It was a big event when I got my first period. The first day I got my period was the first day of seventh grade. We went to a new school. We went to Morningside, and we had been in France the year before. Everything was very new, and here was something very new on top of it. I already must have known about it because I knew what it was when I saw it. I remember my mother had a little package all made up. It had pads and pins and things like that, and a little booklet that she had been saving, thinking that when the time came she would give it to me. I think I remember my mother explaining to me before. I know I talked about it with friends. I had one friend who started menstruating at the age of eleven, so we knew about it from her. For her, it was a terrible experience because we were still in elementary school. All the kids knew she had something secret in her locker. I don't remember who exactly was the first person to tell me about it.

It's funny, because I think of myself and all of my friends as very enlightened, but I don't really know how I found out about sex to begin with. My nephew was born when I was fifteen, and I knew by then. I don't remember exactly when I learned about babies, but it was when I was in elementary school. I heard a lot about childbirth. I was around my sister-in-law when she was pregnant. I had some vague notions of what it was all about. I thought it was a very difficult thing to go through. We didn't think about childbirth so much at that point—about the actual phenomenon of childbirth.

We were more concerned about having boyfriends at that age than about getting married to them. But I think we all felt that we would get married someday and have a family and have a house. We had a pretty stereotyped picture of what it was all about.

Zober remembered her early ambitions. She accepted traditional gender distinctions; her father discouraged a career in medicine. She participated in political causes.

My parents influenced me a lot. I think a lot of what I am and what I believe in is because of their help—pushing or not pushing and doing the right thing or the wrong thing. I think my entire family had a lot of influence. My mother expected me to be a nice girl—I don't think she had any specific expectations. She never said what she expected any of us to be. My father told me not to be a doctor. He said it didn't go with my personality. I think he was right. Whatever I wanted to be, they went along with, unless it was something outrageous.

When I was sixteen, I thought I would be a simultaneous translator. I guess I expected to travel a lot. And I expected to go to college and eventually get married. I wanted to be like Joan Baez, a great and famous folk singer. I thought she had the same principles as I did; I liked a lot of the singing and the peace movement, the liberation and equality. I related to those kinds of feelings, and a lot of my friends did too. I liked to sing and play the guitar with friends. I still play, but poorly. I read a lot. I recall that I liked Kurt Vonnegut a lot, and I still like him.

During Vietnam, my friends and I were very antiwar. Of course, we watched on television. We marched in all kinds of protest marches. We were all members of Another Mother for Peace and organizations like that. Very antiwar. In college I did a lot of marching and petitioning to get out of Vietnam. I went to the University of Michigan. We went to Washington a couple of times. Every time there was a march, we went on the march.

I think that John F. Kennedy, for my particular generation, for my particular group of friends around my age, was a great hero. I remember his death very well. And now it is very disappointing. I was also going to school when everybody was beginning to question the whole American ideal. I think this was very complicated for most of us. I think Americans have had too high an expectation of what their government is. A lot of it was trained and rammed into us about democracy when we were children, and we would still like to believe that we are somehow purer than the rest of the world.

In college, Zober worked in both paid and volunteer jobs. Her father's influence did limit her career choice. His death was traumatic for her.

I went to the University of Michigan in Ann Arbor for four years. I decided against translating, and I majored in elementary education, but I didn't like teaching thirty-five kids. I've always been interested in helping people and switched to social work. I had thought at one time of becoming a doctor, but my father didn't approve of that for me. He felt I would become too involved with my patients, and he was right, because even as a social worker, it happened.

My father died when I was a freshman. That was a very important happening. It was very bad. It was a very shocking kind of thing. He was a young man—fifty-six. It was very unexpected. I was just home for Christmas vacation of my freshman year. I didn't want to go back to school at first, because I didn't want to leave my mother by herself. Well, I had a brother who was here at the time, but I still didn't want to leave my mother. I did go back. At the beginning of the term I was very depressed. I moped a lot. I didn't feel like talking to people, and I think even today—it's been eight years—it's still a very hard part of my life.

I was still with the peace movement. I was still interested in folk music and singing. I worked as a switchboard operator in the dormitory where I was living. I was a volunteer at a mental hospital a couple of days a week. I worked with adolescents for a while; then I worked at a halfway house with emotionally disturbed patients. That was pretty much my week.

When I graduated college I was almost twenty-two, and came back to Pittsburgh. I looked for a job, couldn't find one, and then started graduate school in the University of Pittsburgh's Graduate School of Social Work. I went to school every day the first term. The second term I worked three days a week at St. Francis Hospital and went to school two days. I taught Sunday school every Sunday at Rodef Shalom Temple. Monday nights I did volunteer work at Council House with resocialization of mental patients. And I spent some time with friends. I liked doing social work, and I liked school.

There were some changes because of my father's death. I helped out at home a lot more than when I was younger. I was living with my mother and my brother in my mother's house. I did a lot of the shopping and cooking. We shared responsibilities. My mother worked and my brother was in school. My mother and I had always been very close, and I think our relationship matured along with my own maturity.

Zober recalled her courtship and marriage. Like her, her husband was Jewish and idealistic. When they met he had served four years in the Peace Corps in Africa and India. The newlyweds left for Europe and for Israel. Their experience was repeated by many young people of their generation.

I met my husband the year I came back to Pittsburgh. We started to date in January 1972. He was twenty-seven when I met him. He was sort of idealistic and fun to be with. In a way he was a romantic figure. He had spent all this time overseas. He and my brother were good friends, and he and my mother were also friends. My mother worked at the graduate school where he was enrolled; she was happy that he was Jewish, and she liked him.

He was going to the University of Haifa to do his field work for his master's degree. He said, "I'm going to Israel in August. If you would like to come, we could get married, and if you want to wait here for me, I might come back, but I might not!" I decided to go with him [laughter].

We were married on August 6, 1972. We left two weeks later for Israel. We spent two months in Europe on the way. We were in England, France, and Spain. In Spain we bought a motor scooter with a sidecar. We traveled on the motor scooter through Italy and southern France. When we got to Venice, we put the motor scooter on a boat and went on the boat to Israel. Then we spent six months on a kibbutz, learning Hebrew and picking grapefruit. I worked in the kitchen. The beginning of May we went to a small town in northern Israel with a mostly north African population. My husband was a community worker, and I was a social worker. We were married a year when the war [Yom Kippur War, 1973] broke out. We went through a lot of traumatic things that tied me to Israel. When you wake up in the middle of an afternoon, when you're taking a nap and you awaken to the sounds of being bombed on this holy day of quiet throughout the country—that shock never leaves you.

The Zobers' first child was born in Israel. In Ruth Zober's family, relatives had always helped with new babies. Zober and her husband were alone.

We were married two and a half years when I became pregnant. It was pretty well planned. As soon as I was sure, we called my mother and called his mother. We told friends. I had a pretty good pregnancy, but I had some high blood pressure, so I was under the care of a specialist. We watched it carefully, and it turned out to be no problem. I worked every day up to the day the baby was born. That day I left work a half-hour early.

I was going to do natural childbirth; in Israel it is mostly natural childbirth. I had read a lot of books, but I forgot everything I had read when it was time. I don't think childbirth is ever the same as you think it is going to be. I went into labor at three o'clock in the afternoon and went to the hospital at eleven o'clock at night with pains four minutes apart. Then they slowed down and stopped. My husband was more nervous than I was. I was dilating, so they kept me. He slept in the car. The baby was born at ten-thirty in the morning, and at four o'clock they handed him to me and said, "OK, take care of him." Well, I wasn't quite sure of how to take care of him. The baby was fine, but he was a newborn baby and he was quite colicky and very active. He was quite difficult. Most people stayed in the hospital three days. But they sent me home early because it was a holiday. Everybody was going visiting, and friends who had promised to help take care of me were leaving. There was just my husband, the baby, and I. We went home and took care of each other, more or less. It was a little bit traumatic. I would have liked to have had somebody around to help out a little. My husband tried, but he really didn't know. He had never been around a baby at all. I had been around babies, and though I was fairly experienced, it was a little different. He was so little, only two days old!

After those first days, one neighbor and some other friends, who were nurses, helped out quite a bit. The pediatrician in town was an American. I respected him, and he helped when I needed him. When the baby was three and a half months old, we came back here for my husband to go to graduate school. Then my mother, my grandmother—everybody— gave advice.

Zober talked about Jewish identity in terms of her experience with Jewish people from different cultures.

Being Jewish has always been a big part of my life. It's part of what I am. I've always been very aware of being Jewish. Right now, having lived in Israel and lived among Jews who are not like me, not at all like

American Jews, being Jewish is even more significant to me. I think the world in general has its vision of the Jew as the doctor and the lawyer. They would be amazed to see what some of us are like. I met Jews of every color speaking every language imaginable! I always stand in awe of this fact. I think there are a lot of terrible things committed in the name of religion—whether Jewish, Christian, or Moslem, or whatever.

Being Jewish has had meaning in my life, because I made it important. I chose certain friends; I chose to belong to certain groups; I chose to go to Israel.

Zober's greatest personal concern was also one of the central issues of the closing years of the twentieth century: how to combine career and family.

I would like to find a balance between family and work. I am very weary right now of the woman who wants to run away from the family and just work. I don't know if work is so totally satisfying. I like to work, but it's also very frustrating. My work is helping other people. I don't like going out to help other people and leaving my family in a mess. I see a lot of that in my work. I think a balance between the two is needed. I think a woman should be able to have a career and pursue it without having to give up the family half of herself.

I'd like to see more day-care in the United States for this purpose, and not condemnation of women who want to work, because I think you have to be able to work and take care of your family at the same time. There have to be part-time jobs and other arrangements for women in a certain age-group who are raising a family.

I think the women's movement is very important. I think every woman should have the opportunity to achieve as high a level of whatever that she wants. Why not a woman president? But I think a lot of women who are gung ho on women's rights should not forget that it's also a woman's right to decide that she wants to stay home and raise her family and let her husband be the master while she is the mistress. I think that, too, is a woman's right. I think it's important that we have reached this point where we are even talking about women's rights in the United States. There has to be a balance, but I think every woman should have the right, just as a man should have the right, to do what and how they want to do, as long as it doesn't harm others.

Right now I'm going to school, and I leave the baby with my mother one day a week when I go to classes. I don't know what the next ten years will bring. Right now I want to finish my degree, and next year I start a Ph.D. program. That's as far as I can predict.

June 28, 1989, Interview

Since her 1976 interview, much had happened in Ruth Zober's professional and personal life. She had lived in Waltham, Massachusetts, where she gave birth to her second child and earned a Ph.D. in social welfare; in Ithaca, New York, where she taught at Cornell University; and again in Israel, where she had a third child and taught at Tel Aviv and Hebrew universities.

In 1989, she and her husband divorced. At the time of this interview, Zober, forty, was a social worker with the Jewish Children's Bureau in Chicago. She had won a 1989 national award presented by the Jewish Family and Children's Agency Professionals in recognition of her work in organizing a support group for siblings of mentally disabled children. Her closing words summarized a central message of these oral histories: individual lives do matter, for a long time, to the generations that follow.

Last week at my daughter's bat mitzvah, we played Grandma's tape; she spoke to us. I still get choked up when I think of my grandmother. She meant so much to me. She taught me about being a mother, about being a Jewish person, and about being a woman. She took care of us when my parents went away. Sometimes we stayed with her for a week, or for a night, or for a holiday. She wanted me to have shiny hair. Once she washed my hair with an egg; another time it was vinegar. She played a very significant role in my life and even in my children's lives. Even my little son, who was four when she died, remembers her. At the age of ninety-one she baby-sat for him. My mother and I had errands, and we were going to take the baby with us. Grandma said, "Leave the baby here," and we did. She was afraid to put him down, and she sat in the rocking chair and held him the whole afternoon.

My mother and I are very, very close. I tell her everything. We think in a similar way. I didn't expect to be different from my mother and my grandmother. I saw how similar they were to each other, and I expected to be the same. In some ways my life is so different. I'm the most educated; I'm the least stable in where I've lived; I'm the only one who's been divorced. Still, I am similar in very basic ways.

Slavic Families

SIX

*Mary Miroka Laver, Elsie Firka, and Joanne Gereg**

The oral histories of Mary Miroka Laver, Elsie Firka, and Joanne Gereg document a significant and neglected chapter of American history, that of Slavic immigrant women who struggled to survive and raise children in steel-manufacturing towns of western Pennsylvania. Family solidarity, religious faith, and the continuity of ethnic tradition are major themes of this family history.

Mary Miroka Laver was born on March 1, 1901, in rural Austria-Hungary. Her oral history tells of coming to America, reuniting with a father she had barely known, and experiencing a life of poverty, hard work, and marital difficulty.

Elsie Firka was born on September 18, 1924, in Jessup, a coal-mining town in northeastern Pennsylvania. Her oral history continues her mother's story of poverty and hard work but tells also of upward mobility. She and her husband, a steelworker, worked and saved to create an attractive home and to raise their daughter with advantages they never had.

Joanne Gereg grew up living the American dream with loving parents, a nice home, family vacations, even her own horse. She married an ambitious man of similar ethnic background and values.

*Pseudonyms have been used at the request of the respondents.

Mary Miroka Laver,
b. 1901
November 23, 1976, Interview

I lived in a small town in Austria-Hungary with my mother and my grandmother and my sister. My father was in the United States. I don't know how many years he worked here before he sent us passage to come to this country. Do you want me to tell you something about the European country, how it was?

It was pretty hard, because my mother had to go out and work on the land, and my grandma took care of us. It wasn't an easy life. My mother went out in the morning at four or five o'clock and came back after it was dark in the evening. She worked on land somebody else owned, and they gave her a part of the harvest.

She brought wheat and took it to the mill to have it ground into flour, so she had her own flour for her own use. My mother baked the bread. My goodness, it was moldy half the time because it was maybe once in two weeks that she got time to bake. There was an old-fashioned stove built into the wall where she baked bread. They used to heat it up with wood, lots of wood. When the temperature got so high . . . with a long, wooden paddle she would shove it in there and bake the bread.

Living in Europe wasn't very good at all. We had one big room. We had a section against the wall where my grandmother and my mother slept. I slept with my sister on top of the stove where we baked the bread. It was solid on the top, and on the bottom was the opening. My mother made our mattresses from straw, and she would put them on top of that oven when she wasn't using it to bake. So one section was a kitchen; one was a bedroom; and the other, low like a fruit cellar, right alongside of it. We didn't have bathrooms or anything; we had to go outside on the ground. When I think back on it now, I can't think how people could put up to live like that.

I didn't do anything—just played around because I couldn't go to school, because my mother wasn't able to pay the tuition for me to go to school. My father couldn't send us any money, because work was bad in this country. So I didn't go to school until I got here. My sister was three years older than I was. She was at home, too, but she went to school certain times. Whenever my mother had a few extra dollars, she would send her to school.

We ate the bread mother baked. She used to toast us a piece of bread on the top of the stove and put some water on it and a little bit of salt, and this was our toasted bread. We didn't have butter, even though we had a cow. That cow had to support us. My mother always tried to make a few pennies, and she sold the milk and butter so she could manage to buy other things that we needed—more vegetables than anything else.

We hardly had any eggs to eat, because we only had a few chickens. And she'd sell what she could. We had chickens, a cow, and a pig. In Europe in the fall, they slaughtered the pig and that took care of meat and bacon for the entire year. What you slaughtered at home, you kept. If you were able to raise it. If you can't buy the hay in the fall, you have nothing to feed the cow in the winter. So you just have to do without it. This is how my mother struggled to raise us until we came to this country.

I never had shoes on my feet until I was coming to this country. Always barefooted—winter, summer, I was always barefooted. We couldn't afford shoes. People had their shoes made, see? Shoemakers made the shoes. My sister had them because she went to school, but they were kept only for that purpose. At home she was barefooted just as I was.

I remember that when the harvest time came, my sister and I had to go out in the fields and we would have to pick the leftovers of the wheat. They cut the wheat off and then the ladies come and they pick up that wheat and put it in bundles. Whatever is left, what they don't pick up, it's just like—you would say "scrap." One piece of wheat would be left here and there. Well, we would go and pick that up. That would be our work. It was hard work for little girls—you bet your life it was. Naturally, we had to walk barefooted because we didn't have no shoes, and we walked on the stems and they were hard and they used to cut our feet. Our feet would bleed, because when you cut a piece of dry twig, it's real hard and it cuts you. It wasn't easy for us to live there.

My grandmother raised us. My father was her only son, and after my mother was married to him, my mother lived with my grandmother. My father came back to Europe and then went back to the United States. Poor soul—he had to borrow the money to bring us here so we could have life a little bit better than in Europe. My grandmother stayed in Europe when we came here. I remember she didn't want to come. My father wanted to bring her over, and she wouldn't leave the land. My mother had a lady come in to take care of her. My mother gave the lady the house so she would take care of my grandmother. My grandmother only lived about two years after we left. After she died, the other woman sold the land.

I remember getting ready to come, and I remember the trip. We had to get shoes to make the trip. Some man made me shoes. This is the first time that I had shoes on, when I was coming to this country. And we had to get shots. We had to go from one place to another to get shots, get papers. It was something. I enjoyed it because I was never anywhere.

The only thing bad was that we were on the ship for twenty-four days, and we were sick on and off for twenty-four days. Most of the people, even the grown-ups, were sick. The people used to lay in those beds downstairs and—well, the ships weren't very clean. I don't want to be on one again.

This was our first time out anywhere. We ate stuff that we never ate before. It was funny for us to see fruit. At the ports, small boats came up alongside our big boat and they were selling fruits . . . oranges and apples and grapes and bananas. Well, we didn't know what an orange was and we didn't know what a banana was, because they don't grow in Europe. My mother bought a little basket of bananas and she gave them to us. I'll never forget. Some lady—she lived here in Homestead—saw us eating those bananas with the skins. We didn't know any different. She said, "Oh no, no! You don't eat them with the skins. You take the skins off." We looked at her like dummies. She said, "Now, wait. Let me show you." She showed us how to peel the orange, how to peel the banana. I said, "Oh my God!" When I think of it now, I can't believe we were so dumb!

We were able to talk to a lot of people on that boat because they were Slavish* too. A good bit of them were coming to this country to work. Some came to New York; some came to Pittsburgh. So they were our class of people. Their husbands worked in the mills.

When the ship landed, we all had our bags and our baskets. We came to New York, and there was a platform and all the people were waiting for whoever was coming from the ship. Families were waiting, and our dad was there too. Everybody had to sit in the corner until they passed the inspection. I remember we sat there with these bundles. Well, my mother brought three feather ticks. They're like quilts, but they're made with feathers. Well, everybody told her to bring them so we would have enough covers. So, each bundle was tied together real tight and we each had a bundle to hold. There we were with three bundles, plus the basket that she brought. We were sitting there waiting for somebody to come to take us to get checked out. Finally my father came with all the cards, and they allowed us to get on the train.

My father brought us to Homestead. We lived where the mills are now, on Heisel Street. We boarded with my godmother in two rooms for a while. Then from Heisel Street we went to City Farm Lane, which went from Eighth Avenue all the way down towards the mill.

*Slavish is a colloquial term used by several women in their oral histories to refer to various related Slavic peoples and languages.

Laver spoke about her father, a kind, hardworking man.

To tell the truth, I didn't know my father that well. I was born when he was here. Then he came back to Europe once when I was about three years old. Then I didn't see him until I came to this country. I was a stranger to him, and he was a stranger to me. My sister remembered him more because she was older. He was a stranger to me, but we got close when we got to this country, because my father was a good, kindhearted man. He was very, very fond of us, and we got close right from the beginning. He was a very good person, a good man.

He worked in the mill all night long. He was kind. He made sure that we got what he could afford to give to us. If he couldn't give it to us, he'd always promise us, "on payday." He'd say, "On payday I'll give you a *grajsa* [penny] for candy." So we would always look for it, and when that payday came, he would give us a *grajsa* for candy. A good pay [for two weeks' work] was twelve dollars. One pay[day] he brought eight dollars, because it was a hard time at the mill. But he still kept his promise that he would give us that *grajsa*. He always tried to please us very well. I don't think he ever hit us.

When he was home in the day, he slept, because his work was from nine or nine-thirty in the evening until nine-thirty in the morning again. When he came home from work, he'd have his breakfast. Then he would go up to Seventh Avenue—there used to be wholesale stores there—and bring boxes so we would have fire for my mother to put in the coal stove to keep us warm during the wintertime and to cook on in the summer. Of course, you could have bought coal if you had the money, but if you didn't have the money you had to substitute the wood.

My dad didn't have to pay for the wood. From his pay we had to pay rent . . . seven dollars a month when we first came, and later thirteen dollars. My mother did the shopping because there was a store right next door to us. It was two cents for this, a nickel for this; we were used to budgeting. It was hard to manage on eight or twelve dollars every two weeks.

Laver described the neighborhood where immigrant workers lived in Homestead. Her perception contrasts with that of writer Margaret Byington.

It was different from Europe. At least we had shoes, anyhow! We didn't run around barefoot. The bathrooms were outside—there were sheds with commodes in them, so that was different. The meals were different, because our mother didn't have to go out and earn the stuff and milk the cow and do all those things like she did in Europe. So that was a little bit different for us, to live a life like that. To us it was like luxury, you know, because we never had anything back in Europe like that.

It was just an ordinary two-room house. That's all—two rooms, one downstairs, one upstairs. It was in a row of houses with different families living there, and each house had two rooms. So we all slept upstairs in the bedroom and we had a kitchen downstairs, and that was it. The neighbors were very, very good. They were all Slavish people. They were all our kind of people. To me, looking at how it is now and how it was then, they were closer than they are now. It was like a family living together. It was a very nice place to live because we all got along fine. There wasn't anybody who lived there who thought they were any better than one or the other. The men all worked in the mill.

In the evening we'd sit outside. All the ladies would come out. They would bring their little stools out, and they would sit and talk together about their European situation—how they worked there and what they left behind and all that. This is what was interesting to hear. Each one had something to say, and even the young people who were born here were anxious to listen.

I was about nine or ten years old. I found it interesting because I felt it was something that I had lived through in Europe. I knew what they were talking about. Even now, when we get together, the ladies from the church, how we talk about Europe! No matter where you go, you find people that still remember.

My mother didn't have to go to work when she came here. She cleaned the house, but that was no problem for her, because she was a hard-working woman. There was dirt, because we lived right by the mill. There was our house, and an alley, and there was the mill. It didn't seem bad to us. My mother said she went through so much in Europe that life here was a little bit easier for her, and she felt good because she knew what she left behind. She enjoyed life here. She enjoyed every bit of it.

My mother couldn't talk English. And as many years as she was here, she could say only a few words. Our older people weren't interested in getting to know [the] English language. They were always together and nobody else came in to talk to them, so, naturally, all they spoke was their own language.

If our mother needed a dress, my dad used to go out and get it for her. He went up on Eighth Avenue [the main street of Homestead], and he took her and he took us, and he bought clothes. My father could speak good English because he was here so many years.

Laver recalled traditional foods and old-world Slovak holiday customs.

Christmas was special because we had a Christmas tree; we had ornaments; we had some little candies, or maybe a gift put under the tree if somebody could afford it. My father put everything—the ornaments and everything—on the Christmas tree. That was his job, to decorate the Christmas tree. And he always put at least a candy cane for us on the tree, to make sure we had our Christmas present from him. Christmas Eve, my father would bring us straw. In Europe our people put straw under their table for Christmas. Then they put nine different tools under the straw; that's because these tools are used all year for the work in the home—you know, a hammer or saw or nails or a chisel or something like that. Then we looked forward to the European food that my mother made for Christmas . . . *bolbalkies* and mushroom soup and nut rolls and poppy-seed rolls. This is what we were looking forward to, because it was only once a year that we got that treat. Then, before Christmas Eve, she would put a pan of water out—on a chair or somewhere—and she would put nine pennies, or different coins, nickels or dimes, in that pan, and we were supposed to wash our faces with that water while the money was in it so it would bring us good luck for all the year round.

Just before we ate our Christmas dinner, our dad would say his Christmas prayers and then he would take honey and he would make a cross on our heads. All the family was sitting by the table. Then we would have to eat a little piece of garlic. Each person had to dip it in honey, and we ate that before we ate our dinner.

We looked forward to Easter because we were going to have Easter eggs, all colors. And for Easter our mother would bake a *paska* bread; it would be a loaf of round bread. Then she would make poppy-seed roll and nut roll from the dough. Then she'd have the ham and she would have *kolbassi*. She would make a piece of bacon and cook it and put it in to bless in the basket. Then she'd make an egg ball. I still make that. I beat it like an omelet and put it into boiling milk and stir it and it curdles up. Then I take it in a towel and I squeeze it, and it makes a ball. That's called a *sirok*. So we were looking forward to Christmas and Easter because we had all these goodies. Through the year we didn't have it, so, naturally, Christmas and Easter were very interesting to us. Easter Saturday night, we had the blessing of the basket up at our church and we put all that stuff in the basket. We put butter in a little dish; we put salt in a little salt shaker, and we would take all that up to the church and Father would bless it. Then we would come home, and we wouldn't eat anything out of the basket until Sunday dinner. That was our Easter dinner. We went all together to get the basket blessed. This is what Easter always was for us. We were looking forward [to] something.

Laver recalled going to school and to church for the first time.

I went to school when I came here. Well, it wasn't a very pleasant thing for me to go to school, because I didn't know how to talk in English. Our parents talked to the kids only in Slavish. At school the kids would laugh at me and they would call me all kinds of names and shove me around . . . and I didn't do nothing but listen and look as if I was a wild animal, because I didn't understand what they were saying. But I had a good teacher. I was already nine years old when I started school. I was fortunate to have that teacher. She would teach me after school. She taught me how to write, until finally, little by little . . . she was very kind. She tried to explain to us and tried to help us. There was another girl there who knew a few words in Slavish and she was good in English. She told her mother, "We have greenhorns in our school." That's what they used to call us, "greenhorns." So her mother said, "Why don't you try to help them? They came from Europe. Your people came from Europe too. . . . You have to help one another." Her mother said, "Go and bring her here after school and you show her how to do this and that." And this girl showed me so much. I'll never forget her; she's still living. She was so close to us in school. If somebody would try to hit us—there were bad kids, too—she would stand up for us and say, "Now, you shouldn't do that because these kids just came from Europe. They don't understand. Don't be like that." Then the teacher would get after them and she would explain it to them. I wanted to learn because I saw that what I knew in Slavish wasn't good where I was in school. I had to try to learn, and after I got the reading, I caught on pretty good.

Sundays we went to church. And coming home from church we'd have dinner. I liked going to church. At first I didn't understand much, because in Europe I never went to church, but after I started I wanted to go. I saw all these people and I looked forward to getting that penny for the basket. My father would always say, "All right. Now here's a *grajse* for you," to my sister. And then to me, "Here's a *grajse* for you. Take it to God and ask him to pray for me. I had to work all night and I'm too dead-tired. I can't go." We would say, "Okay, Upo" (we called our dad Upo). We didn't spend too much time with our father on Sundays, because after church he went to sleep so that he could be ready for work at night.

Laver went to work at age twelve.

I didn't stay in school long, only until fourth grade. When I graduated to fourth grade, I got a job for two dollars a week and I went to work. So from twelve years on, I've been working. I worked for some people up on the hill. The lady was sick and her husband was a boss in the mill. I started in the summertime, so I walked there early every morning because the mills used to start at seven. He paid me two dollars a week to stay with his wife. Before he left for work, he made sure that I was there. I stayed all day. I would shop for her if she needed it. I would make her breakfast, do things for her, like scrub the kitchen floor and cleaning up. Then, I would get my meals there also. I didn't prepare the meals. Sometimes she did, and sometimes he would do it the night before and just come home and warm it up. Then I'd wash up the dishes and then I would go home.

I didn't think it was right to leave school, but the works got bad, and my father brought less money, and we needed it to pay rent . . . and there was nothing coming in. It was pretty tough. At the time, it seemed that a lot of kids were doing the same as me. I had a hard time getting out of school, because they don't allow you to quit school unless it's really necessary; it has to be a real hardship on the family. So when my father a couple of times brought home a pay of seven dollars, we were back in rent; we didn't have what we needed, so the principal let me go.

When I was about fourteen, I quit that job and got a better job in a restaurant, washing dishes for four dollars a week. So that helped. I went in the morning to wash dishes, and then in the afternoon, after I got all the lunch dishes washed, I was able to go home for two hours. Then I went back for the supper rush. I got my meals at the restaurant, and I had a very good boss and a good cook. She was a Russian lady, and she gave me anything that I wanted to eat. This Russian lady explained to her boss what kind of situation we were in, and he said, "Anytime there's anything left over, give it to her and let her take it home." I stayed there about two years, and I worked all the time. I didn't go anywhere. Couldn't afford movies.

When I was about fourteen or fifteen, I started to go Saturday night to a dance right on Dixon Street. There was a Jewish lady, Mrs. Lefkowitz, who had these dances on Saturday night. She owned the only hall around our part of town. You paid fifteen cents to go to the dance. Lots of times we didn't have the money to go to the dance, and she'd let us in even if we didn't pay; next time we made sure that we had that fifteen cents for her. If we could hear the music, especially our kind of music . . . czardas and waltz . . . , we were all for that. She'd say, "All right. Come on in. I see your feet are ready to go dancing and you can't get the money." She was very nice to us, yes. I really enjoyed it, and I met a lot of older girls from Europe there. They came here because they couldn't get married there, because the fellows left Europe to come to this country to make money and live. So the girls that were able to come came here and they got married here. I got acquainted and made friends and it was nice. I enjoyed every bit of it.

Lot of times there was a free wedding in the hall. After supper they'd open the doors and anybody could come. We all went. I met my first husband at a wedding. A couple of months later we were getting married.

Laver knew nothing about sex or marriage; she told of a sad and difficult marriage.

I didn't know anything about sex. I didn't even know anything about periods until I got mine. My mother never told me that. When I got my period, I said, "Oh my God, something's wrong with me. Blood's coming. What's the matter?" She said, "Oh well, every girl gets that." So then I knew about periods.

She didn't tell me anything about sex. She never told me to be careful or to watch. They never preached to us that, well, if you meet a boy and you go out on the road and do this or that you might get pregnant or something. They never did that. I didn't know about sex until I was married. My girls learned in school, and I did tell them, "You have to find out for yourself. You can't mingle with men, because you'll get in trouble." Nobody told me that.

My mother and dad didn't know too much about [my husband]. He had an uncle that lived right across the street from where we lived, and his uncle put us together. He used to drink. That's why my father never did like him from the beginning, because my father wasn't a drinker. He would take his drink when he came home from work, but that was his portion. But when my father met him a couple times and saw that he was drunk, he didn't think that he was the right guy for me. But his uncle would say, "Well, don't worry. After he gets married, he'll be on his own, and he could correct himself, you know."

I didn't even think whether I liked him or not. At that time, you didn't have the feeling if you liked him or not. You just met him and times were bad and you're looking for something better to live. You figure if you got married, you had a better life. If you got a right choice, maybe you made a good choice, then you had a better life. If you got the wrong person, then you were going to suffer. My portion was that I got the wrong one. Who knew? We took his uncle's word for it because we figured, "He's an uncle; he should know." We were married in 1916, and in 1925 he picked up and left.

He was Slavish too, but from a different state. He was seven years older than I was. In Homestead we lived in two rooms on Heisel Street down near the tracks. I had to be home, so I stopped working. I packed his lunch bucket—a sandwich, an apple, a piece of cake, a cup of coffee. We used to crochet a lot. That's about all the ladies would do.

I wasn't that crazy about being married, because it didn't work the way I thought it would. I was sorry, but it was too late. And in our religion, you can't get a divorce. It's hard, because our church doesn't accept divorce. But if I had to live life over again, I would have never stayed with him. Even at my young age, I felt that [he] wasn't the right guy for me, but what are you going to do?

They always say, "Maybe he'll change when you have your first child." But that didn't help any. I was married about three months and I was pregnant. I knew when I missed a period. When my time came, I knew to go call the midwife. It was rough. The pains were something terrible. I thought I was dying. The midwife took care of me for a week. She'd come to the house to wash the baby, wash me all up, put clean clothes on me, wash the diapers, and then she'd leave. I was glad to have a little girl. But she lived only ten days. I figured he would turn different, but he didn't change a bit. Then I got pregnant again and that baby came, and that didn't help any. I think it was worse; he started drinking more.

In spite of Laver's efforts and his family's support, her husband deserted her. Laver took boarders and eventually turned to her mother for help.

There was no help. They didn't have marriage counselors like they do have now. Well, if you would go to your priest and ask for his advice, he would say, "Well, try to put up. Try to see if you can't get to know one another better and sometimes give in when he feels he's right. Maybe you might be sometimes wrong." I went up there one time with my mother and I said, "How much could you put up? Whatever he earns, he boozes away." Half the time he doesn't go to work. I pack his lunch; he goes to a beer joint, to the saloons. He comes home at a certain time whenever the men are coming home from the mill. For a long time I didn't know where the heck he was going, but when payday came, I didn't have any money to pay my bills. If it wasn't for my mother to give me food, I don't know what I would have done.

Then after the first child came, the second child came, and where in the hell are you going to go with kids? I was stuck. And I always figured, "Give him a chance." How many times can you give him a chance? Didn't he realize he was married and that he was supposed to support the family and give them a shelter? We all make mistakes, but sooner or later we get straightened out. But not him.

I had to move from here to the coal mines because he lost his job here through drinking . . . damaging the steel property, so he had to leave Homestead steel mill. Then he couldn't get work anywhere, because he was blacklisted. He couldn't get a job in any U.S. Steel mill anywhere. So he went to the coal mines in Scranton, in the hard-coal region. He went there, and I was back here with my two kids. Then I went after him to Scranton. We lived there for a while, and he picked up and went some other place. He left me, and by that time I had three kids. Then he came back and we tried to make a go of it again. We bought a lot and we built a home and still we tried to make a go of it. We were able to do this because at the coal mines, if you bought a lot for a hundred fifty dollars, they would build a house. His sister bought the lot and loaned us money for the house. And that's how we built. His sister said, "Well, maybe if he would have a property, maybe if he would have some mortgage on him, maybe he wouldn't be doing this." But it didn't work. We had a home. He stayed in the house for about seven years—it was 1925 or 1927. Then he picked up and left again. I had four kids by then. When he left, I didn't know where he was.

In the meantime, I had to work and support myself and the four kids, and the only thing I could do was keep boarders. So I had six and seven men, keeping a boardinghouse to support myself and my four children. The last time he left and didn't come back, I figured, "Well, there I am." I was not going to put up with this no more. I had all this work with these men. I had to wash clothes by hand. I cooked their meals. I packed their lunch buckets.

Then they were threatening a strike out there in the coal mines. The guys were leaving because they had to go somewhere else to find a job. I wrote to my mother, and she said to me, "Well, pack up your clothes and come back home." My mother lived on City Farm Lane by the tracks, and she had a four-room house and she accepted me with the four kids. I couldn't find where the heck he was. I didn't get a penny from him to support my kids. I raised them . . . gave them as much as I could give them. I figured after he left and he never contacted me, I didn't want to bother with him.

I went to the Welfare and I asked the Welfare to help me out. Well, they used to give me two dollars a week on each child. That was in the depression.

Then a neighbor of my mother's got me a job for eight dollars a week. I was washing and ironing and cooking and cleaning and everything for the house—there were eight or nine people in the family. There was an awful lot of work to do, but still, I had no choice, because my mother couldn't afford to give me anything more than the shelter over her head, because she was a widow. Anyhow, I started in that place, and they were very nice to me. He was a boss in the mill, and she had two daughters that were teachers. I stayed with them for nine years. I helped my mother out as much as I could and bought the food, paid the utilities, and tried to do the best I could.

Laver remarried in 1937. Her second husband was a responsible worker, husband, and father.

I met my second husband in my mother's home. He used to board in my sister's house and come down to my mother's to help her to do little odd jobs. He was a very kind person. He said, "I'll take care of the children and I'll feed them and I'll give them shelter. You don't have to worry about that." My mother talked me into it; she felt that he might be the right person, a kindhearted person. And I said, "Well, maybe I might have my break now." I left Annie [her second daughter] with my mother so my mother wouldn't be left all by herself. Annie was sixteen or seventeen years old, and she worked daytimes.

So I moved to Neel Street down on Seventh Avenue; it will be thirty-seven years I've been right in this section. He was a good man and he raised my kids, gave them a home where their own father didn't give them a home. Even to this day, my youngest one will say, "This is the only father that I know."

I had a nice life with him. A lawyer helped find my husband, and I got the divorce so I could marry again. My daughter went with me for a witness, and she said, "My dad never came to see us. He never sent us anything. . . . There was never a penny sent to my mother all these years. She was the one that raised us." I got the divorce one-two-three. Then I married him in the justice of the peace office. He gave me a home; he gave me everything. I had a roof over my head, and I had a nice family, and he supported them. And I had two babies with him.

Mr. Laver died in 1955, and Mary Laver entered a new stage of life. In her midfifties, Laver became a citizen and worked in both paid and volunteer jobs in her church.

I got my citizenship paper right after my husband died, twenty-one years ago. I didn't know what year we came; I didn't know what ship I came on. My dad died in 1936. My mother couldn't read or write, and she didn't know. The ladies that came to Homestead at the same time we did went to other places. After my husband died, I saw in the paper that Mrs. Kelty was having a class at Munhall School for seniors to get citizen papers. So I went there and I registered and she told me she would look into it. She got all the information for me, and finally she found out what year I came, what line I came on, and everything. She went to a lot of trouble. I was fifty-six when I got my citizen paper.

I was glad I went. Mrs. Kelty was glad to find out that I could talk in English, because she had Polish people there and she had Slavish people and she had Mexicans and other people that couldn't understand English. She used to say, "Wait. Don't you leave. You stay here with me because you're the only person that understands me here." And I said, "OK." And then I would explain what she had to say to the Slavish people and the Polish people. I could explain it because even though the Polish language and the Slavish are a little different, you can always understand one another. I couldn't explain to the people who spoke Spanish, because I didn't know their language. I got the citizenship, and I vote all the time.

Whenever [the older girls were] on their own, and my son and Rosie [the two youngest children] got married, I was about fifty-seven, and I went to work for the church. Father knew me because I belonged to a quilting club with the ladies. We made all the quilts to sell at the bazaar every October. About twenty years ago they wanted to start a quilting class, and I knew something about sewing. I handled those bazaars down at the church for about seventeen or eighteen years. I took care of the sewing circle. We went to town; we bought stuff; we brought it home; we cut the pieces; we quilted them at home so we'd have them ready to sew together at the church. I used to bake with the ladies, make different pirogies and food for our Friday dinners. You ask anybody! I took care of practically everything. That's how I got acquainted with Father closer than just Mass on Sunday.

Father asked me if I would take care of the church. So I accepted, and I worked for twelve years there. Scrubbing, lugging those buckets of water up and down steps to clean that church—oh, what I didn't do in that church! I stopped doing the cleaning because my pressure was high and I got sick. I kept doing the altars until this year, when I reached seventy-five. I really felt bad when I gave it up, because my heart and soul was in that church.

Laver discussed her current activities and what it meant to her to be an American with strong ethnic ties. She concluded her oral history with a touch of humor; she was a survivor.

They all call. Sometimes they can't make it to come, but if I have anything that I bake, I ship it right over to them. Whether they come or not, I'm just so close with them as if they were here. The phone is good because you can say a few words over the phone. They don't have to hurry to come down here, and I don't have to worry as long as they call me. Elsie calls to take me bowling; Annie calls to take me shopping.

Now I have my Rosie and my grandson living with me. When her husband left her, Rosie moved back here with me. She works for the county and I have her twelve-year-old son. I cook for the three of us, and I still shop, and I still do the washing, and I still do the ironing, and I'm still managing the house. And my Helen's husband died three years ago, and I call her to come and eat all the time.

I was born Slavish and this is what I am. I can't be anything different. I still make everything for the holidays. Annie married a Catholic fellow and Elsie married a Hungarian fellow and Helen married a Polish fellow, and they all go to different churches. I wasn't against it. I felt that I didn't care where they went, as long as they belonged to the church where they wanted to belong. I'm Slovak, but I think since you are in this country, you should be according to this country. I feel that I'm part of this country now. I had nothing good back there. You know, I feel this way—I would rather be American already.

Looking back at old times, life now is altogether different. I always had the sad time. I never had it easy, and I never felt that life was happy for me. Even now I'm glad I can help, but it's a lot of work with my daughter and the boy. I enjoy life more now, because there's a lot of improvements in everything, and nothing but heartaches at the old . . . years back. Now, as long as I have my health, this is happiness for me. And I take care. I eat my meals. I rest, and like they say, I take Geritol!

On March 1, 1989, Mary Laver celebrated her eighty-eighth birthday. She was keeping house for her daughter and grandson. Her daughter Elsie had suffered a stroke, and Laver spoke to her on the phone every day. Granddaughter Joanne Gereg's added this bit of information about Mary Laver:

My grandmother can whip off fifty pounds of noodles in a day. She has certain customers who call her for noodles. They only want Mary Laver's homemade noodles! And you don't bother Grandma on her noodle day! She's already worn out one dough board, and she's gone through three noodle machines. She's hard on noodle machines, and she has to have a new noodle machine so she can continue her business.

Elsie Firka,

b. 1924

December 1, 1976, Interview

I can remember that we lived on a dirt road, and the coal mines were on the opposite side of the road. Right in back of us were the railroad tracks, so we had to be very careful. My mother had boarders, and that's how she was able to provide for us. My father had a drinking problem and just refused to work.

The boarders were very friendly. . . . A lot of them were married men, and sometimes their wives would come out there to visit. Just about everybody in the coal-mining district that had homes had boarders. This is the way they could live. I remember that a bunch of neighbors would get together, and they would kill a pig and roast it. Then they would have the food for the rest of the year . . . make their own sausage and all. They made the fire in an iron oilcan. I was only about four years old when we left Jessup and came to Homestead, but I can still picture that.

Elsie Firka's perception of life near the Homestead mill differed from that of her mother. She remembered a "mean" grandmother. We can only imagine how difficult that grandmother's life must have been.

We came on a train to Homestead to stay with my grandmother on City Farm Lane. Her house was the last house down next to the railroad tracks. I remember when a train would come by, my goodness, it shook the whole house. There were six of us sleeping in one room. Upstairs were two bedrooms. Grandma's boarder was on one side and the six of us on the other side—my mother and my grandma and the four of us. She had one boarder there, and he had the other bedroom. Grandpap was dead—I don't even remember my grandpap. The house had two rooms downstairs—a kitchen and a living room.

I had a mean grandma. Only on Sunday was the living room door opened. You never were allowed to listen to the radio. That room stayed closed six days a week, and Sunday, after church and after you ate your dinner, you were allowed to go into the living room and listen to the radio. They'd have Slavonic programs on, and this is what they listened to. But during the week, that living room was not opened to nobody.

I don't remember a thing I could say that was good. It was hard. We had to wash; we had to iron. There was a little shanty outside, and she had another boarder. After school, we'd wash clothes and iron, because we tried to help my mother out. My mother did housework for a school-teacher and her family. She'd go in the morning, and we went to school. Then we'd go up about six-thirty to meet her and we'd walk home with her. It's so hard when I think of my life . . . I mean, mostly for my mother. My mother didn't have an easy life.

At this point, Elsie Firka began to cry. She stopped, apologized, and then continued with painful memories of her childhood.

It never hit me until you came here how hard it was to live there. I think it's the part about Grandma. She was mean. She hit us. Oh, did we get it! And my poor mother, we never told her. We'd try to do all the work so our mother wouldn't have it. Because when she came home, if Grandma couldn't do the washing and ironing, my poor mother would be in that shanty washing and cleaning after the boarders.

My mother taught us everything. When we cleaned, it had to be just so, and it had to be in the corners, and everything had to shine. I remember at Grandma's house, my mother got on a scaffold and painted the house. The steelworkers would be coming from the mill and they'd be whistling and saying, "That's not for you," but there was nobody else to do it. And today, I can get on a scaffold and paint a house, because I'm not afraid of it.

My mother was a good worker, a very good worker, very good cook and all. The people she worked for were both schoolteachers, and she did cook for them. She learned a lot of fancy ways of cooking. Even today—and she's seventy-five years old—when my mother puts out a meal, she could top the best. She does cook wonderful.

In those days, before my mother would go to work in the morning she would give us a nickel. At lunchtime we'd go into this store and buy a nickel's worth of jumbo [bologna], and the four of us would lunch on that. One thin slice, and this was our lunch. Even though we stayed with Grandma, our mother bought our food. Grandma wouldn't put a penny out for us. I remember Grandma saying she wasn't going to feed my mother's children.

I do remember there used to be a little meat market up there, and my mother would buy a bone and maybe a little piece of chuck plate and she'd make a pot of soup. When she came home from work, she would cook our supper for us. She made such good stock, and it was made out of hardly anything. My mother was just a wonderful cook.

We got clothes from the Welfare. It was funny. If the Welfare package came in one day, next day at school just about everybody had on the same thing. They must have sent every family the same kind of package. You'd get stockings or a dress or blankets or shoes. But it was new, and you wanted to hurry up and put it on, and you went to school. But you didn't think about it. Nobody looked and said, "Well, she got the same thing on that I have on"; they didn't think that way. Even today, when I meet some of my girlfriends we laugh and say, "Remember those Welfare stockings we wore," or "Remember those Welfare blankets."

My mother worked five days; she would have Saturday and Sunday off. We always looked forward to Saturday because that was her payday, and she used to go up the street and buy the groceries we had to have for a week. And she'd always go to Wohlfarth's Bakery, and they specialized in strawberry cream cake. It was probably so hard for her to pay for that, but she made sure that every Saturday we got that cake for Sunday. Because we held Sunday highly then. We worked on Saturday, and we prepared for Sunday, and we did nothing on Sunday.

We had a wooden porch in the back, and we had to scrub it with lye because people believed in white wood. And I remember our bathroom was—it wasn't a bathroom, it was just a commode in the cellar, and we had a wooden seat on it. But it was scrubbed with lye until it was white. It had to be white. And if it wasn't white, Grandma would holler at my mother. My grandma was pretty meticulous and very careful and clean. Everything was scrubbed down with lye. We had fun scrubbing that porch and hosing it down. I guess we didn't realize how dangerous that was.

In the hot summer, we jumped in the tub that had the rinse water from the laundry. It was a picnic to jump in the tub and get cooled off and all. They didn't waste water! If you took a bath, two people took it in the same tub to save that. And then the next two. Nobody would have a full, fresh tub. We bathed in the tub in the kitchen near the coal stove.

Church every Sunday was a must. You didn't live in that house if you didn't go to church. My mother and my grandma were very religious. . . . I still follow the tradition and so does my daughter. Now my little granddaughter—she's six—wants to go to church too.

Laver's second marriage made life more pleasant for her children. Then the depression brought hard times. Firka left school in eleventh grade to work full-time.

When my mother married Mr. Laver, we moved out of Grandma's house to an apartment in West Homestead. I was twelve years old. My little brother and sister were born there. It was depression time. Nobody was working. My dad—we called him Dad because he really was a dad to us—was home out of work.

With the little kids at home, my mother couldn't go to work every day. But she would take in washing and ironing. The kids would go to the people's house and pick up the wash. We'd bring it down to Seventh Avenue and she'd wash and iron it, and then we would take it back up.

One time my dad came home pulling a little wagon for Ernie, and he had the wagon loaded with food. It had everything, even candy. "Where did you get it?" my mother said. She got scared—did he steal it? He said, "Don't worry. My credit is good and this man trusted me." When my mother remarried, that's when we knew what it was to really live. He worked hard in that mill, and he was a good worker, and he just provided wonderful for all of us. He had a heart of gold. That was a stepfather that's maybe one out of a million. Then with defense and the war, the steelworks picked up. I don't think my mother had to work too much after that.

After a while we moved to a better building. I was going to school, and after school I would work in a Chinese laundry. My cousin made her living working in the laundry. We went there to see her after school. I used to sit and watch, and she'd say, "Well, if you iron these hankies or if you iron these sleeves on these shirts, Tommy Yee will pay you." And this is what my sister Helen and I did when they needed help on wash days. They were wonderful to us and very appreciative, and even after I was married I worked for those Chinese people for twenty-five years.

The summer before I would be in eleventh grade, I got a job at Pittsburgh Coal Company. I'd accept the money when people came to pay their bills. I gave my pay to my mother, and she'd give me what she could out of it. We all turned our money in, and we didn't mind it. We had a little money, and if we asked her or my dad for something, they'd have it for us. When it was time to go back to school, I wanted to go, but my dad was laid off, and the man at the Pittsburgh Coal Company asked me to stay on the job. I really wanted to go back to school, and I talked it over with my mother. She said, "That's something you have to make up your own mind to do." I knew that the money I was making was helping, so I stayed with the job. But the owner got sick, and the business folded about six months later.

I still envy that I didn't finish high school. How many times during my married life I would think, "Go to night school and finish up and get that diploma." I really wanted it, but I never did it.

Then I found out that a restaurant in Braddock was looking for a waitress. So I went. I think I was sixteen years old. It was a Greek restaurant called the Rialto Restaurant. I had to get up at five o'clock in the morning because I'd be on the streetcar at six. I'd work from seven to two.

There wasn't too much social life. The only thing we did was go to Eighth Avenue Saturday nights. The stores would be open and we walked up and down the streets. One time when a boy asked me to go to his prom, I refused because I was afraid to ask my mother. I knew she didn't have money to buy a gown.

Elsie married John Firka on February 15, 1942. She was seventeen years old. He was Hungarian and belonged to a different church. The weddings of Firka and her sister illustrate religious divisions within the Slavic community.

I met my husband when I was seventeen years old. I liked him a lot. He said, "Do you want to get married?" We came home and we told my mother. She said, "No way. You're too young." But he was just a lovable guy. Even my mother accepted him. He wanted to get married, and my eyes lit up because he was a young kid, a good-looking kid, and he had a brand-new 1941 Chevy. I knew he had to be a good kid because he was so nice with Rose and Ernie, my little brother and sister. I'd baby-sit Rosie and Ernie. I had little Rosie one time, and I was supposed to have a date with my husband, and we picked up little Ernie and we took them for a ride. The kids were always with us. He came from a family with all brothers. They didn't have a sister. And he fell in love with Rosie. Even today, he's just wild over children.

He got into the steel mill when he was sixteen years old. He was Hungarian—very strongly Hungarian. His mother and dad always spoke to them in Hungarian. He was Byzantine Catholic under the pope, and I was Greek Rite, so that created a little bit of a problem as far as getting married. My sister and I planned a big double wedding at St. Nicholas, where we were brought up. My sister's husband was Roman Catholic, and his family told her she had to go to St. Ann's to get married. I know it broke my mother's heart, but she said, "I'm not going to interfere. It's your life and you're going to live it." Annie asked me to come up there and get married in the double wedding at St. Ann's, but I just couldn't. My husband's parents said to him, "Do you want to get married in Elsie's church? Go ahead!" I had a wonderful mother- and father-in-law. They liked me, and I liked them. Annie got married at St. Ann's and I got married in St. Nicholas Church, but we had the reception in our home together. My sister and I had our double wedding in the house. My mother hired a woman to come and do the cooking. We had a big sit-down meal, starting with chicken soup and stuffed cabbage and chicken and all for about fifty people.

Firka described her marriage and the joy of childbirth. Then tragedy struck.

John was just unbelievable. We must have got along like two young kids. Only one time we had an argument, and I went back to my mother's. Well, John came over and he said he was going to join the navy if I didn't come home. And he wouldn't go home. My mother said, "Go back already." So I had to go back. He's like he is—a wonderful person. I don't know what else to say about that.

I was married six months when I was pregnant. I felt real good. I was happy. After going through that hard labor and all, and they bring that baby to you, you just can't believe that you had something like this. It's just the most precious thing, I think, in the world. I think the first feeling with your first child is a feeling that's indescribable. Marlene was born at Homestead Hospital, with Dr. Hughes. I lived upstairs and my sister lived downstairs. We both helped one another. I think living together did a lot for us. We cooked together, ate together, went out together. We shopped and walked our babies in strollers down the street together. My family, I must say, likes a lot of togetherness.

I stayed home, but whenever they were very busy in the laundry, they would call me. Then if John was off, he would watch the baby. He would drive me to the laundry and pick me up.

Just out of the clear blue sky, Marlene went outside and that was it. She had stepped outside, but she was on the sidewalk. A streetcar was stopped and a car zoomed around the streetcar. He came close to the curb and just dragged her under. That was in June. She was four years old [when she was killed]. I was sick for a while, I'd say for about six months. I had suffered a real bad shock.

My sister and her husband were on vacation, and they said, "Let's go up to Canada, to Ste. Anne-de-Beaupre" [a Roman Catholic shrine in Quebec]. We went there, and then I discovered I was pregnant again. That must have been my answer. Why did my sister drag me there? I don't know. It was beautiful. We made the novenas, and it was beautiful going all through them. When I came back, I wasn't feeling well and I knew something was wrong. I was under a doctor's care because I was so nervous after losing Marlene. Then I used to go up to St. Philomena's church [in Squirrel Hill] and make a novena that I wanted a little girl. Joanne was born on June 25, exactly a year after Marlene died.

The Firkas built a new home and worked and saved to furnish it and to give Joanne advantages that they never enjoyed.

I think that brought us luck. We moved from there because I refused to raise my baby there after suffering that tragedy. John's mother had a lot up in West Mifflin, and we built our home there and moved in 1949. Annie was in her own place, and my sister Helen and her husband moved into the house we moved out of on Ravine Street. I went back to work in the laundry, and John's mother watched Joanne. This is how we tried to pay for the new house. In those days, John made money, but not enough. Every little bit I made, I tried to help. I always wanted to help get furniture into the house, because we couldn't get everything at one time. We lived there until we built this house in 1964.

War bonds helped us. John got the bonds at the mill, and that helped with the down payment on our house and on things we bought. John was a pretty good saver. He joined a credit union in the mill, and that helped too. For a dining room, I went to a secondhand store and bought an old table and four chairs. I stripped them down to the clear wood, and I refinished it, and I had the prettiest dining room table and chairs. It took a while until we got the carpet; we bought it on time. My mother- and father-in-law had a garden and chickens, and they brought us fresh eggs in the morning.

Firka explained her allegiance to St. Elias Hungarian church. She made a strong statement about family solidarity.

We have lots of friends. We belong to St. Elias, the Hungarian church, and I worked with the bingo and met a lot of people. After Marlene died, Father Orris at St. Elias gave me such comfort; he really did console me. Then I decided that I would remarry in St. Elias, because they didn't recognize the marriage in St. Nicholas. I think the church did something for me from the tragedy that I suffered. Now I think I would die for St. Elias.

The whole family—the sisters and their husbands—get together every holiday, for the Fourth of July, Christmas, Easter. If I have Thanksgiving here, Annie will have Christmas. Now since Joanne has her own house, sometimes it will be at Joanne's. We alternate and we get together for birthdays . . . the family is just together.

Our family just can't break apart. What is it that holds this family like this? Nobody does anything without one another, even my stepsister and stepbrother. We're only about ten or fifteen minutes apart from one another, so we always get together. If we're going to go here or there, we'll call Annie and Hank to see what they're going to do. Or we call Queenie. We don't leave my mother out of anything. My mother is "Queenie"—that's the queen in our family.

My mother-in-law lived directly in back of me, so I never had to leave Joanne. I bowled, and I got pretty good and joined several leagues. Then I traveled with the bowling. If I was going for a weekend tournament and had to stay over, then she would come and stay with Joanne. Joanne was pretty fortunate because she was never left with strangers. She was left either with my husband or with my mother-in-law. I never had to have a baby-sitter. My husband is a family man. He doesn't drink. He goes out occasionally, but mostly he stays home and tinkers with cars or something like that.

I think the world of Joanne. If I could give her the world, I would. They are all I have. But I didn't think that she would be so close to me. She just can't detach herself from me. Her husband's pretty nice, and he said, "Boy! I didn't only marry Joanne; I married her mother, too!"

When Joanne was married she could have lived with us, but I told her, "There's room here, Joanne, but I'd sooner see you go into an apartment and try it. Buy your furniture; learn how to pay for it." They did; they moved into their own place, but they came home every day and ate here, so I didn't lose. I gained.

Firka described her weekly schedule in 1976. She spent a lot of time at St. Elias church. In addition to cleaning her house and shopping, she took her mother to the doctor's, bowled, worked at the laundry, and occasionally worked at her son-in-law's print shop. She cleaned the church and worked at the bingo games (paid jobs); played bingo on the night she didn't work; and cooked pirogi and noodles (volunteer jobs) with other women who sold them to benefit the church.

When I feel down, I turn to God. I'll go to the church; I get a lot of answers there. The church is Hungarian, but there are a lot of Slovaks there. Joanne married right in the church. Her husband's mother is Slovak and his father Hungarian, so we're all St. Elias. I didn't think it would happen, but it just happened. I'm glad it went that way, but I would never be against somebody that she loved. The most important [thing] is they believe in God—have some faith. If she had married out of it, I would have to accept it, because everybody has to live their own life today.

My cooking is Slovak, and I like the music and the dancing. You can't beat the foods, the traditions of the church, or the holidays. I built my life around that, and I'm going to keep it that way.

Elsie Firka spoke about her marriage in terms of an equal partnership. She expressed strong support for equal opportunity for women. She spoke, too, of her own unfulfilled ambitions.

It's good working and sharing together—housework, anything that comes along. I'll tell you, while I'm on a ladder painting the house, he's in there making our supper and washing up the dishes and cleaning the dishes. See, he won't go up to the roof, so if I have to go on the roof, I say, "You have to take over here." And he does. Many times I've had my brother here and we'd be painting together. We'd come in the kitchen and here the table was set just so, and he had our meals ready. Then we'd just get up, go back to our painting, and he'd have the kitchen as spotless as ever.

I think marriage comes first for women, but if they have the brains for it and the knowledge, then I wouldn't stop anybody from getting ahead. As for a woman president, if she could run this country as well as any of the presidents we had, I wouldn't object to that either. It's the knowledge. You need the knowledge, and if you have it, I don't care what human being it is . . . what race or color or what sex they are. I don't think that anybody should begrudge anybody if they have the capacity and mentality to do a better job.

If I had my choice, I'd love to have been an artist. I love artwork. I do. Even after I was married, I went to Pittsburgh to the YWCA and I took some art lessons there. When the schools had art classes, I went there for painting class. I was interested in decorating and creating. Yes, this was my desire. Even today, how many times I think I would love to do this because I just love it. I love to create. I went to ceramics class. I made the plaques on the wall. I'd like my house really beautiful.

I hope I can keep on doing what I'm doing now. Bowl and bingo and go and shop . . . just have good health and be able to do what I'm doing now.

In March 1984 Elsie Firka suffered a massive stroke and has been confined to her home since that time. Her husband retired, and after his wife became ill, he managed the household and cared for her. Daughter Joanne Gereg visited daily, did the ironing, and frequently brought cooked meals to her parents' home. Firka talked on the telephone daily with her daughter and her mother.

Joanne Gereg,

b. 1948

December 1, 1976, and January 19, 1989, Interviews

I was born in Homestead in 1948 and grew up in a house on Lincoln Avenue in West Mifflin. One of my earliest memories is of my grandfather taking down a chicken coop we had in our backyard. I remember them killing chickens in the alley, and plucking feathers. My other early memory is of family vacations. We went to Conneaut Lake and rented a cottage. My best friends were my cousins. My mother's sister had three daughters who were close in age, and we all played together. My other aunt had two daughters, so we were all girls in the family and we did a lot of things together as a big family. We went on picnics on Sundays, and swimming. We spent all our Christmas holidays, Easter, and Thanksgiving together as a big family, not just the three of us.

Thanksgiving, we ate at my grandmother's—my father's mother. My mother worked, and she usually made the turkey. Christmas Eve, my mother would have everybody over after Midnight Mass. We'd have a snack, and that's when we'd open our presents. Christmas Day we'd go down to my Grandmother Laver's, and she would have a turkey. The traditional Christmas Eve dinner is hard—I couldn't make it. We usually sit down to eat *bolbalky* and sour mushroom soup before we go to Midnight Mass. My Grandma Laver still makes it. Easter, everything surrounds the church. We go to church the whole week. And we make our baskets at home, and in that basket is a *paska*, kielbasa, an Easter cheese, horseradish, dyed Easter eggs, butter, a ham. We take it and get it blessed. That's the first meat we eat, the ham on Easter morning. My grandmother's the one that really holds it together; that was their custom. Now, today, it's a thing of the past unless you are really a tight family.

At home in our house, we spoke all in English. My father would talk to my grandmother in Hungarian. When my mother and her mother and the rest of the sisters would get together, they would talk in Slovak. I knew no Slovak or Hungarian. I can't speak or understand either.

My father and mother went to church every day. I think when my sister was killed, it brought them closer to the church. And it was a must that we went to church on Sunday and on all the holidays and on all the holy days. No matter what we did or where we were to go, we were to go to church first. When I was smaller I resented it. But today, I think it really brought me closer to church. My husband is also that way, because it's a must that we go to church on Sunday. We belonged to the same church. I grew up with him . . . not as a friend, but I knew who he was, and I met him in church and we were married in the same church. We grew up with the same customs. He's Hungarian also. His mother's Slovak; my mother's Slovak. They knew one another for many years. They belonged to church societies together.

Joanne Gereg added information about her mother's interests and activities and spoke about her neighborhood and her relationship with her father.

My mother bowled, and she went to painting class with the two neighbors across the street. They played cards and went to classes together. Also, she worked two days a week at the Chinese laundry on Eighth Avenue for many years. And she got involved in church work. She started working when I was in kindergarten. My grandmother would take care of me. She lived behind us, so I was always home. She would baby-sit at home, or I would go down there.

I wasn't expected to do any work in the house. Not the dishes or the ironing, but I had a dog and took care of the dog. We lived on an older street. The homes were older; the people were older. Their children were married and grown up. I did have a girlfriend down at the end of the street. She came from a large family, and I grew up with her. My uncle lived on the side of us and his parents in front of them, so it was sort of a family street. I would say the people were mostly Slovak and Hungarian. The girlfriend I played with was Slovak.

My dad and I did everything together. I had a horse, and that was our favorite pastime. From when I was in about fifth grade until I was in eleventh, we owned a horse, and I would ride it and he would take care of it. We had it out in South Park. That was our biggest activity together. It was just my dad and I—my mother wasn't included; that wasn't anything she wanted to get involved in. That's what kept us close. I think that's why we're close today, because I grew up more with him. He'd go out to work and I'd go to school and come back, and we had nothing in common, really. But we found something, a horse.

We would clean the house on Saturday. That was a must. Go food shopping. I'd go to a girlfriend's, or we'd listen to records. We'd go to dances; we would go shopping. We played tennis and rode bikes. Maybe Saturday would be a date or whatever. Sunday, church. Probably have the family over, and that would be it.

In school I was in Y-Teens, a pep-rally group, and I was in Beavers, an organization of girls selected to be secretaries to their teachers. And I worked in the office of the principal. I made Bs on my report cards. I had two girlfriends who came over a lot, and we usually studied together.

At school, my favorite activities were sports. I liked basketball, calisthenics, and gymnastics. I think that stemmed from my mother and my aunts. They were very athletic. They always played badminton. They played baseball when we went on picnics. They swam a lot. I still enjoyed my horse, but when I started driving I became interested in boys and cars and we sold the horse.

Gereg knew very little about menstruation and sexual intercourse when she was growing up. Her testimony suggests that she did not want to know; reticence about sex may have been related to old-world taboos.

I think I was twelve when I got my first period, I was told about it, but I was too dumb to really realize what happened. The school and my mother had told me about it, and my girlfriends. But when it finally did happen, I didn't know what it was. First I put up with it for a few days; then I realized something was wrong. Then I went to my mother, and she explained in more detail about it. Still, I was anxious for it to happen, because it gave me a little "growing up" feeling, really.

I didn't really know about sexual intercourse until I was married. Even my mother said I should have known. She never really did sit down and tell me the whole thing; she never did. I had general ideas about it from books and magazines, but when I was a teenager, girls didn't talk that much; that still was very personal, and only you knew about it. I was shocked, I can remember, on my honeymoon. It wasn't until after I was married that I really knew. It was sort of a hard way to learn. I'm sure I'll tell my daughter a little more than I knew. Now with the outlook I have and the outlook that the kids have, and the commercials on TV, they tell you to tell your children, so I'm sure she'll know. Even now, I really don't enjoy seeing a lot of sex on the screen. I'm still embarrassed to go to a show with my husband and to see those types of movies. I still am reserved about that.

I knew about how babies were born in about tenth grade. As far as growing up, I was always told it was from heaven. So, mommies went to the hospital and they had babies from heaven, but that was it. And I don't really remember a pregnant person standing out in my eyes. I really don't remember anything.

Gereg started to date at about seventeen. She graduated from high school in 1966 and worked in an office. She started to date her husband, Bill Gereg, a

young man from a similar background. They were married in September 1968.
She discussed her courtship and early years of marriage.

I didn't know what I wanted to do. As far as seeking a career, it really wasn't my ambition to do that. I wasn't thinking of being a doctor or a secretary. I wanted to be a housewife. I wanted to have my own home. I also wanted to do things outside the house. I have all that now.

As a teenager, everybody looked to get married. Girls that I knew didn't work. Married people cleaned and did dishes and took care of kids and that was it. Nobody in our family worked outside, other than my mother, who worked two days a week.

I was a collection secretary at Family Finance in town. I worked there for three years, up to a year after I was married.

I met Bill the first three months that I worked; that [job] was part of a high school program before graduation. I think he waited for me to mature. He's six years older than I am. I did see him at church, and I felt an inkling that he would ask me out—I could tell in his eyes. He was really my first love involvement. I remember that I first knew him when I was in sixth grade and I went to his high school graduation party. He was an altar boy, and he was also very close with the church. His parents always went to church, and they were involved in Hungarian organizations.

He keeps the tradition more than I do. He has Hungarian records. He gets a Hungarian newspaper. He's more interested in traditional dances and folk art than I am. His father was interested in that. His father played the violin and he played the cimbalom. He now owns two of them. I listen to KQV [contemporary music]; he listens to a Hungarian record.

He went to college and night school and IBM school. He's a printer and he has his own business. He's very ambitious. He knew what he wanted out of life and he had an ambition and he had a goal. He wasn't satisfied, not as far as money and material things—he always has to do more. Now he has two cimbaloms and two antique cars. When I was going with him, he had a small orchestra that played at weddings. He played czardas and polkas, and he has always been involved in music.

We had a typical Hungarian wedding. We even had a cimbalom player. My husband went up and started to play with the orchestra. He forgot he was part of the wedding! It was a traditional large wedding. First was a church service, then a big "hunkie" [Slavic] wedding; we had the traditional bridal dance; then everybody did polkas and czardas. It was the orchestra that made it that type of wedding. There were a lot of older people, and everybody really had a good time.

Learning to manage bills and money and having her own home were important to Gereg and reflect values that were emphasized in the oral histories of many Slavic women.

I worked for a while. At that time Bill worked four to twelve and I worked daylight. It was just too hard coming and going that first year of marriage. It took a lot of adjusting. We decided I should quit, and then we decided to have a baby. I became pregnant right away. Then we were both at home until four o'clock, and I spent my evenings by myself or I would go to my mother's. I would do my cleaning at night or maybe baking. I would see my mother every day. I had a lot of growing up to do, like learning to cook on my own, and to manage bills and money.

The baby came, and it turned out to be a girl. I really wanted a girl. We lived in an apartment for ten or eleven months, and I moved back with my mother before Lori was born. We didn't like apartment life, and we decided to buy a lot and build a house. Lori had her first birthday in my mother's house. Right after that we moved into this new house that we built. I always lived in a new home, and this neighborhood is new; the people are young and have children. It's different from my mother's, because we lived in an older neighborhood. The custom there was that you washed on Monday and you ironed on Tuesday. And if you had wash out on Wednesday, the neighbors would talk because they were older and that's how they believed. Now, nobody hangs out! They all have washers and driers and they're going all hours of the day. The generation is different. Plus it's a nice neighborhood because of the children.

Gereg returned several times to the theme of family closeness and generational continuity.

My relationship with my family didn't change. Lori is seven now, and we're still close. It's because we want to be close. I see my mother almost every day, and I call her if I don't see her.

She's here for dinner, or I go there for dinner. It's like I never really left, but yet our family got bigger with my husband and daughter.

When I go out I usually leave Lori with my mother or Bill's mother. I don't depend on baby-sitters; I really don't have to. We're a tight family and we're close. We all sit down to supper—we did that at home. We all go to church—I did that at home. I'm raising [Lori] with her grandparents just the way I was raised with mine. We still have family picnics, but now they're bigger. I still do a lot with my cousins, and Lori still likes them and goes over to their house. The cousins her age are on Bill's side of the family and live in a different area, so we don't get to see them that much. Lori still has interests that I have. She likes to bowl, and when she's nine she's going to get a horse.

We were a happy family together. We are still a happy family. We think of each other and we do for each other and we're still together. Nobody really pulled apart.

Improvement in economic circumstances was the major difference between Gereg's life and that of her mother and grandmother. Gereg's husband is self-employed; her father and grandfather were hourly workers. Gereg referred to the printing business as "his" job, never as "ours." Although her views differed somewhat from those of her grandmother, she expressed traditional ideas about male-female roles.

I am involved with my husband's job. I go to the shop almost every day. I come and go as I need to. I leave after Lori goes to school, and I'm home before she comes home. I work when I have my things done here first. Or, if I have to go somewhere, I don't have to run down to the shop. It's not a set schedule. I can go when I can and leave when I can. But sometimes I wish he had a nine-to-five job. Being together all day and breakfast, lunch, and dinner is just too much togetherness.

Working makes me feel useful. It's because of me that the bills get paid and different things get done. It's not because of me that we have what we have, but I'm helping it to run smoothly. I'm happy with anything that I accomplish on my own, with things that I can do without the help of someone else.

My grandmother still believes that the husband is the king: even if you have a full-time job, when he comes in the door, you put that meal on the table. When I look in the rearview mirror and Bill's right behind me, I can't do that. I do take care of him, but he has to wait. I see nothing wrong with a woman working, as long as she thinks of her family first and her job second. If she's going to think of her job as her first life, I don't feel she's capable of being a housewife or a mother. If a woman feels that she can work and she can take care of her family, I think she should go out and get what she can. If it's bettering yourself and you feel you can handle it, I feel you should be out there doing it.

But as far as equal rights . . . I still feel that there are some things women should leave to men. I don't think she's capable of being a president. I don't feel that a woman should be down in the mill doing manual labor. I think that's a man's job, and I feel a man should be able to do that.

January 19, 1989, Interview

With her mother-in-law's death and her mother's illness, Joanne Gereg became the responsible woman in her immediate family. She visited her mother daily and spoke on the telephone at least twice a day. She reminisced about her grandmother and mother and introduced her nineteen-year-old daughter, Lori.

My grandmother, like millions of others, came here for a better life. She achieved that herself, and each generation has enjoyed a better life than the previous generation. I didn't have everything I wanted, but there was always heat in the house. I think it would be good for my daughter to know what her grandmother went through. I think she should be honored that each one of us has bettered ourselves.

My mother worked in a Chinese laundry. I saw how she worked and stood on her feet. It helped us own our house on Lincoln Avenue. And my father worked in the mill in the bitter cold. I respected them for that so that we could have a better life.

My goal was to get married. Lori is preparing to support herself. People who didn't prepare are looking at minimum-wage jobs. I want her to do better. Now we're concentrating on getting her through college. She is working toward a degree in business to prepare for a career in hospital administration.

I'd like to see Lori get a good job. I'd like to see her be happy. Someday I'd like her to have a family. I want her to respect how hard it was for us to come this far. I don't want her to take this for granted.

The traditions are really important to me and to my husband too. We want to make a videotape of Grandma in the kitchen cooking her special dishes. We don't know how to make her mushroom soup and her *bolbalky;* we want to videotape Grandma so we can learn and carry it on. Grandma is the matriarch. We all cling to her, and she holds us all together.

Great-grandmother, grandmother, and mother: Mary Grajewski, Mary Sypniewski, and Eva Carey, Pittsburgh, 1918.

Immigrant Court in Second Ward of Homestead, 1910. From the Eastman Collection. Courtesy of Historical Society of Western Pennsylvania.

Eva Carey, 1989.   Mary Lou Olmo, 1983.

SEVEN

Mary Grajewski Sypniewski, Eva Carey, and Mary Lou Olmo

Oral histories of three generations trace the process of assimilation from grandmother to mother to daughter.

Mary Grajewski Sypniewski was born in 1887 in Nanticoke, Pennsylvania, to Polish immigrant parents. She and her husband, a Polish-born lawyer, lived in Pittsburgh and were involved in Polish affairs and in the Polish-American community.

The Sypniewski's daughter, Eva Carey, grew up in a home in which Polish identity was very important. She graduated from medical school, became a radiologist, married a midwestern Protestant, and joined the Episcopalian church. Carey's oral history speaks to the problems faced by a woman professional from the 1930s to the present and to the difficulties of combining a profession with family obligations. Although she did not identify publicly as Polish, Carey's commitment to serve her husband, clean her house, help with grandchildren, and care for her mother—and to do it all herself—reflects Polish values concerning the home, work, and the domestic role of women.

Third-generation Mary Lou Olmo never identified with her Polish heritage. She married a man of Spanish background and converted to Roman Catholicism. In 1976, she devoted her time to family, volunteer activities, and sports. When Olmo was reinterviewed in 1989, her children were grown and she was a graduate student anticipating a career in sports psychology.

Mary Grajewski Sypniewski,

1887–1977

January 16, 1976, Interview

I was born on April 2, 1887, in Nanticoke, Pennsylvania, in the heart of the anthracite mining region. Nanticoke is near Scranton and Wilkes-Barre. There were about twenty thousand people in the town, and the main occupation there was coal mining.

My parents came from Poland to the United States on their wedding trip, and they decided to stay. My mother's sister and her husband lived in Nanticoke. They had a meat business. My father was a tailor. When they came here, my father bought property. It was a double building—I think a nine-room house on each side. Two stores were in the front of the building. My mother's sister got them started buying the property.

My father learned the tailoring trade in Europe. Then when he came here, he got a job. Then one of the men said, "My goodness, but you're pretty good. You ought to go into business by yourself." He told my father to go to New York. So he went to New York and learned how to cut the suits. He did that, and then he set up a tailoring establishment. He was very prosperous. He had a lot of people come in. They didn't have ready-made clothes then, so everybody had their clothes made. Later, when they started to have ready-made clothes, they still came. The stores needed alterations, so they used to send their ready-made clothes in to my father's place for alterations. But my father had his customers. Men that wanted custom-made clothing came to him. He had about seven men working for him, and one woman. The woman made the trousers, and the men did everything else. They did the sewing—there were three sewing machines. My mother's brother was a tailor, and he lived with us. The others came in to work each day.

[My parents] came here on their wedding trip, and I was born a year later, in 1887. Our living quarters were in back of the store. We had a living room, dining room, and kitchen; upstairs we had five bedrooms and a bathroom. My father was busy in the store all the time. He'd come back and the children would come home from school, and we'd have lunch and dinner together. My mother had nothing to do with the business. She had a maid and she supervised her.

The friends my parents had were from Poland. And there were relatives. My mother had cousins. Mostly my mother's relatives came to Nanticoke to live and to associate with each other.

My parents were part of a Polish club. The men would sing; they had concerts and we would go to them. They used to have little plays in one of the halls there. They would sell tickets and use the money toward a library. It was a library club, and you could get any kind of books. They put on plays in Polish. Everything was in Polish, and we spoke Polish at home. I went to public schools and learned English, and my father spoke English. I went to Catholic school until I had my First Communion, and after that to public school.

We went to a Polish church. They had two in Nanticoke. By the time I got married, there were three Polish churches in the town. We observed the customs. Like Christmas and Easter—we'd celebrate. My mother would invite some friends and some of her cousins for dinner. We had the priest come and bless the table for Easter. We'd all go together to church every Sunday—all the children and my parents.

My parents were active in the Polish clubs. They'd get all the people of Polish descent to come. They had different entertainments, and they all got acquainted. They helped the new people get started. They had classes with different professors to teach them English when they came here.

Our neighbors were from different backgrounds. The parents of the family next door came from Poland. They had children born here, just like my parents did, and we all associated. They were all in business, most of the people of Polish descent. The next-door neighbors had a grocery store. Then there were shoemakers; in later years, one of the shoe-maker's sons was a judge in Pittsburgh. In the neighborhood there were American people from Ireland and from England and from everywhere. And they used to associate nicely. When I got to public school, I got to know the American people. We'd go to each other's homes, usually on Saturday. We would invite each other; we'd take turns to go to each other's houses.

Mother supervised the household. She always had a maid who dressed us in the morning and got us ready for school. We all went to school. My parents were very strict in raising us. If you didn't come straight home from school, they wanted to know why. Some children stayed around and played tag and got home late, but I always got home in time from school. I'd go to school and come home and study in the evening. Some-times we would have our classmates come and study with us.

I played the piano. My first teacher was a nun; later, a man came to the house to teach me. My brother played the violin, and we played together. I was in some clubs, and there was a place where I learned how to sew. One of the churches had some women who gave lessons in sewing. Later, I had sewing in public school. I was very young when I started to sew—I don't remember exactly, but I could have been five or six or eight years old. I went to sewing class on Saturdays for a little while.

On Saturdays we'd go to the movies with my mother. She would always go with us. Movies cost a nickel then, and they were the silent movies. On Sundays we would go to church and stay at home. Sometimes friends came to visit us.

I asked Mary Sypniewski how she learned about menstruation, pregnancy, childbirth. Her immediate reaction reflected a cultural taboo that persisted to some extent over the generations.

About what! We didn't talk about those things. I think one of our maids told me about babies. She said, "You don't know where you come from?" I said, "No." Well, she told me. When I first got my period, I was visiting my mother's sister. I said, "I'm going home." I ran so fast because I was frightened; I didn't know what was wrong. Then I came home and told my mother, and my mother said, "You'll get that now [that you are] a certain age." Then she said I shouldn't be frightened. I was bleeding, and I didn't know what was happening to me. I was not told about it. My daughter was told about those things; she didn't have to go through what I did.

Sypniewski continued with an account of her family and of her own satisfying work, which utilized her skills and benefited the Polish-American community.

My sister died when she was only sixteen. When she died, we had lots of friends come in. My father was pretty well known, and the children had friends and they all came to the funeral. Our neighbors were very nice. They arranged all the flowers nicely in a room. They were very helpful.

All my brothers went to college. One brother wanted to be a dentist; one wanted to be an accountant. So they took courses for that. Then they opened their own offices. I decided what I wanted to be. I wanted to go to the Wyoming Seminary to learn to be a secretary, so my parents sent me there. I knew I wanted to go further with school. My next-door neighbor was going to Wyoming Seminary, and I thought it was nice and decided to go there too. It was in Kingston, Pennsylvania. I had to take a streetcar and transfer two cars to get there. I never thought about a different kind of college. The courses I wanted were there, and they were handy.

When I finished school, I was a bookkeeper and I took care of an office. I worked at an insurance and real estate office close to my home. They asked the seminary if they had someone. I was asked to go and work there, so I did. It was just two blocks away from my home. On the same street, my father had his business place and they had their real estate and insurance company.

I sure did enjoy my work. And then, I spoke Polish: that's another reason they wanted me. They wanted somebody who could speak Polish. They had a lot of Polish people coming in that were sending money to Europe, to Poland. I was able to speak Polish to the people and to translate letters and documents for them. They needed to know what the English meant and what the American government rules and regulations were. So my knowing Polish helped with all that.

There were a lot of people that were interested in Poland. My father was, and all the people who came from Poland. I wasn't born in Poland, but I was interested. I was, naturally.

Sypniewski reminisced about her courtship and the early years of her marriage, which meant moving to Pittsburgh.

I didn't go out with boys until I went to a wedding. I was a bridesmaid, and my husband was one of the groomsmen. I met him there, and a few years afterward he started to call on me. My parents approved. Boys came to the house sometimes. We had parties and went to parties, but I didn't have anyone steady and I didn't go out on dates. It was more in a group.

I was twenty-four when I met my husband, and he was thirty-four. We got married four years after we met. He came to Nanticoke a lot during that time. He used to come up from Pittsburgh to see me. He traveled by train every weekend. He'd take the night train, stay a few days, and then he'd leave. He'd go to a hotel and spend the day with me at my home. He would send me bouquets of flowers before he'd get there—and candy too. I had a nice courtship.

I liked him right away. We talked for a little while at the wedding where I met him. He seemed like a nice person, and I liked him. He liked me. He told them all that he liked me, but he wanted to know more about me. We saw each other for four years because he wanted to know all about me, and he didn't know me, see? We were engaged for one year.

He was born in Poland. I think he was only five years old when he came here with his parents. He was going to be a priest, so he went to a seminary. Then he changed his mind and decided to study law. First he was a professor. That's right—he used to teach the priests in the seminary at Orchard Lake. Then he changed his mind and he took a course in architecture, and finally he took up law. When I met him, he had been practicing law for five years. He came to Pittsburgh from Chicago. He was a partner with another lawyer, Frank Piekarski, at that time. His partner later became a judge. They had law offices in the Berger Building in downtown Pittsburgh. His family were all from Chicago or LaSalle, Illinois. His parents weren't living; his mother died when he was in college, I think.

He was very kind and very nice, and my parents liked him. Oh, if they didn't like someone, I wouldn't let them come. I always did what my parents were satisfied with. It was all right. We always got along all right. I knew what would please them. I did have a nice courtship. Beautiful.

Our wedding was on June 27, 1911. We were married in Nanticoke at the Polish church that our family went to. I had a very nice wedding. I had about two hundred people, and I had bridesmaids, just like at the wedding where I met my husband. He had his brothers as groomsmen.

In Pittsburgh, the Sypniewskis moved into their own home in a middle-class white Protestant neighborhood on the eastern boundary of the city, near Wilkinsburg.

I left home with him and came to live in Pittsburgh. For two weeks we stayed with my husband's law partner and his wife on Beechwood Boulevard. Then we moved into the home my husband had bought. It was a nice home on East End Avenue—something like this house [two-story brick]. He had already bought some furniture to have in the bedroom. We had it all set, right away, when the house was finished.

I didn't miss Nanticoke at all. I liked to be with him. I was very happy with him. I miss him very much—because he was so good to me. I did very little. I used to belong to a club with a group of married women. Judge Piekarski's wife was in it. She was from my hometown too, from Nanticoke. Once a month we'd have lunch at each other's homes and discuss certain things. We talked about going to plays, about some of the nice plays. We'd get together with our husbands and go to the plays, and go for dinner somewhere, or for supper. We used to go to the Nixon Theater on Sixth Avenue.

Family from Nanticoke joined the Sypniewski household.

I kept house myself, but I had help every week to do the laundry and cleaning. My father was dead, and my mother and the boys all came here to live. My father died just about six months after our engagement. He dropped dead in the store. And then my mother sold everything, building and all, and she came to live with me. At that time my brothers were rooming somewhere. My mother came to live with me as soon as I was settled in my own home.

Then my brother the dentist lived in Carnegie, and my other brother worked with Pittsburgh and Lake Erie Railroad and he lived with his family in Monroeville. They died about five years ago. We used to see them often—we used to entertain them, and they entertained us. My daughter and the dentist's daughter were pretty close. We only had one daughter, and he had one daughter.

I had no expectations, and I don't know if my husband did. I just took things as they were coming. I never gave planning a family one thought. I just said, just as God gives whatever He wants, that's the way we'll have it. I left everything to the Good Lord.

As for church, we joined Saint James Church right here in Wilkinsburg because that's where we lived. East End Avenue, where we first lived, was about eight blocks from where we are now in Wilkinsburg. Then we did join the Polish church when we moved away from here. I lived right on Craig Street [in Oakland]. I owned an apartment house, the Craig Manor Apartments, and I sold it when I came here to live. I'm here seven years.

I was pregnant after about a year and a half. My mother was the first one to know. I had my baby at Columbia Hospital, and I was very, very happy. I had no experience with babies, but I had a book, a baby book that I went by—my husband got it for me. My mother was in the house if I went out; otherwise I took care of the baby. I never thought about having more, to tell the truth. I didn't think of it. If they'd be here, they'd be here, that's all. I just took things as they came.

Of course, my daughter was different from me. She went to medical school. She had her different kind of friends. They were all in her class; they were taking the same courses. She went to Park Place Elementary School, just a block from where we lived. I had one of the girls a little older come with her from school. She always came home with her, and I'd watch for them.

Sypniewski and her husband were leaders in the Polish-American community. Men and women had separate organizations in all of the ethnic communities.

I used to meet a lot of people. We'd always have little entertainments going on at that Polish National Alliance Lodge. Different people belonged to the lodge and certain groups would meet.

All of us were interested in Polish independence. My husband didn't serve in the army in World War I, because he was too old. After the war, when Poland became independent, he talked about living there. He was delegated to investigate certain things in Poland. He liked it, but things didn't pan out that way. We went to Poland together with Eva—she was a little girl—and I enjoyed that. We visited, but we came back here to live.

My husband was very active. He was supreme head of the fraternal, the Polish National Alliance. He was head of that big national organization besides his law practice. It's an insurance fraternal. They take insurance policies and they come and have meetings. The offices are in Chicago. He'd go to those meetings, but then he was home with me a good bit. My husband also started an English class for immigrants from Poland. A lot of people used to come, and that's how they got to be known.

I organized a Polish girls club. We celebrated our fiftieth anniversary [in 1975]. Some of the girls are still here; some are not. But they still like it. That was fifty years ago. I'm eighty-eight now, so I must have been thirty-eight years old when I started it. It was a club for single girls. Later they changed that, because they got married and they liked having the club, so they had married girls and they changed the name to Women's Club.

My husband was very active with the clubs with Polish people. They still have them. They wanted to hold the people together. He started his own branch of the Polish National Alliance. He went to meetings with the men, and I went with the women to the women's club. It was part of the Polish Women's Alliance. The women were separate. We had our meetings on a different day. The parents of some of the girls in the club I organized were there. We've known each other for years and years.

The topic turned to her daughter, Eva Carey.

Eva—Dr. Carey—grew up quite differently from the way I did. She knew about growing up and the facts of life. I think I told her; in fact, I did tell her what happens when she gets a certain age. I didn't expect anything for her; she chose medicine herself. She met a woman doctor from Poland here once. She happened to be of Jewish descent, but she spoke Polish. Well, she got acquainted with Eva and talked her into taking medicine. She said, "Why don't you take up medicine and find a cure for cancer?" I remember. I said, "That's up to her." I wouldn't stop her, because there was no reason to do that.

I had no reason to worry about her. She was a pretty good girl. She came right home at the right time, and I always knew wherever she'd go. I'd know all about it. Then many times, I'd just go with her. I wouldn't let her go alone for certain activities. We had different clubs where girls became better acquainted. I showed you a picture of the girls in a club; they were all younger. Well, we would all go together to these. In the beginning she belonged to that club too. That was something we did together. My mother lived with us, but she did not go; she was too old.

I didn't do too much besides that. I was active in the churches. I took part in charities and fund-raising and donating things. I wasn't loafing. Best of all, I had my husband, and now I have my daughter and Mary Lou, my granddaughter. I think that's about enough.

Mary Sypniewski died August 23, 1977. She was ninety.

Eva Carey,
b. 1913
November 24, 1975, and January 23, 1989, Interviews

I was born in Wilkinsburg in 1913. As far as I can recall, I had a very happy childhood. My father, Casimir Sypniewski, was an attorney and very involved in Polish affairs, and he was the head of one of the largest fraternal insurance organizations in this country, representing—I'm not exact on this—at the time, about fifty thousand Polish-Americans. As I recall my childhood, he always came home with a briefcase full of work. So when I was thinking about what I wanted to do when I grew up, I thought that the one thing I don't want to be is a lawyer; I don't want to have to work at night. He always worked at night. I always had to be quiet. "Ssh, Daddy's busy."

Eva Carey remembered the presence of extended-family members in her child-hood home. She grew up in a bicultural milieu, Polish Catholic at home, American Protestant in school and neighborhood.

In our family there was my mother, my father, my maternal grand-mother, my maternal great-uncle, and two of my mother's brothers. My maternal grandfather died before my mother was married, and her youngest brother was only thirteen. So when my mother was married, her mother and this youngest boy came to live with her and my father. [Eventually the boy] grew up and moved out. When I was an infant, they were all there. My mother was a housewife; my grandmother was a housewife. In those days, a maid did the cleaning, ironing, cooking, and everything for a few dollars a week.

I remember very little as a very small child. I do remember that after World War I my father went back to Poland. We all went—my mother, my grandmother, and my father. At the time, he intended to stay in Poland. Independent Poland had just been reestablished after the war, and he always loved his native land. My mother and he sold everything, intending to stay there. Well, he went back there and found that the stock company he was representing was a hoax. We came back to the United States and started over again.

Then he became very active in the Polish National Alliance. Of course, I was always interested in what he was doing. Then, when I was in high school, I became even more interested and we became pals. I tried to learn the Polish language, and I did some translations. I was a guest at the Polish Embassy in Washington, D.C., when I was a girl. The men at the embassy all remarked that I spoke Polish with an American accent. I haven't used Polish for years now, and I've forgotten the language. I think the war made the difference; I thought we should all be just American.

My parents spoke English at home. They spoke Polish only occasionally. My grandmother was born in that part of Poland that was ruled by Germany, and as a result, she spoke German much more fluently than Polish. She tried to talk to me in German and Polish, and, just like all children, I resented that. You know, you want to be like everyone else on the block. I refused to learn German, which was my grandmother's language. So I didn't learn German and I have forgotten Polish.

I used to think that we should all be Americans and forget the nationality differences, but I feel differently now. It's nice to know where your ancestors came from and to know about your heritage. I'm sorry I've forgotten Polish. I remember that I was embarrassed because my grandmother spoke Polish. That was a different time.

We lived in Wilkinsburg on Wood Street, not in a typical Polish community or in a Polish neighborhood, although most of my parents' friends were of Polish extraction and all of their social events were with Polish people. Being raised in Wilkinsburg, my friends were mixed. Some of the parents had come from Germany; some came from Switzerland or from England. I was raised as a Roman Catholic. My parents belonged to the Catholic church in Wilkinsburg, not to a nationality church. With my school friends, religion and national origin meant nothing; the ethnic part wasn't an issue. Of course, a lot of people would make fun of my name, but that was later. I didn't notice that so much in high school. In fact, every once in a while I'll have a patient who was a classmate and they'll call me by my maiden name. They say, "It's easier for me to remember you as Dr. Sypniewski than by Dr. Carey." That's funny!

Carey recalled her teenage years in Wilkinsburg. Memories of sex education were vague. She referred to her father's dominant role several times throughout her interview.

I don't even remember how I learned about menstruation and reproduction—I suppose my mother told me. I came home from school and said I had the bellyache. And my grandmother decided that it was something we ate for lunch. I felt so bad I went to bed, and then, of course, I saw blood. I wasn't surprised; I knew about it. As far as sex education and having babies, it seems to me I just always knew. I don't recall my mother sitting me down and giving me a lecture. It might be difficult for me to remember because, being in medicine, I've known this for so long that I don't remember anybody telling me.

Before college, I really wasn't much of a social butterfly—partly because my father didn't allow it. I never had a date until I went to college. I used to study, maybe go to the movies once in a while. No sports—that was not ladylike. My own daughter was a physical education major, so you see how things change. I used to read a lot, mostly historical novels, I believe. I used to try to read all the Polish novels that were translated, because I couldn't read them well enough to enjoy them in Polish. My reading of Polish was only fair. We did get a Polish newspaper in the house, but I don't think I read much of it.

I did know a lot of what was going on, being around my father. And I did go along with him on several of his trips, and I met a lot of people, because after all, he was the head of this whole national organization. He would take me along where he had his meetings and he'd put me on the sight-seeing bus while he was busy, and then afterward we'd go to dinner. When I was out of school in the summertime, I'd go with him and my mother wouldn't go. He always took her when he went on business ventures.

Carey was unique among the women interviewed in that she was committed to a professional career from a very young age.

When I graduated from Wilkinsburg High School in 1931, I graduated with highest honors and I went to the University of Pittsburgh. I was pretty happy. I had a great goal in mind. I made up my mind that I was going to study medicine when I was a sophomore in high school. I think I was always interested in medicine, and when I was in high school I did research with a woman doctor in the summer. There was just nothing that was going to interfere with that. That was it!

I didn't let anything interfere; medicine was my goal. Even when I started dating in college, if I thought some fellow might have an "in" to get me into medical school, why, I sort of clung to him, you know. I was absolutely not interested in anything except getting into medical school.

In college, Carey first experienced prejudice.

I did enjoy college very much. Socially, I was more with the nationality group. In fact, that was the time when they were raising money for the nationality rooms at the University of Pittsburgh. I served on committees helping to raise the money for the nationality rooms, and in that way we did get together. I stuck with nationality groups, which I did not do in high school. I was with the Polish and Czechoslovak and Italian groups, and we used to have a lot of meetings and parties at the International House on Dithridge Street. It was maintained by the YWCA. That's when I first started dating, and most of the dates I had were the boys from the Polish group. I guess most of them were Roman Catholic. But there was never any thought of marriage. I wouldn't have anything to do with it . . . I had to be a doctor.

When Carey applied to medical school in the 1930s, very few women were admitted. People with ethnic names also encountered discrimination in admissions. Competition was keen, and it was generally agreed that influential friends could be helpful to potential applicants.

It was very difficult to get into medical school. I was so surprised when I received my news that I was accepted. I think it was the biggest thrill that I ever had in my life. I don't know whether I can say somebody helped me or not. I had everybody working! . . . I always felt that I was fortunate to have my interview with Dr. Huggins, the dean of the medical school. He was a gentleman, a good doctor, a great man. And, I don't know—after I had my interview with him, I just felt real good. I felt, "I think maybe he liked me." You get that impression. I believe he said when I was leaving, "Well, I wish you all the luck, and I'll be seeing you." And then, when he had the reception for the freshmen class in medical school, he especially said to me, "Do you recall what I said to you?" I said, "Well, I didn't think you meant it." So I think that maybe he had something to do with it.

There were three girls in my class of eighty-five or ninety. The other two girls were married in school, so I was really the only single woman. The boys were nice. I studied with three of my classmates all of the time. The boys used to take turns taking me out Saturday to the movies. We were friends—nothing about love or anything; they called me "one of the boys." Everybody went out on Saturday night in those days. But out of the four or five of us that studied together, there'd always be one of them who would sacrifice himself that Saturday night to take me (laughter). They rotated. Most of those boys had a different type of girl they went out with on Saturday night.

The professors were all very nice. In fact, I dated a couple of them. And my internship was a very happy time. I interned at the University of Pittsburgh Medical Center. It was a tough but very happy time. I used to go thirty-six or thirty-eight hours without even sitting down, especially when I was in obstetrics.

It was difficult. I got awfully tired. But it was a happy time. I liked everything in medicine. And I dated, too. That's what I shouldn't have done, though. A lot of times, instead of going to bed I went out. I can't recall exactly what we did. Most of the people used to go to dances, boat rides, movies. I lived at home.

Dr. Carey recalled her courtship and her marriage, which represented a major break with her Polish Catholic heritage.

In 1938, during my internship, I met my husband. I fell in love. He happened to be a technician working in the X-ray Department at Presbyterian Hospital. He was thirty-three years old and I was twenty-four. And then all my good intentions of nothing to interfere with my medical career came to an end. Anyway, we got married. We didn't even date very long—we first went out in February and were married the following August [1938]. I've often wondered what it was that made me fall in love. I had no rational reasons. You just fall in love and that's it; against your better judgment, you get married.

Mr. Carey was born and raised on a ranch in Kansas. His mother was Irish and his father was English. He was Presbyterian, and we decided to go halfway, so we became Episcopalians shortly after we were married.

I don't think my mother particularly liked my leaving the church, but she adjusted. She liked him; everybody liked him. When he was a young man, he was dashing and charming, and we had a lot of common interests. I thought he was a nice guy, and I enjoyed his company. I remember asking my father whether he thought I was making a mistake getting married, and he said, "I sure do. If I had it to do over, I wouldn't have gotten married!" So I knew he was kidding me. If he had objected, I'm sure he would have made it very, very definite in no uncertain terms, because that's the way I was brought up. I wasn't allowed to go out; I wasn't allowed to do this, and there were no questions asked—although my father did say, "Now, you understand it's going to be very difficult to have a career and a marriage." I said, "Yes, I know."

Carey recalled the difficulties she faced as a woman trying to establish a career in medicine.

I wanted to go into gynecology, but I could not get a residency. The excuse for not giving women residencies was that they didn't have the facilities. That's what I was told when I applied for gynecology: "We have no facilities to house women."

I think World War II made the difference for women in medicine. Before the war, a woman could stand on her head and wiggle her toes and they wouldn't give you a job. Then, when male doctors were away in the service, hospitals were critically short of help. Dr. McElroy, dean of the University of Pittsburgh Medical School, asked me to get all the women doctors together. We met at my house and he recruited them for jobs at the hospitals. I remember one doctor, in particular; she was a highly trained neurosurgeon, and she was sitting at home because she couldn't get a job or get on a hospital staff.

It was my husband's idea that I go into radiology. He worked with Dr. Henderson at Magee Hospital. They were just starting a program in radiology at the University of Pittsburgh hospitals. Dr. Henderson offered me a residency in radiology, and I couldn't turn it down. So I was the first resident in radiology at the university.

When I decided to go into radiology, I thought I'd better have a baby first. Many people suggested that if I ever expected to have a family, I should do this first because of the danger of radiation.

Carey described her pregnancy and feelings about pregnancy that she did not fully understand.

Mary Lou was born just before our first wedding anniversary. In fact, it was a surprise. I just felt sick to my stomach one morning, and I thought, "When was my last period?" I told my mother right away. Everybody at home knew right away, although I didn't care to publish it. During my pregnancy I did some examinations at the YWCA, and some school examining, and a little general practice.

It was a very normal pregnancy, but I hated being pregnant. I never heard of anybody before or since who had that problem. I was extremely sensitive. I didn't want anybody to know I was pregnant. Although my mother and all my friends knew, they also knew that I didn't want to talk about it. Some women get sick to their stomachs; some get bleeding gums; some get congestion of the mucous membranes. Well, I think I got congestion in my brain. Maybe I do know why. A friend of mine, a doctor at Bell Telephone, told me that if you were pregnant, they wouldn't let you work. You didn't flaunt your pregnancy. She said, "Don't let anybody know you're pregnant until you start showing." Well, I hid it pretty well. I think the last three months I just stayed home and pouted. I just hated being pregnant. I just hated it.

At that time Judge Lois McBride was running for reelection. She was responsible for the blood-test law in Pennsylvania and at that time was working for premarital blood tests and for sex education in schools. And she asked me to go out and make some speeches for her. Her office set up appointments, and I went to schools, women's clubs, Rotary, etcetera, talking up these things and trying to get her reelected. I camouflaged myself pretty good, with suits and blouses with lots of ruffles, and went out and made speeches [laughter]. I saw the doctor, and I had a very uneventful pregnancy but quite a hard labor. Mary Lou was delivered at

St. Margaret's Hospital. After that, I never got pregnant again. I was careful for about a year. After that, I didn't do anything but I never got pregnant. After Mary Lou was born, I went right into my radiology residency.

Despite the demands of her profession, Carey assumed full responsibility for all housekeeping. Her mother helped with child care.

I was brought up in a home where the husband does nothing around the household. I managed to take care of the house. I insisted that just because I was a career woman, I wasn't going to accept any help. I was going to see that I got it done myself, somehow. I was going to do it. Whether I could or I couldn't, I was going to do it.

My mother saved the day. We lived in the same apartment building, so that I could do most of the things for the baby. When I had to leave, I took her to my mother's. I'd leave her over there during the day, and then when I'd come home I'd wheel her bed back to my apartment. My mother watched her during the day when I worked. Then all my mother had to do was give her [her] noon bottle. Of course, as [the baby] grew up, Mother had to do a little more. So I had a built-in baby-sitter. Without my mother, I couldn't have done it.

Being a resident in radiology, I had pretty regular hours. Except for a conference, I worked from nine until four or five o'clock. While Mary Lou was an infant, I used to get her formula all ready, and bottles sterilized, and give her a bath and everything before I left. In the evening I gave her a meal, gave my husband dinner, and we had playtime with Mary Lou, and I'd clean house. I had day help one day a week.

My husband was very old-fashioned. When Mary Lou was a baby, he did very little for her. I don't think he ever changed a diaper. As she got older, he used to do a lot of chauffeuring. When she was in high school, she was very much interested in the basketball team and he'd take her and all of her girlfriends to all the basketball games. No matter where they were playing, he'd drive them. And she went to dancing school, and I guess he would do that.

Carey taught her daughter the facts of life in a rather academic way. Like most mothers, she avoided explicit discussion of the sex act.

I remember telling Mary Lou about menstruation and reproduction. I think I just got the book out and we studied the differences between the male and female, and how things grow. In fact, I had all her little friends in here one time, too, and gave them all a little lecture. They all thought that was great!

I think I taught her very gradually, though. Whenever she asked a question, I'd answer it the best I could, without any specifics until she was old enough to sit down and look at the pictures. And then I went over the whole—not "the birds and the bees" business but the physiology of the female and the male—and showed her pictures of how a baby develops in the uterus.

I don't think I ever went into how that sperm got in there, though. Not until she was much older. All her little friends wanted to know something more about it. I think that's when I hedged, skirted the intercourse idea, quite, well, around the bush. I figured we wouldn't go into that in detail, although I think they realized how the sperm got in there.

My father told my mother, and my mother told me, and I told my daughter, "Sex is something you don't talk about. You don't discuss what happened in the bedroom. You don't discuss it with your girlfriend. You don't discuss it with anybody." That's your own private affair, and that's the way I feel. That's private.

Mary Lou had the usual teenage problems: you know, "I want to go out," and Mommy says, "You can't go out," [and Daughter replies,] "You're a mean mommy"—which she laughs at now. She thought I was a little bit too strict. She knows now that it was for the best. My husband was very strict. That caused a lot of conflict. In his eyes, no boy would ever be good enough for her. Even when she was teaching, he didn't want her to go out. There was always tension.

Carey was ambivalent about her Polish background. Although she claimed that being Polish had no real effect on her life, her remarks about sensitivity to ethnic slurs and exposure to prejudice suggest otherwise. Avoidance of confrontation was standard behavior for her generation.

My husband and I were from different backgrounds, and we didn't know what to expect from each other. It caused a lot of arguments when I was first married. He would make a joke about the Polish, and it hurt a little. And then you say, "Well, all right, you Irishman," and then the fight is on. You get used to that as you get older. It takes a long time to get to know somebody you're married to. In fact, you can be married to him for fifty years and still not know him.

Because my name is Carey, many people say, "Oh, you don't need to tell me you're not Irish. You've got the map of Ireland all over your face." I just sit there and grin to myself. I never say anything. Why embarrass people? I really do have very Slavic features. If you've ever studied any Polish physiognomy, it's very typical. Recently there are Polish jokes. I don't have a problem with that; I never say a word. If my grandchildren came home with them, I think I'd consider the source and just say nothing. After all, there are a lot of Jewish jokes, a lot of Irish jokes. I think I would ignore any jokes.

My daughter was well aware of her Polish heritage. She never could speak, although there are still quite a few words that we use every once in a while, because it's sort of a joke. *Comforter,* for instance: a real heavy lamb's wool comforter was *prezynka.* Well, we still call our comforters *prezynka.* Even my son-in-law calls it that. And the little kids call it that. That doesn't mean they can speak Polish. A lot of little words.

We never did observe a lot of customs like some Polish families did. Like on Christmas Eve, they put straw on the windows. We never did that, although I guess my grandmother used to bake the doughnuts and the poppy-seed cake at Easter. But that was about it. We were not traditional. We were more toward doing things the way that it was done here. The tie was to the pride of heritage rather than the heritage itself.

I don't think that my Polish background has ever really been a part of my life. It was part of my father's life. If somebody asks me what I am today, I would never think of saying, "I'm Polish." I mean, I always say, "I'm American." Unless somebody pushes me and says, "Well, where did your ancestors come from?" why, I don't even think about it. Although I'm not ashamed of it—I'm proud of it. We used to joke about it. We'd talk about "the fighting Irish of Notre Dame—Cheslevsky, Snisnewski . . . !" That's always been a joke.

Talk about prejudice when I was in school [college and medical school]! Not only was I Roman Catholic, but a girl, and with a Polish name! It's a wonder I survived. Once I had a feeling—in fact, I was told that the reason that I wasn't accepted in a sorority was because of my name and my religion. That hurt a little bit. Then I thought, "Phooey on you."

Career and family are interwoven in Carey's account of the period from 1939, when she started medical practice, to 1976, when she reflected on her history.

After Mary Lou was born, I started my residency at Magee Hospital. As I said earlier, if it had not been for my mother, I don't think I could have done this, because she took care of my daughter during the day for the two years I was a resident. Of course, my mother and father both enjoyed their grandchild.

When I finished my residency, then came the time for an assistantship, which I had at West Penn Hospital under Dr. Alley. She was in charge of the diagnostic department at West Penn Hospital, and she asked me to come to be her associate. For the first time in my life I was making a little money—two hundred dollars a month. I felt like Rockefeller! I spent two years there, and it was time for me to take my examinations to be accredited by the College of Radiology—which was a harrowing experience. Anybody who has ever taken board examinations to qualify for a specialty knows what a nightmare it is, but fortunately I passed.

During this time we still lived at the apartment. My daughter was growing up. At the age of two she started to nursery school at the Frick Training School in Oakland. The teacher's name was Miss Hahn. I remember the day I left her. She had a little pink dress on and little curls and I was heartbroken. I could hardly leave her, and Miss Hahn said, "Go, go, go!" Before I could turn around, she was jumping in the sandbox and starting to play with the other kids. It was an excellent setup. It was the entire day. They got their lunch. They took a nap. So I would drop her off in the morning, and my mother would pick her up at three o'clock.

After the two years at Frick, I enrolled her in another nursery school, and she went there for two years. By the time she was ready for kindergarten, we were sort of crowded in the apartment and we started to look for a house. We bought a beautiful home in Point Breeze, on Carnegie Place. It was a remodeled Andrew Carnegie coach house with a two-story living room. We just loved the place. The next seven years were spent there and were very happy years.

My mother was still my main baby-sitter. Weekends, we always had a lot of things to do. Either I was having guests, or we were invited out— every weekend was full of social life. So I always took Mary Lou over to her grandmother's, usually Friday night, and then I'd pick her up Sunday morning. They enjoyed having her. My mother always had something planned. They either went downtown or my father would surprise them and take her to see Blackstone the Magician. It was a real treat for her. Maybe that's the reason she started leaving her kids here. She remembered how much fun she had.

I was working at McKeesport Hospital at that time. The position became available and I got it. For the next seven years, I was the radiologist at McKeesport Hospital. The work was challenging and satisfying, but that was a terrible trip to make every day, especially in the winter. I hated the drive. I usually started at eight in the morning and got home about four or five, and if it wasn't snowing, it was raining, or it was fog or ice. I think one winter I wore out five pairs of chains, which, of course, nobody uses anymore.

Well, my husband had changed jobs and decided he wanted to go into business for himself. Prior to this, he was working for Westinghouse and then for General Electric in commercial X ray. I decided I wanted to open an office for the private practice of radiology. So we bought this house which had been made over into three apartments on South Avenue in Wilkinsburg. We put my office on the first floor and put our living quarters on the second and third floors. We shared the office space, and this worked out very well. I could be there when Mary Lou came home from school for lunch and for dinner. Even though I was in the office, I had one eye and one ear open.

In discussing her career, Carey touched on some of the difficulties experienced by women in medicine. She also expressed a feminist conviction that women must support one another.

It's always difficult to start a private practice. I realized that patients were not lining up to get to my door and I needed to pay the grocery bill, so I found a few odd [part-time] jobs. One job at Doctors Hospital ballooned into a bigger job. I continued my private practice and the work at Doctors Hospital, which was later reorganized as Podiatry Hospital.

Of course, at first all my friends were women physicians. I was friendly with the group in the Women's Medical Society in Pittsburgh. We got together for dinner every month before the Allegheny County Medical Society meeting, to console one another. We were all having the same kind of problems—difficulty getting your practice going; none of the men wanted you on the staff of a hospital. We just consoled one another.

I recall that when I started the practice of medicine, other women wouldn't particularly refer work to me. Most of my work came from men. Now it's just the opposite. I do have a lot of women referring [patients] to me. Recently I brought that up at one of the women's medical society meetings. I said, "I'm not particularly interested for me now. I have enough work. But if you don't stick together, who's going to help you? If I can do just as good an X-ray examination as Dr. Z. down the street, why not send your patient to me instead of Dr. Z.?" I was never very shy about saying what I thought!

I suppose that my career did create problems in my marriage. We're still married, but it's not easy. I know that it takes a certain type of man to be married to an active career woman. It was awfully hard to take that "Doctor." They always call him "Doctor" and call me "Mrs." There are a lot of embarrassing situations that a lot of men can't take. When we were with strangers, someone would say, "This is Dr. Carey," and they would invariably go over and shake his hand. I'm so used to it I just think, "Well, poor people, they don't know any better." You know, they're look-ing right at you; right at you, but they'll go shake hands with the guy over there who isn't even anywhere near. They just can't accept the fact that maybe a woman could be a doctor.

I don't think things have changed so much. I had a patient the other day who said, "You know, I never knew there were women doctors." I said, "Well, your day is complete. You learned something today."

I'm sure my career would have been different if I had been a man. I'm sure I would have gone a lot further—maybe a teaching job at a hospital or something. I like private practice better, but I am sure that I would have gotten a lot further ahead. I'm not talking about financially; finances were not really a problem. But it would have been easier.

Eva Carey never separated work and family in her mind or in her activities. The traditional Polish value placed on the domestic role of women and the lasting influence of her dominant father are reflected in her work and in the stress she experienced.

I was always sort of torn between my work, my parents, my husband, and my child. It always seemed that one of them needed me all the time and I had no place to hide. I was stubborn, too. I had to do it all.

I waited on my husband. I always had his breakfast ready, even in his last year, when he was so ill and the nurse came every day. In my mind I had something to prove. When I decided to become a doctor, my father told me, "You can't do both. It's impossible to be a professional and to be a wife and mother." I decided that I was going to prove that I could. I even ironed shirts. I don't know why I was so stupid. But he said, "You do them so much better than the laundry." I got up at five in the morning to iron his shirts. I proved it to myself. I know a lot of times I'd be down scrubbing the floor, I'd say, "For this I went to medical school!" Would I do it today? Sure, if I had to!

I think my father was right. You can't really do both. I'm sure I short-changed somebody. When my daughter was sick, I was torn, because I had appointments that I had to keep. Even now, if Mary Lou isn't well or if the kids are sick, I'm torn. I feel that I should be there to help.

Eva Carey voiced her long-standing commitment to increasing the public role of women, and she explained what membership in an executive women's organization meant to her.

I think the legal rights of women are important. And I think the movement should get women interested in politics, push them a little bit. I think the leaders in the women's organizations ought to get together and find some great, outstanding woman and push her for an office—a capable woman to push for office, and everybody stay with her. I'm sure it's a mistake, but a lot of times I go to vote and I never have time to see who is running, you know, for the little offices. But if I see a woman's name, I'll vote for her.

I belong to Zonta, which is a women's service club similar to Rotary or Kiwanis. They meet monthly, and it's a very relaxing relationship because this is a group where each woman has to be in an executive position in a different field. There are women lawyers and a lot of people in the education field and fashion and retailing and architecture. So it makes for a nice relationship among the group: you find there are good women in other fields besides medicine, and it gives you sort of a glow.

Dr. Carey spoke of her current activities and contrasted her life with that of her mother and daughter.

I usually start here in my office about seven-thirty in the morning. We have office hours until about five-thirty or so. Two days a week I go to a small hospital in East Liberty called Doctors Hospital. It's a nice little hospital. I do the radiology there. I go there on Mondays and Fridays from about eleven o'clock until two o'clock. The rest of the time I'm here in my office. Then I go home and fix dinner. And tonight, if I'm not too tired, I'm going to clean the living room. Yesterday I did the dining room—for Thanksgiving. Anyway, every evening I make myself up a schedule, and half the time I get it done. Most of the time I don't. I do my own cleaning because I've just not been able to get help.

I have Mary Lou's kids here every weekend. They usually come on Saturday afternoon and stay overnight with me, and then on Sunday my daughter and son-in-law come to have brunch and then they go home. Mary Lou gets a little break, and we have a great time. We paint pictures; we make Christmas ornaments. We used to make little figures out of pipe cleaners. We have a regular routine. Often on Sundays I deliver the X rays to certain doctors. We do that early Sunday morning. We'll get in the car and go down Graham Boulevard, which is a yellow brick road. So we sing the song from *The Wizard of Oz*, "Yellow Brick Road," and we just have a lot of fun. Sometimes it's a little too much for me. I enjoy them, but they're awful hard to handle at times. I'm too old to bring up children. That's why God made young ladies.

January 23, 1989, Interview

Eva Carey's mother died in 1977. Carey closed her office in Wilkinsburg and sold the building in April 1987. Her husband died on May 6, 1987, after a long illness. When I visited her in 1989, Carey not only filled in the events of the intervening years but also offered some further information about her mother.

My dad died on January 7, 1958. My mother stayed in the apartment in Oakland and continued to manage the building until it got too much for her. In about 1969 she sold the building. Then we moved Nanna—we called my mother Nanna—to 746 South Avenue, into the apartment above my office.

After she died, I found letters in which she wrote, "I'm so unhappy here. Although I'm glad to be near Eva and helping her, I'm so unhappy." And then a year later she wrote, "I finally got adjusted." She never said anything to me. She always said, "I'm so happy." She used to wash the gowns for my office, and she felt she was doing something. I had these crinkle-cotton gowns, and the laundry used to just wreck them. I had a washer and drier there, so it was no problem to do them myself. When she moved to the apartment, she said, "Let me do that." And then she used to keep Andy [her great-grandson, Mary Lou Olmo's child] overnight, usually on Wednesdays.

An interesting thing about my mother: she could amuse children with two toothpicks; she was marvelous. I remember one time my daughter and her husband went away. They asked me to watch the kids, so I took a week off, went to their house. It almost killed me. They were just at the wrong age. Andy was picking on Kari and she was crying—it was more than I could handle. So about the third day, I called my husband and I said, "Please get my mother over here; I don't think I can make it." So she came over and I said, "I just have to sit down." And she said, "Why, they're just little angels. They're just little angels. Why would they be bothering you?" And they were! When she was there, they were just perfect. She made toys out of spools, and out of neck bones, and any little thing that was handy.

I know I hurt my mother's feelings once. She felt as though this was her place, her apartment. When she'd have company, she'd bring them down to show them my office [laughter]. Well, I might be doing a barium enema or something, and in she'd walk! I didn't want to hurt her feelings, but I said, "Grandma, I just can't have you coming in here anytime when I'm working on patients." She said, "Whoops, I didn't know you were busy."

Then one time she said, "I'm having Betty over. Is it all right if I bring her down and show her your office?" I said, "No, it isn't." And she was so hurt. And I am so sorry. She just didn't understand—that that's my office, and I just can't have her wandering in there anytime she wants to. And I'm sorry I hurt her, but I had to, because she would just wander in anytime at all. She just didn't understand . . . out of pride, she wanted to show her friends my office. [With a laugh] And I hope if she's listening, "I'm sorry."

I'm happy in my widowhood. I'm busy. I hardly have time to do the things I'm supposed to. I see Mary Lou and her husband and the kids every weekend. They're here either for dinner on Saturday or brunch on Sunday. Andy is a sophomore in college and Kari is a junior in high school, and they're great kids.

I now spend half of every day at Podiatry Hospital, and I chair the Credentials Committee. The hospital is doing a good job now. And I'm grateful for it, because I'm retired from private practice and that gives me something to get out of bed for in the morning. I became associated with Doctors Hospital about 1955 [later changed to Podiatry Hospital]. I do all their radiology, and now I have someone helping me. I'm on the board of directors at the hospital. I'm sort of a fixture there now.

What do I want in the next ten years? I just hope I'm still alive. I hope to enjoy my semiretirement. I enjoy going to the hospital every day for four or five hours. I plan to stay at Podiatry Hospital as long as I can walk—as long as they'll have me.

Mary Lou Olmo,
b. 1939
January 29, 1976, and January 26, 1989, Interviews

Mary Lou Olmo began her oral history with a denial of any ethnic content in her life. Her grandfather's strict separation of religion from ethnic custom, together with the emphasis in the family on professional success, may have contributed to assimilation.

I'm totally unethnic. We never followed any traditions. In fact, it's something I would have liked to have done, now that I think back on it. What is a traditional Polish Christmas dinner? I have no idea. I cook strictly American. My mother didn't follow any customs at home. In fact, they didn't celebrate Christmas, because my grandfather believed in it as strictly a religious holiday. My mother just told me this not too long ago. For my grandfather, Christmas meant going to church, and that was it. All I can remember as far as Christmas when I was little would be at my mother's. Everybody would come for the traditional turkey.

My grandmother did get the Polish newspaper. About the only thing I can remember about that is that Tarzan was in it, and we used to save it and my grandfather would read it to me in English translated from the Polish. My grandparents spoke Polish only when they wanted to talk about things without me knowing.

My father is English all the way back. When anybody asks me, I usually say that I'm English and Polish, married to a Spanish man. But I don't really think of myself in those terms. Since my mother was a professional woman, the whole social structure of the family was a lot different. Most of the acquaintances were doctors or associates of my father's from various backgrounds. My mother married a non-Polish person, so there was no reason to be ethnic. I don't think she wanted to be ethnic. She said it was a definite disadvantage to be in a minority group and she was in three minority groups. She was a woman; she was Polish; and she was Catholic. Trying to get into medicine wasn't an easy job. I think it was because of this that she just broke away from all that.

Olmo's mixed feelings about her working mother were probably influenced by the negative view of professional women that prevailed when she was a child.

My mother was a radiologist. I was proud that she was a doctor. It wasn't that I was ashamed that my mother was [a] doctor and not a housewife. When I would say, "Well, my mother is a doctor," people were always surprised. Today it's not so unusual. When I was little, in grade school, it was frowned upon. The principal and the teachers gave her a rough time. I remember her making comments once that at the open houses at school, they said she should be home with her child instead of out in the world.

She was a doctor and worked all the time. I never really thought about it until I was a teenager. Then I thought the communication lines that I thought should be there weren't there because she wasn't home. It's lonely to come home after school to an empty house when you are a teenager. Coming home to an empty house was a very big thing to me. Years later, when I had my own children, I told my mother how I missed her after school. She told me Grandma wasn't there for her; she said that Grandma always had a committee meeting or something and was usually not at home.

When I was in high school, I used to clean up the house and cook dinner when I came home from school, because my mother was late. I'd get my allowance for cleaning the house. We had a constant menu of hamburgers and green beans [laughter].

Olmo enjoyed a special relationship with her grandmother. Her grandfather is remembered for his single "surprise" treat.

When I was younger, I had my grandmother. Because my mother practiced medicine, my grandmother more or less raised me for the first five years. Whenever I was sick, I wanted my grandmother. One year I had a really bad ear infection and missed a month of school. My grandmother came and stayed with me. She would take me to dancing school. She would take me shopping. Everything that a mother and her daughter do when you're six, I did with my grandmother. I wanted to ice-skate; she would take me to Duquesne Gardens. I wanted my own ice skates, so we went to Gimbel's basement. She bought me a pair of ice skates to grow into—I had to be seven or eight years old. Those ice skates are still too big for me!

She would take me downtown on the trolley to the Diamond Market to do grocery shopping. My grandfather surprised us with tickets to see Blackstone the Magician. Well, she took me downtown shopping. Then she took me to Grandpa's office, and he took me to see the magician show. My grandmother was terrific with little kids. She could do anything with children. If you didn't have a toy, she could make something. She could take anything off the desk and make a way to play with it. I have really good memories of my grandmother.

Olmo's account of her mother's lesson in sex education presents one example of a tension-laden mother-daughter relationship.

My mother taught me all about menstruation and reproduction. It was represented totally as a lecture, very early, before it ever happened. I was the big informer for all my girlfriends. We used to sit around and talk about menstruation and childbirth and intercourse and all this jazz. I was twelve, I guess, in seventh grade. It was a shock. She said, "You're starting to grow up, and when women start to grow up certain things happen to them physically, and this is what happens." I saw pictures in the medical books. It was a very good way to introduce it, but it was a little shocking! It could have been a little softer, I think. I think I was aware of menstruation before she explained it to me, because I can remember Kotex. I asked her about it, and she told me it meant she's not pregnant. That was when I was little. I think my daughter, Kari, will know about menstruation much sooner before it happens than I did. The timing for me was very close. I got the explanation and three months later, there it was.

When I was pregnant with Kari, Andy, who was three, wanted to know how babies got there. I bought him a Time-Life book about how babies grow and let him look through it. When he asked a question, I answered it. My mother said, "I don't think you should tell them those things. They're too young. They won't understand." My parents were very conservative. Sexually conservative.

202

Mary Lou continued with a chronological account of going to high school, attending college, and choosing an occupation.

As I look back on those days at Wilkinsburg High School, they were a lot of fun. But it was hard for me personally. I didn't like myself as a teenager, because I was overweight. That was always a problem. I'm tall, and I've always wanted to be lithe and flowing, and I have never been [laughter]. It's still a problem.

I've always been athletic, and that's what I did in high school. I had a group of friends, and we all played basketball. We went to basketball games and football games. In the summertime, we'd go swimming.

My mother sort of wanted me to be a lawyer like my grandfather. She still wants me to go back to law school and become a lawyer. I didn't feel that a professional career like law was for me. My father never expressed any expectations for me. I guess he just wanted me to turn out good.

I liked athletics best. I thought I wanted to teach physical education, but when I heard that kids give a lot of trouble to student teachers, I changed my mind.

I went to Hood College, which is a women's college in Maryland. I started out in home economics, but after one semester I changed my major to political science, and by the end of my sophomore year I had changed my major four times. I finally decided that I would teach physical education. They didn't have a physical education major at Hood, so I transferred to Pitt and finished my work there in 1961.

Then I got a job teaching at Mount Mercy [parochial school for women], which is now Carlow. I taught high school freshmen and grade-school students until 1967. At the same time I got my master's degree in education. I was very happy. I lived in my own apartment in Shadyside, and I loved it.

Mary Lou Carey met Ray Olmo in 1963, and they married in 1965. Their first serious conflict centered on the children, Andy and Kari, who were born, respectively, in 1969 and 1972.

I was very happy being married, but I didn't think marriage was going to be as hard as it turned out [laughter]. People always say you have to work at having a happy marriage. I think that girls that grew up in my generation all had a lovely picture of marriage being a bed of roses and all happiness. It isn't. If I were growing up today, I would think very hard about getting married. If it wasn't for having children . . . being married is a very difficult thing. There are days when I would rather be free and loose and go out on my own. But then, there are days—most days—that I'm very happy where I am.

My parents like Ray a lot. And my mother-in-law is a very warm and accepting person. Ray's background is Spanish and he's Roman Catholic. It was my decision to convert before we were married; I felt that two people getting married to raise a family should have the same faith.

I was married about three years when I became pregnant. It was a terrific pregnancy. I felt fine. I got very fat. I stayed very fat. My mother recommends all my doctors; I went to a woman gynecologist. And I do think that women physicians in her age bracket are a lot more dedicated.

Labor was hard. I was ecstatic when the babies were born. I wanted children, and I was very happy I was having them. I never had any postpartum depression. My mother came for a couple of days to help me after Andy was born. It had been a long time since she had a baby, and I'd say it was like the blind leading the blind. But we did it!

Having kids was the hardest thing to get used to in marriage. My husband is a very social person and he liked to entertain a lot. When you have no children, it's very easy to go out a lot and have parties. Now, with children, it's more difficult to go out; you can't get a sitter at the last moment. I think it was harder for him to adjust than for me. We are very big hockey fans and we have been going to hockey games since we were dating. We still go out a lot, but he had to get used to the fact that he couldn't come home Friday afternoon at five o'clock and say, "We are going to the game tonight. Get a sitter." He had to realize I needed a day or two to dig one up. We had a lot of heated discussions about that!

I have always been a person who feels a need to get away from every-thing, do something on my own. My ice skating, for example: it's me accomplishing something. There were times when I needed to go out in the evening for skating this past couple of weeks. He had to baby-sit. I don't like that expression, *baby-sit*. They are his children too. If he consid-ers it baby-sitting to stay home with the children, that means that my job is baby-sitting all day long. That's the biggest bone of contention we have now. He doesn't feel that he should have to stay home with the children.

Olmo's remarks about holidays and foods suggest how far she has moved from ethnic tradition.

We don't celebrate any customs. Ray's situation is similar to mine. His mother and father are Spanish. However, they were divorced when Ray was very young, and his mother's husband is not Spanish. She speaks Spanish fluently, and Ray does too if he gets a chance to practice. We were in Puerto Rico, and after a day there, Ray could speak good Span-ish. There are a couple of things that he likes that are Spanish. There is a special way to make rice. His mother makes rice this way. It took me a long time to learn how to do it. Some Spanish foods he likes are hard to find here. A kind of *frito* that he likes, I won't make, because I don't know how it's supposed to taste, feel, or smell.

Olmo summarized her weekly routine, which includes volunteer teaching and secretarial work for her mother. She talked also about her relationship with her mother.

I skate every day. I took it up seriously in September and just passed my preliminary dance steps. I was very pleased. Ice skating is my very own thing; that's what I feel best about accomplishing. On Saturday mornings I teach ice skating.

In the mornings, I teach first- and second-grade gym at my children's school, and I teach CCD [Catholic Christian Doctrine] classes at church. That's after school, to eleventh- and twelfth-grade students.

Thursday afternoons I usually type for my mother. I do her billing and everything from her office. I don't want her to pay me. If I do need some extra money, she'll give me a dollar here and there. She doesn't want to have to hire someone to do this little bit of typing. It's not worth it—it's just sending out the bills and insurance forms. I said, "I'll do it." The kids visit Grandma while I do the typing. Then we go up to her apartment for lunch.

My relationship with my mother is very close. I'm still a little girl to her, and I sort of act the role for her. It's always like mommy and little girl. We've never reached the point where it's woman to woman. My husband tells me that when I'm on the phone, he can always tell when I'm talking to my mother. I feel "down here" while she's "up here" [with gestures] I've never gotten up to the point where I feel I'm not a little girl.

Her own experience and the experience and philosophy of her mother helped to shape Olmo's ideas about women. She compared her life with that of her grandmother.

I have some mixed feelings about the women's movement. I think equal pay for equal jobs is right. I don't think you should be discriminated against for a job opportunity because you are a woman. If you are qualified, you should be equally considered no matter what—not only for women but for everyone.

I definitely feel that if you are going to raise a family, you should be obligated for those children until they start school. Once they're in school, then you can do what you want with your time, to a point.

My grandmother, from what I understand, was a really involved person in a Polish women's group. From stories my mother told, she was always out doing this and doing that. That's sort of what I do—I'm out doing this and doing that. I think my life differs mostly from my mother's because she was a career woman. Probably my life and my grandmother's parallel each other more because we both stayed at home. But I'm freer to do a lot of things. I can go skating and skate with a man at the skating rink. Back in my grandmother's day, that would have been totally frowned upon.

I value my time and my choice. It's nice to say I have my time to do with as I wish. If I want to go to work, I can. If I want to stay home, I can. I guess that's what I value most in my life. I enjoy being able to choose my own life.

January 27, 1989, Interview

Mary Lou Olmo became an accredited judge for the U.S. Figure Skating Association. In 1984 at age forty-five she returned to graduate school to study sports psychology and in 1989 was completing requirements for her Ph.D. Ethnicity played no role in her life, and she no longer attended church. Always remembering her own childhood need for someone to talk to after school, Olmo spoke of her efforts to encourage communication with her children, who were nineteen and sixteen in 1989.

Now I'm in graduate school, and I'm not at home after school either. But my daughter will talk to me about everything; she'll tell me exactly what's going on in school and with her friends. About the only thing she doesn't talk about openly to me is something that she thinks will disappoint me, and I make her talk about it. I keep saying, "What's the matter?" until she tells. Then I can help her. I worked very hard to build that relationship. I love my mother a lot, but I remember really needing somebody to talk to. And my daughter does talk to me.

Conclusion

In these pages grandmothers, mothers, and daughters in six families recorded the stories of their lives. They spoke of their parental families and the families they established as adult women. They talked about work and recreation and about experiences and attitudes that were important to them. They recalled Italian, Jewish, and Slavic customs that were a part of their lives. They talked about relationships between themselves and their mothers and their daughters. And in the process they each contributed previously unpublished information about change and continuity in women's lives in twentieth-century America.

In personal terms, immigrant women remembered loneliness, alienation, and feelings of inadequacy. Women who successfully adjusted to the United States recorded memories of unfamiliar situations in a strange culture in which people spoke an unknown language. Although the absence of much that was familiar compounded the difficulty of adjusting to the new land, there were people who made the transition less painful—a father, a mother-in-law, a cousin, a teacher, a classmate. Networks of relatives, the building of their own families, and improvements in the material conditions of life provided welcome supports, as did the continuity of tradition through ethnic neighborhoods and ethnic church.

These oral histories document the central function served by the ethnic group. In the ethnic neighborhood were familiar foods, a European bakery, a church or a synagogue where the native language was spoken. In the neighborhood immigrants found people who knew Slovak or Polish or Yiddish or Italian and who could speak English as well. These were the mediators who helped find a place to sleep, a place to eat, a job. They showed the new arrivals what was expected on the job, how to count money, where to shop, and what to buy.[1]

Daughters of immigrants, the second-generation "mothers" of this book, understood from childhood that a degree of assimilation was essential in order to feel at home in American society. They wanted above all else to be American. Most of their children, the third-generation "daughters," expressed a longing for ethnicity, even though ethnicity no longer served the pragmatic purpose it had for their grandparents. Instead, ethnicity for most third-generation women had nostalgic and psychological value. Comfortable in their American identity, "daughters" looked to the ethnic group to satisfy a need for intimacy and belonging. That need was heightened by changing economic realities and by geographic mobility that took young people away from home to live and work among those whose backgrounds differed from their own. Although there are significant differences, a possible parallel can be drawn between the experience of the granddaughters and their grandmothers.

Ethnic neighborhoods and ethnic churches and synagogues lost some of their importance as families moved away from the immigrant settlements. Of the third-generation women whose oral histories are included in this book, only Joanne Gereg continued to pray at the ethnic church in which she and her husband had been baptized, confirmed, and married.

Over the generations, specific ethnic behavioral patterns and attitudes diminished. This lessening was to be expected as daughters and granddaughters of immigrants associated with people of varied backgrounds at school and work and in the general life of the community.

In some cases, class proved to be a deciding factor affecting gender roles and family relationships. Class influenced where people lived and what their aspirations, education, and relationships were. Power within the family was also influenced by class. The oral histories suggest that in the first and second generations, a working woman whose economic contribution was essential to the household held a greater degree of power relative to her husband than a middle-class woman at home did.[2] The oral histories indicate that in some instances class affected ethnic identity. Emphasis on upward mobility sometimes promoted assimilation.[3] Other publications suggest that, for some working women, class consciousness replaced ethnicity as the primary group identity.[4]

Nevertheless, among women of all social classes, ethnicity maintained significant meaning. Social networks for all but a very few of the women interviewed tended to remain within the ethnic group. Volunteer activities and often paid work took place in an organized ethnic setting, such as a church or social service agency.[5] Ethnic identity lost its relevance for only a few of the women interviewed.

In the areas of family and personal values, evidence of ethnic values persisted even among women who professed no strong sense of ethnic identity. The focus on family was integral to the design of the project and touched a responsive chord among the women who were interviewed.

Women wanted to talk about family. Their accounts of family life confirm studies that have identified distinctive cultural patterns in Italian, Jewish, and Slavic families.[6]

Italian-American culture has been distinguished historically by the central importance of the family unit. Even though the contemporary family has relinquished much of its economic function, the social interaction within the Italian family has remained intensive. As illustrated particularly in the Profeta/Fastuca/Dorio oral histories, frequent interaction and extensive patterns of visiting and exchanging services have continued to characterize the Italian family.

Over its long history, the Jewish family has developed a basic set of values and behavioral patterns designed for survival. Most striking is the generational structure of the family with its focus on children, for children represent the future. Although relationships with extended-family members are valued and interaction between siblings is frequent, the primary responsibility in the Jewish family is that of parents to children. Sociologist Marshall Sklare writes that Jewish parents see their children as extensions of themselves and, like Eva Dizenfeld, Belle Stock, and Naomi Cohen, take pleasure when the achievements of their children go beyond their own.[7]

The Slavic family has been distinguished historically by stability and by a great deal of mutual reciprocity between the generations.[8] Sociologist Michael Novak has described a Slavic conception of the family in which nourishing takes place "both of the generation of the elderly and the generation of children."[9] The oral histories of two families of Slavic background in this book document this tradition of reciprocal support of the generations.

Paid work played a significant part in the lives of almost every woman interviewed. In fact, all of the daughters and 50 percent of the mothers were working in 1989. Yet the women spoke little about the specifics of their work. Except for a very few, work was an economic necessity.

Betty Friedan identified the difficulty of reconciling family needs and the need to work as the greatest challenge to the women's movement in the 1980s.[10] In each generation and ethnic group, women did two jobs; they worked and they cared for families. And in each generation and ethnic group, women voiced serious reservations about working and raising children at the same time. This concern was articulated by all the women interviewed, including young professionals who were committed to feminist goals. Ruth Zober voiced the problem succinctly when she said, "A woman shouldn't have to give up the family part of herself." Women questioned whether it was feasible to expect to work and to raise children properly. Mothers, regardless of their generation, considered family their primary responsibility. Tensions between work and the care of children constituted a constant source of stress for women with children.[11]

The lasting tie between the generations stands out as an overriding theme of the oral histories. This tie is expressed in affectionate bonds and in conflict as well. It can also be discerned in the persistence of strengths and weaknesses from one generation to another. Conflict was frequently a part of mother-daughter relationships.[12] Among daughters of immigrants, the desire to escape ethnicity and to be "real" Americans was often a source of conflict. Marriage to someone outside the ethnic group provided an avenue of escape, and in the second generation such marriages increased significantly. Although many of the women who chose husbands of a different ethnic background claimed a continued attachment to their native culture, "marrying out" represented a noteworthy break with tradition.

Personal conflicts between mothers and daughters often persisted after young women married. Frequently, middle-aged mothers voiced unsolicited opinions on such topics as housekeeping, raising grandchildren, budgeting, and working. As one would expect, daughters resented such interference. In later years, roles were sometimes reversed. As mothers aged, daughters offered unsolicited advice on a wide range of subjects, such as where to live, what to eat, and what activities to pursue or relinquish. Just as young women resisted parental domination, aging parents often refused the advice of solicitous children. Even harder for an aging mother was the realization that she was no longer capable of living independently and really did need the "parenting" of her daughter. The daughter's time and attention were frequently divided between obligations to children and obligations to aging parents. Their very position as the middle generation subjected the second generation to great emotional stress, for they were expected to give support to both the older and the younger generations.[13]

In spite of conflict, in most families interviewed, ties of intimacy and responsibility between generations remained strong. The three generations of women genuinely cared about one another and acted to keep bonds intact. Most mothers and daughters communicated about family-related issues with frequent visits and daily telephone conversations. Maintaining connections was vital to grandmothers, mothers, and daughters. Because they did care deeply, they were profoundly disturbed by disagreement or misunderstanding, as well as by the physical or mental debility of a loved one. Affection and caring coexisted with tensions. This combination of emotions contributed to the ambivalence and complexities that characterized mother-daughter relationships.

These oral histories also offer information about a less explored relationship, that between grandmothers and adult granddaughters. Here, granddaughters expressed a love and respect for grandmothers that superseded wide gaps in experience. And there is much evidence of the devotion of grandmothers to granddaughters. The close grandmother-granddaughter relationships developed in the absence of cultural and linguistic barriers that had separated the generations in the period of immigration early in the century.

The oral histories in this book tell a great deal about relationships between the three generations of women. Yet there is much about interactions within families that the oral history accounts do not adequately explain, because information about the male role is missing. In this book we know about men only from the perceptions of the women. How much more we would understand about family history did we also have access to the oral histories of the grandfathers, fathers, and sons.

Here is history from the perspective of women. Women have opened their hearts to talk about personal relationships, aspirations, grief, childbirth, love, marriage, divorce, and their dearest hopes for their children. In these oral histories women have admitted to superstition, ignorance about important and intimate aspects of life, prejudice they felt and prejudice they experienced. Their oral histories tell personal stories that dramatize and humanize the history of twentieth-century America. Their words demonstrate that oral history can enrich the meaning of more traditional narrative history and that it can simultaneously individualize the findings of quantitative social history.

Oral history also highlights the central influence of time and space. The profound impact of the steel-based economy was felt by every woman whose story is told in this book. Each generation grew up in a distinct cultural and historical milieu; each oral history shows the influence of a particular time in history. The experiences of three generations of ethnic women help the reader to understand changes in the lives of women in the twentieth century. The oral histories also document continuity. The strengths and weaknesses, the values and beliefs of grandmothers frequently find expression in contemporary form in the lives of their daughters and granddaughters.

Time, place, ethnic culture, class, and gender—all significantly affect the course of history. Above all, people make history. The oral histories in this book demonstrate the historical significance of individual lives. Each woman who recorded her oral history for *Grandmothers, Mothers, and Daughters* contributed to the fund of historical knowledge about women. Each woman has become a part of history.

Notes and References

Introduction

1. John Higham, *Send These to Me: Jews and Other Immigrants in Urban America* (New York: Atheneum, 1975), 8–28; Maxine Schwartz Seller, ed., *Immigrant Women* (Philadelphia: Temple University Press, 1981); Cecyle S. Neidle, *America's Immigrant Women: Their Contribution to the Development of a Nation from 1609 to the Present* (New York: Hippocrene Books, 1975).

2. See Judith E. Smith, "Gender and Class in Working-Class History," *Radical History Review* 44 (1989):152–58; Christine Stansell, *City of Women: Sex and Class in New York, 1789–1860* (New York: Knopf, 1986); Virginia Yans-McLaughlin, "Italian Women and Work: Experience and Perception," in *Class, Sex, and the Woman Worker,* ed. Milton Cantor and Bruce Laurie, (Westport, Conn.: Greenwood Press, 1977), 101–19; Miriam Cohen, "Italian-American Women in New York City, 1900–1950: Work and School," in Cantor and Laurie, *Class, Sex, and the Woman Worker,* 120–43; Alice Kessler-Harris, "Organizing the Unorganizable: Three Jewish Women and Their Union," in Cantor and Laurie, *Class, Sex, and the Woman Worker,* 144–65; J. L. Newton, M. Ryan, and J. R. Walkowitz, eds., *Sex and Class in Women's History* (London: Routledge and Kegan, 1983); Susan Estabrook Kennedy, *If All We Did Was Weep at Home: A History of White Working Class Women in America* (Bloomington: Indiana University Press, 1979); S. J. Kleinberg, *The Shadow of the Mills: Working-class Families in Pittsburgh, 1870–1907* (Pittsburgh: University of Pittsburgh Press, 1989); Elizabeth Roberts, *A Woman's Place: An Oral History of Working-class Women, 1890–1940* (Oxford and New York: Blackwell, 1984), Joan Wallach Scott, *Gender and the Politics of History* (New York: Columbia University Press, 1988); Elizabeth Ewen, *Immigrant Women in the Land of Dollars: Life and Culture on the Lower East Side, 1890–1925* (New York: Monthly Review Press, 1985).

3. Corinne Azen Krause, "Grandmothers, Mothers, and Daughters: An Oral History Study of Ethnicity, Mental Health, and Continuity of Three Generations of Jewish, Italian, and Slavic-American Women" (New York: The Institute on Pluralism and Group Identity of the American Jewish Committee, 1978)

(referred to hereafter as "Grandmothers, Mothers, and Daughters" [1978]). This publication describes the research methodology and procedure of the study and reports the results. Interview data were coded and analyzed with the SPSS (Statistical Package for the Social Sciences) program. Results of this analysis are part of the report. The original cassettes and transcripts are housed at the Historical Society of Western Pennsylvania; the Archives of Industrial Society, Hillman Library, University of Pittsburgh, holds copies of the transcripts. See also Krause, "Oral History in Pittsburgh—Women, Ethnicity, and Mental Health: Rationale, Procedure, and Methodology," in *The Italian Immigrant Woman in North America*, ed. Betty Boyd Caroli, Robert Harney, and Lydio Tomasi (Toronto: Multicultural Historical Society, 1978), 260–72.

4. Rae Carlson, "Understanding Women: Implications for Personality Theory and Research," *Journal of Social Issues* 28 (1972):17–32; K. Anderson et al., "Beginning Where We Are: Feminist Methodology in Oral History," *Oral History Review* 15 (Spring 1987):185–207.

5. Carol Gilligan, *In a Different Voice* (Cambridge: Harvard University Press, 1980).

6. Gilligan, *Different Voice;* see also Cohen, "Italian-American Women," in Cantor and Laurie, *Class, Sex, and the Woman Worker,* 120.

7. Daniel J. Levinson et al., *Seasons of a Man's Life* (New York: Ballantine, 1978); Erik Erikson, *Childhood and Society* (New York: Norton, 1950).

8. Helene Deutsch, *The Psychology of Women,* 2 vols. (New York: Bantam, 1978); Juanita H. Williams, *Psychology of Women: Behavior in a Bio-Social Context* (New York: Norton, 1977).

9. On assimilation, see Milton M. Gordon, *Assimilation in American Life: The Role of Race, Religion, and National Origins* (New York: Oxford University Press, 1964). The classic work on cultural pluralism is Horace M. Kallen, *Culture and Democracy in the United States* (1924; New York: Arno Press, 1970). For definitions and theories on this topic, see Michael Novak, *The Rise of the Unmeltable Ethnics* (New York: Macmillan 1971) and *Further Reflections on Ethnicity* (Middletown, Pa.: Jednota Press, 1977), 55–62.

10. Roy Lubove, ed., *Pittsburgh* (New York: Franklin Watts, 1976), 109; Corinne Azen Krause, "Urbanization without Breakdown," *Journal of Urban History* 4 (May 1978):291–306; Krause, "Ethnic Culture, Religion, and Mental Health of Slavic-American Women," *Journal of Religion and Health* 18 (October 1979):298–307.

11. Lloyd A. Fallers, "A Note on the 'Trickle Effect,' " in *Class, Status, and Power,* 2d ed., ed. Reinhardt Bendix and Seymour Martin Lipset (Glencoe, Ill.: Free Press, 1966), 402–5.

Chapter 1

1. Oscar Handlin, *The Uprooted,* 2d enlarged ed. (Boston: Little, Brown, 1970), 3, 33.

2. Leonard Dinnerstein and David M. Riemers, *Ethnic Americans: A History of Immigration and Assimilation* (New York: Harper and Row, 1975), 11; Leonard Dinnerstein and Frederic C. Jaher, eds., *Uncertain Americans: Readings in Ethnic History* (New York: Oxford University Press, 1977), 135.

3. Madlyn Allen Jones, *American Immigration* (Chicago: University of Chicago Press, 1960), 94–96, 193, 198–201; see also Alan M. Kraut, *The Huddled Masses: The Immigrant in American Society, 1880–1921* (Arlington Heights, Ill.: Harlan Davidson, 1982), 39–40.

4. Lubove, *Pittsburgh*, 75–76, 108.

5. Elizabeth Beardsley Butler, *Women and the Trades: Pittsburgh 1907–1908* (New York, Charities Publication Committee, 1909; reprint, Arno and the New York Times, 1969), 339–45.

6. David Katzman, *Seven Days a Week: Women in Domestic Service in Industrializing America* (New York: Oxford University Press, 1978), 44–58.

7. Susan Kleinberg, "The Systematic Study of Urban Women," in Cantor and Laurie, *Class, Sex, and the Woman Worker*, 20–42; also Kleinberg, *The Shadow of the Mills*.

8. Lubove, *Pittsburgh*, 107–12, 117.

9. Corinne Azen Krause, "Italian, Jewish, and Slavic Grandmothers in Pittsburgh: Their Economic Roles," *Frontiers* 2 (Summer 1977):18–28.

10. Ewen, *Immigrant Women in the Land of Dollars*, 202.

11. William H. Chafe, *The American Woman: Her Changing Social, Economic, and Political Roles, 1920–1970* (New York: Oxford University Press, 1972), 55, 155.

12. Eugenia Kaledin, *American Women in the 1950s: Mothers and More* (Boston: Twayne, 1984), 214.

13. Chafe, *American Woman*, 135–50.

14. Colleen Johnson, "The Maternal Role in the Contemporary Italian American Family," in Caroli, *Italian Immigrant Woman*, 239; see also Francesca Colecchia, "The Italian Woman, Impressions and Observations" in Caroli, *Italian Immigrant Woman*, 252–59.

15. Richard Gambino, *Blood of My Blood: The Dilemma of Italian-Americans* (New York: Anchor, 1975).

16. Gambino, *Blood of my Blood*, 144–66; A. Parsons, *Belief, Magic, and Anomie: Essays in Psychosocial Anthropology* (New York: Free Press, 1969).

17. Johnson, "Maternal Role," in Caroli, *Italian Immigrant Woman*, 234–44.

18. Krause, "Women, Ethnicity, and Mental Health," interviews I–3A, I–19A. References to specific interviews in the "Women, Ethnicity, and Mental Health" collection are cited by the word *interview* and the code number.

19. Virginia Yans-McLaughlin, *Family and Community: Italian Immigrants in Buffalo, 1880–1930* (Urbana: University of Illinois Press, 1982), 150, 247–48, 253.

20. Krause, "Grandmothers, Mothers, and Daughters" (1978), 56; interviews I–5A, I–22A, I–22B.

21. Ewen, *Immigrant Women*, 192.

22. Butler, *Women and the Trades*, 21; Cohen, "Italian-American Women in

New York," 123; U.S. Congress, Senate Immigration Commission, *Immigrants in Cities*, vol. 1 (Washington, D.C.: U.S. Government Printing Office, 1911), 220.

23. Virginia Yans-McLaughlin, "Patterns of Work and Family Organization: Buffalo's Italians," *Journal of Interdisciplinary History* 2 (1971): 299–314.

24. See also interviews I–8A, I–8B, I–3A.

25. Sydney Stahl Weinberg, *World of Our Mothers: The Lives of Jewish Immigrant Women* (Chapel Hill: University of North Carolina Press, 1988), 23.

26. Weinberg, *World of Our Mothers*, 134–47; Susan Weidman Schneider, *Jewish and Female: Choices and Changes in Our Lives Today* (New York: Simon and Schuster, 1984), 285–86.

27. Mark Zborowski and Elizabeth Herzog, *Life Is with People: The Culture of the Shtetl* (New York: Schocken, 1962), 131.

28. Interviews J-2A, J-9A.

29. Interviews J-2A, J-2B, J-4A, J-5A, J-6A, J-8A, J-10A, J-12A, J-14A, J-16A, J-24A.

30. Charlotte Baum, Paula Hyman, and Sonya Michel, *The Jewish Woman in America* (New York: Dial, 1976), 123.

31. Marshall Sklare, *America's Jews* (New York: Random House, 1971), 87.

32. Helena Znaniecki Lopata, *Polish Americans: Status Competition in an Ethnic Community* (Englewood Cliffs, N.J.: Prentic Hall, 1977), 97–98; Helen Stankiewicz Zand, "Polish Family Folkways in the United States," *Polish American Studies* 12 (July–December 1956):77.

33. John Bodnar, "Schooling and the Slavic-American Family, 1900–1940," in *American Education and the European Immigrant: 1840–1940*, ed. Bernard J. Weiss (Urbana, Ill.: University of Illinois Press, 1982), 78.

34. See Thomas Bell, *Out of this Furnace* (Pittsburgh: University of Pittsburgh Press, 1976); also Helen Znaniecki Lopata, "The Polish-American Family," in *Ethnic Families in America: Patterns and Variations* ed. C. H. Mindel and R. W. Habenstein (New York: Elsevier, 1976), 15–44.

35. Paul Wilkes, *Six American Families: An Insider's Look into the Families Seen on National Television* (Nashville: United Methodist Communications, Seabury/Parthenon Press, 1977), 30; Corinne Krause, "The Work of Ethnic American Women, 1900 to 1970" (Paper presented at the Duquesne History Conference, October 18, 1979, Pittsburgh).

36. Lubove, *Pittsburgh*, 109.

37. Leonard Irwin Kuntz, "The Changing Pattern of the Distribution of the Jewish Population of Pittsburgh from Earliest Settlement to 1963" (Ph.D. diss., Louisiana State University, 1970; Ann Arbor, Mich.: University Microfilms, 1979), 63; Franklin Toker, *Pittsburgh: An Urban Portrait* (University Park: Pennsylvania State University Press, 1986).

38. Diocese of Pittsburgh, "Ethnic Parishes (City)" and "Ethnic Parishes (Outside City)," unpublished lists provided to the author by Father Edward McSweeney, archivist, Diocese of Pittsburgh, May 1989.

39. Bruce Skud, "Ethnicity and Residence" (Unpublished seminar paper, Department of History, University of Pittsburgh, 1975).

40. Interviews I-25A, I25-B, I-2B, I-2C, I-3A, I-19A, I-19B.

41. Toker, *Pittsburgh*, 215–16.

42. Allen F. Davis, *Spearheads for Reform* (New York: Oxford University Press, 1967); see also Mary Ellen Mancina Batinich, "The Interaction between Italian Immigrant Women and the Chicago Commons Settlement House, 1900–1944," in Caroli, *Italian Immigrant Woman*, 154–67; in the same volume, Richard N. Juliani, "The Settlement House and the Italian Family," 103–23.

43. Kuntz, *Distribution of Jewish Population*, 43. Kuntz estimated the Jewish population of Pittsburgh in 1910 at thirty thousand.

44. Weinberg, *World of Our Mothers*, 4.

45. "Address given at Jewish Educators Assembly Convention" [1979], cited in Schneider, *Jewish and Female*, 257–58.

46. Krause, "Roots and Branches"; Sklare, *American Jews*, 101.

47. Kuntz, *Distribution of Jewish Settlement*, 122–124, 162, 169.

48. Marshall Sklare and Joseph Greenblum, *Jewish Identity on the Suburban Frontier* (Chicago: University of Chicago Press, 1979), 8–11; Deborah Dash Moore, *At Home in America: Second Generation New York Jews* (New York: Columbia University Press, 1981), 235–37.

49. Howard F. Stein, "A Dialectical Model of Health and Illness Attitudes and Behavior among Slovak-Americans," *International Journal of Mental Health* 5 (1976):117–37.

50. Caroline Golab, *Immigrant Destinations* (Philadelphia: Temple University Press, 1977), 41, 43–50.

51. U.S. Twelfth Diennial Census, vol. 3, *Population*.

52. "Slavic Organizations in Homestead: Patriotic Statement by a Slav," in Margaret Byington, *Households of a Mill Town* (Pittsburgh: University of Pittsburgh Press, 1974; reprint of volume in the Pittsburgh Survey, 1909), 271–76.

53. Byington, *Homestead*, 131.

54. On the psychological support provided by a shared, ethnic, working-class culture, see Ewen, *Immigrant Women*, 267.

55. *Homestead: The Story of a Steel Town, 1860–1945,* pamphlet (Pittsburgh: Historical Society of Western Pennsylvania, 1989), 25.

56. Byington, *Homestead*, 132–36.

Chapter 2

1. Total lack of information about childbirth was reported frequently by immigrant women. Several repeated an anecdote similar to that of Mrs. Profeta. A midwife or a mother or a mother-in-law told them, "The way it got in is the way it will come out." Two women, both born in southern Italy, were told that the midwife would cut a slit in the knee and the baby would come out of the knee. (Interviews I-22A and I-17A).

2. Rose Colecchia, in "Seventy-seven and Still Going Strong," a videotaped interview. (Pittsburgh: American Jewish Committee, 1976), Hillman Library, University of Pittsburgh.

Conclusion

1. Interviews S-2A, S-7A, S-10A, J-8A, I-1A, J-3A.

2. Smith, "Gender and Class in Working-Class History," *Radical History Review* 44 (1989):152–58. Ewen, *Immigrant Women,* 268–69.

3. Ewen, *Immigrant Women,* 267.

4. Kessler-Harris, "Organizing the Unorganizable" in Cantor, *Class, Sex, and the Woman Worker,* 144–65.

5. See Gordon, *Assimilation in American Life,* 158–59.

6. See Monica McGoldrick, John K. Pearce, and Joseph Giordano, *Ethnicity and Family Therapy* (New York: Guilford Press, 1982); Andrew M. Greeley, "Ethnicity as an Influence on Behavior," in *Ethnic Groups in the City* ed. Otto Feinstein (Lexington, Mass.: Heath–Lexington Books), 3–16; Michael Novak, "The Family Out of Power," *Harper's,* April 1976, 37: Marshall Sklare, *The Jews: Social Patterns of an American Group* (Glencoe, Ill.: Free Press, 1960); Judith E. Smith, *Family Connections: A History of Italian and Jewish Immigrant Lives in Providence, Rhode Island, 1900–1940* (Albany: State University of New York, 1985); Johnson, "The Maternal Role," in Caroli, *Italian Immigrant Woman,* 234–44; Lopata, "The Polish-American Family," in Mindel and Habenstein, *Ethnic Families in America,* 15–40.

7. Sklare, *America's Jews;* Betty Yorburg, *The Changing Family* (New York: Columbia University Press, 1973); Zborowski and Herzog, *Life Is with People;* Zena Smith Blau, "In Defense of the Jewish Mother," in *The Ghetto and Beyond,* ed. Peter Ruse (New York: Random House, 1969), interviews J14A, J15A, J15B, J16A, J22A, J22B.

8. Lopata, "The Polish-American Family"; Danuta Mostwin, *Differential Values and Attitudes among Families of Eastern and Central European Background: Implications for Mental Health and Social Services* (New York: Institute on Pluralism and Group Identity, 1976); Howard F. Stein, "An Ethno-Historical Study of Slovak-American Identity" (Ph.D. diss., University of Pittsburgh, 1972); Zand, "Polish Family Folkways," 78.

9. Michael Novak, "You Can Go Home Again: A Conversation," *Journal of Current Social Issues* 14 (Winter 1977):54–58.

10. Betty Friedan, *The Second Stage* (New York: Summit Books, 1981); see also *American Woman 1988–89,* 341–42.

11. Krause, "Grandmothers, Mothers, and Daughters" (1978), 69–74.

12. See Nancy Chodorow, "Family Structure and Feminine Personality," in *Women, Culture, and Society,* ed. M. Z. Rosaldo and L. Lamphere, (Palo Alto, Calif.: Stanford University Press, 1974), 43–66, and *The Reproduction of Mothering: Family Structure and Feminine Personality* (Berkeley: University of California Press, 1977); Nancy Friday, *My Mother/Myself* (New York: Delacorte, 1977); S. Hammer, *Daughters and Mothers* (New York: Quadrangle, 1975); Sonya Michel, "Mothers and Daughters in American Jewish Literature: The Rotted Cord," in *The Jewish Woman, New Perspectives,* ed. Elizabeth Koltun (New York: Schocken, 1976), 272–82. See also literature by daughters of immigrants, such as Anna Yezierska, *Bread Givers* (New York: 1927).

13. Krause, "Grandmothers, Mothers, and Daughters" (1978), 167–69.

Bibliography

Adler, Ruth. "The 'Real' Jewish Mother." *Midstream* 23 (October 1967):38–40.

Baum, Charlotte, Paula Hyman, and Sonya Michel. *The Jewish Woman in America.* New York: Dial Press, 1976.

Bell, Thomas. *Out of This Furnace.* Pittsburgh: University of Pittsburgh Press, 1976.

Bertaux, Daniel, ed. *Biography and Society: The Life History Approach to the Social Sciences.* Beverly Hills, Calif.: Sage, 1981.

Bloch, Harriet. "Changing Domestic Roles among Polish Immigrant Women." *Anthropological Quarterly* 49 (January 1976):3–10.

Bodnar, John. "Schooling and the Slavic-American Family, 1900–1940." In *American Education and the European Immigrant,* Edited by Bernard J. Weiss. Urbana: University of Illinois Press, 1984.

Butler, Elizabeth Beardsley. *Women and the Trades: Pittsburgh 1907–1908.* New York: Charities Publication Committee, 1909. Reprint. New York: Arno and New York Times, 1969.

Byington, Margaret. *Homestead: Households of a Mill Town.* 1909. Reprint. Pittsburgh: University of Pittsburgh Press, 1974.

Campbell, D'Ann. *Women at War with America: Private Lives in a Patriotic Era.* Cambridge: Harvard University Press, 1984.

Cantor, Milton, and Bruce Laurie, eds. *Class, Sex, and the Woman Worker.* Westport, Conn.: Greenwood Press, 1977.

Caroli, Betty Boyd, Robert F. Harney, and Lydio F. Tomasi, eds. *The Italian Immigrant Woman in North America.* Toronto: Multicultural Historical Society of Ontario, 1978.

Chafe, William H. *The American Woman: Her Changing Social, Economic, and Political Roles, 1920–1970.* New York: Oxford University Press, 1972.

Chodorow, Nancy. "Family Structure and Feminine Personality." In *Women, Culture, and Society,* edited by Christina Rosaldo and Louise Lamphere. Palo Alto, Calif.: Stanford University Press, 1974.

————. *The Reproduction of Mothering: Family Structure and Feminine Personality.* Berkeley: University of California Press, 1977.

Chudakoff, Howard P. "The Life Course of Women: Age and Age Consciousness." *Journal of Family History* 3 (1980):274–93.

Cohen, Miriam. "Italian-American Women in New York City, 1900–1950." In *Class, Sex, and the Woman Worker,* edited by Milton Cantor and Bruce Laurie. Westport, Conn.: Greenwood Press, 1977.

Colecchia, Francesca. "Women, Ethnicity, and Mental Health: The Italian Woman, Impressions and Observations." In *The Italian Immigrant Woman in North America,* edited by Betty Boyd Caroli, Robert F. Harney, and Lydio F. Tomasi. Toronto: Multicultural Historical Society of Ontario, 1978.

Cornelisen, Ann. *Women of the Shadows.* Boston: Little, Brown, 1976.

Degler, Carl. *At Odds: Women and the Family in America from the Revolution to the Present.* New York: Oxford University Press, 1980.

Deutsch, Helene. *The Psychology of Women.* 2 vols. New York: Bantam, 1978.

Diner, Hasia. *Erin's Daughters in America: Irish Immigrant Women in the Nineteenth Century.* Baltimore, Md.: John Hopkins University Press, 1983.

Dinnerstein, Leonard, and Frederick C. Jaher, eds. *Uncertain Americans: Readings in Ethnic History.* New York: Oxford, 1977.

Dinnerstein, Leonard, and David M. Riemers. *Ethnic Americans: A History of Immigration and Assimilation.* New York: Harper and Row, 1975.

Elder, Glen H. "History and the Life Course." In *Biography and Society: The Life History Approach to the Social Sciences,* edited by Daniel Bertaux. Beverly Hills, Calif.: Sage, 1981.

Erikson, Erik. *Childhood and Society.* New York: Norton, 1950.

Ewen, Elizabeth. *Immigrant Women in the Land of Dollars: Life and Culture on the Lower East Side, 1890–1925.* New York: Monthly Review Press, 1985.

Friday, Nancy. *My Mother/Myself.* New York: Delacorte, 1977.

Friedan, Betty. *The Second Stage.* New York: Summit Books, 1981.

Gambino, Richard. *Blood of My Blood: The Dilemma of Italian-Americans.* New York: Anchor, 1975.

Gilligan, Carol. *In a Different Voice: Psychological Theory and Women's Development.* Cambridge: Harvard University Press, 1980.

Golab, Caroline. *Immigrant Destinations.* Philadelphia: Temple University Press, 1977.

Gordon, Milton M. *Assimilation in American Life: The Role of Race, Religion, and National Origins.* New York: Oxford University Press, 1964.

Greeley, Andrew. "Ethnicity as an Influence on Behavior." In *Ethnic Groups in the City,* edited by Otto Feinstein. Lexington, Mass.: Heath–Lexington Books, 1976.

Greenwald, Maurine Weiner. "Women and Class in Pittsburgh, 1850–1920." *In City at the Point: Essays on the Social History of Pittsburgh*, edited by Samuel P. Hays. Pittsburgh: University of Pittsburgh Press, 1989.

Hammer, Signe. *Daughters and Mothers*. New York: Quadrangle, 1975.

Handlin, Oscar. *The Uprooted*. Boston: Little, Brown, 1970.

Hartman, Mary, and Lois Banner, eds. *Clio's Consciousness Raised: New Perspectives on the History of Women*. New York: Harper and Row, 1974.

Higham, John. *Send These to Me: Jews and Other Immigrants in Urban America*. New York: Atheneum, 1975.

Howe, Irving. *World of Our Fathers*. New York: Harcourt Brace Jovanovich, 1976.

Hyman, Paula. "Culture and Gender: Women in the Immigrant Jewish Community." In *The Legacy of Jewish Immigration: 1881 and Its Impact*, edited by David Berger. Brooklyn, N.Y.: Brooklyn College Press, 1983.

————. "The Other Half: Women in the Jewish Tradition." In *The Jewish Woman: New Perspectives*, edited by Elizabeth Koltun. New York: Schocken Books, 1976.

Johnson, Colleen. "The Maternal Role in the Contemporary Italian American Family." In *The Italian Immigrant Woman in North America*, edited by Betty Boyd Caroli, Robert F. Harney, and Lydio F. Tomasi. Toronto: Multicultural Historical Society of Ontario, 1978.

Jones, Madlyn Allen. *American Immigration*. Chicago: University of Chicago Press, 1960.

Kaledin, Eugenia. *American Women in the 1950s: Mothers and More*. Boston: Twayne, 1984.

Karp, Abraham J., ed. *Golden Door to America: The Jewish Immigrant Experience*. New York: Viking Press, 1976.

Katzman, David. *Seven Days a Week: Women in Domestic Service in Industrializing America*. New York: Oxford University Press, 1978.

Kennedy, Susan Estabrook. *If All We Did Was Weep at Home: A History of White Working-class Women in America*. Bloomington, Ind.: Indiana University Press, 1979.

Kessler-Harris, Alice. "Organizing the Unorganizable." In *Class, Sex, and the Woman Worker*, edited by Milton Cantor and Bruce Laurie. Westport, Conn.: Greenwood Press, 1977.

Klaczynska, Barbara. "Why Women Work: A Comparison of Various Groups, Philadelphia, 1910–1930." *Labor History* 17 (Winter 1976):81–95.

Kleinberg, Susan J. *The Shadow of the Mills: Working-class Families in Pittsburgh, 1870–1907*. Pittsburgh: University of Pittsburgh Press, 1989.

————. "The Systematic Study of Urban Women." In *Class, Sex, and the Woman Worker*, edited by Milton Cantor and Bruce Laurie. Westport, Conn.: Greenwood Press, 1977.

Krause, Corinne Azen. "Grandmothers, Mothers, and Daughters: An Oral History Study of Ethnicity, Mental Health, and Continuity of Three Generations of Jewish, Italian, and Slavic American Women." New York: American Jewish Committee, 1978.

————. "Italian, Jewish, and Slavic Women: Their Economic Roles." *Frontiers* 2 (1977):18–28.

————. "Urbanization without Breakdown." *Journal of Urban History* 4 (May 1978):291–306.

Kraut, Allen M. *The Huddled Masses: The Immigrant in American Society, 1880–1921.* Arlington Heights, Ill.: Harlan Davidson, 1982.

Kuntz, Leonard Irwin. "The Changing Pattern of the Distribution of the Jewish Population of Pittsburgh from Earliest Settlement to 1963." Ph.D. diss., Louisiana State University, 1970; University Microfilms, 1979.

Levinson, Daniel J. et al. *Seasons of a Man's Life.* New York: Ballantine, 1978.

Lopata, Helena Znaniecki. "The Polish-American Family." In *Ethnic Families in America: Patterns and Variations*, edited by C. H. Mindel and R. W. Habenstein. New York: Elsevier, 1976.

————. *Polish-Americans: Status Competition in an Ethnic Community.* Englewood Cliffs, N.J.: Prentice Hall, 1977.

Lubove, Roy. *Pittsburgh.* New York: Franklin Watts, 1976.

McGoldrick, Monica, John K. Pearce, and Joseph Giordano, eds. *Ethnicity and Family Therapy.* New York: Guilford Press, 1982.

Manning, Caroline. *The Immigrant Woman and Her Job.* Washington, D.C.: Government Printing Office, 1931.

Marcus, Jacob R. *The American Jewish Woman, 1654–1980.* New York: Ktav, 1980.

Michel, Sonya. "Mothers and Daughters in American Jewish Literature: The Rotted Cord." In *The Jewish Woman, New Perspectives*, edited by Elizabeth Koltun, 272–82. New York: Schocken, 1976.

Mindel, Charles H., and Robert W. Habenstein, eds. *Ethnic Families in America: Patterns and Variations.* New York: Elsevier, 1976.

Modell, John, and Tamara Hareven. "Urbanization and the Malleable Household: An Examination of Boarding and Lodging in American Families." In *Family and Kin in Urban Communities*, edited by Tamara Hareven. New York: New Viewpoints, 1977.

Moore, Deborah Dash. *At Home in America: Second Generation New York Jews.* New York: Columbia University Press, 1981.

Morton, Leah Stern. *I Am a Woman—and a Jew.* New York: J. H. Sears, 1926.

Neidle, Cecyle S. *America's Immigrant Women: Their Contribution to the Development of a Nation from 1609 to the Present.* New York: Hippocrene Books, 1975.

Neisser, Edith. *Mothers and Daughters: A Life-long Relationship*. New York: Harper and Row, 1967.

Novak, Michael. *The Rise of the Unmeltable Ethnics*. New York: Macmillan, 1971.

————. "You Can Go Home Again: A Conversation with Michael Novak." *Journal of Current Social Issues* 14 (1977):54–58.

Parsons, A. *Belief, Magic, and Anomie: Essays in Psychosocial Anthropology*. New York: Free Press, 1969.

Pleck, Elizabeth H. "Challenges to Traditional Authority in Immigrant Families." In *The American Family in Social-Historical Perspective*, edited by Michael Gordon. New York: St. Martin's Press, 1983.

————. "A Mother's Wages." In *A Heritage of Her Own*, edited by Nancy Cott and Elizabeth H. Pleck. New York: Simon and Schuster, 1979.

Rischin, Moses, ed. *Grandma Never Lived in America: The New Journalism of Abraham Cahan*. Bloomington: Indiana University Press, 1985.

Roberts, Elizabeth. *A Woman's Place: An Oral History of Working-class Women, 1890–1940*. Oxford and New York: Blackwell, 1984.

Rothman, Sheila M. *Woman's Proper Place: A History of Changing Ideals and Practices, 1870 to the Present*. New York: Basic Books, 1978.

Rubin, Lillian Breslow. *Worlds of Pain: Life in the Working-class Family*. New York: Basic Books, 1976.

Scharf, Lois. *To Work and to Wed: Female Employment, Feminism, and the Great Depression*. Westport, Conn.: Greenwood Press, 1980.

Schneider, Susan Weidman. *Jewish and Female: Choices and Changes in Our Lives Today*. New York: Simon and Schuster, 1984.

Schwartz, Laura Anker. "Immigrant Voices from Home, Work, and Community: Women and Family in the Migration Process, 1890–1938." Ph.D. diss., State University of New York, Stony Brook, 1984.

Scott, Joan Wallach. *Gender and the Politics of History*. New York: Columbia University Press, 1988.

Selavan, Ida Cohen, ed. *My Voice Was Heard*. New York: Ktav, 1981.

Seller, Maxine Schwartz, ed. *Immigrant Women*. Philadelphia: Temple University Press, 1981.

Sklare, Marshall. *America's Jews*. New York: Random House, 1971.

————. *The Jews: Social Patterns of an American Group*. Glencoe, Ill.: Free Press, 1960.

Sklare, Marshall, and Joseph Greenblum. *Jewish Identity on the Suburban Frontier*. Chicago: University of Chicago Press, 1979.

Smith, Judith E. *Family Connections: A History of Italian and Jewish Immigrant Lives in Providence, Rhode Island, 1900–1940*. Albany: State University of New York, 1985.

———. "Gender and Class in Working-class History." *Radical History Review*, 44 (1989):152–58.

Smith, Zena Blau. "In Defense of the Jewish Mother." *Midstream* 23 (February 1967):42–49.

Sochen, June. *Consecrate Every Day: The Public Lives of Jewish American Women, 1880 to 1980*. Albany: State University of New York, 1981.

Stansell, Christine. *City of Women: Sex and Class in New York, 1789–1860*. New York: Knopf, 1986.

Strasser, Susan. *Never Done: A History of American Housework*. New York: Pantheon, 1982.

Strom, Sharon Hartman. "Italian-American Women and Their Daughters in Rhode Island: The Adolescence of Two Generations, 1900–1950." In *The Italian Immigrant Woman in North America*, edited by Betty Boyd Caroli, Robert F. Harney, and Lydio F. Tomasi. Toronto: Multicultural Historical Society of Ontario, 1978.

Thomas, William, and Florian Znaniecki. *The Polish Peasant in Europe and America*. Urbana: University of Illinois Press, 1984.

Thompson, Paul. *The Voice of the Past: Oral History*. New York: Oxford University Press, 1978.

Toker, Franklin. *Pittsburgh: An Urban Portrait*. University Park: Pennsylvania State University Press, 1986.

Toll, William. *The Making of an Ethnic Middle Class: Portland Jewry over Four Generations*. Albany: State University of New York, 1982.

U.S. Congress, Senate Immigration Commission. *Immigrants in Cities*. Washington, D.C.: Government Printing Office, 1911.

Wanderssee, Winifred D. *Women's Work and Family Values, 1920–1940*. Cambridge: Harvard University Press, 1981.

Ware, Susan. *Holding Their Own: American Women in the 1930s*. Boston: Twayne, 1982.

Weinberg, Sydney Stahl. *World of Our Mothers: The Lives of Jewish Immigrant Women*. Chapel Hill: University of North Carolina Press, 1988.

Weiss, Bernard J., ed. *American Education and the European Immigrant*. Urbana: University of Illinois, 1982.

Wilkes, Paul. *Six American Families: An Insider's Look into the Families Seen on National Television*. Nashville United Methodist Communications, Seabury/Parthenon Press, 1977.

Williams, Juanita H. *Psychology of Women: Behavior in a Bio-Social Context*. New York: Norton, 1977.

Wolfenstein, Martha. "Two Types of Jewish Mothers." In *The Jews: Social Patterns of an American Group*, edited by Marshall Sklare. New York: Free Press, 1958.

Yans-McLaughlin, Virginia. *Family and Community: Italian Immigrants in Buffalo, 1880–1930*. Urbana: University of Illinois Press, 1982.

————. "Italian Women and Work: Experience and Perception." In *Class, Sex, and the Woman Worker,* edited by Milton Cantor and Bruce Laurie. Westport, Conn.: Greenwood Press, 1977.

————. "Patterns of Work and Family Organization: Buffalo's Italians." *Journal of Interdisciplinary History* 2 (1971):299–314.

Yorburg, Betty. *The Changing Family*. New York: Columbia University Press, 1973.

Zand, Helen Stankiewicz. "Polish Family Folkways in the United States." *Polish-American Studies* 12 (1956):77–88.

Zborowski, Mark, and Elizabeth Herzog. *Life Is with People: The Culture of the Shtetl*. New York: Schocken, 1962.

Index

Allderdice High School, 102
Allegheny County Medical Society, 196
Ambridge, Pennsylvania, 12, 117, 118, 120, 121, 122, 125, 127, 128, 133
Americanization of immigrants. *See* immigrants
Anathan House, 122
Ann Street, 12
assimilation. *See* ethnic identity, relinquishing; immigrants, Americanization of

Baez, Joan, 136
Beaver Falls, Pennsylvania, 118, 124, 125
Blackstone the Magician, 195, 202
Bloomfield, 8
B'nai B'rith, 132, 133, 135
boarders, 156, 160
Boswell, Pennsylvania, 84, 90
Braddock, Pennsylvania, 163
Burlington, Vermont, 80–84
Byington, Margaret, 11

career and family, 43, 66, 80–83, 87–88, 98–99, 100–102, 113, 118, 140, 168, 174, 175, 188, 190, 192, 195–97, 201, 205–6; conflict over combining, 44–45, 140, 174, 197
Carlow College, 203; *see also* Mount Mercy College
Carnegie, Pennsylvania, 183
Carnegie Steel Company, 10, 12; *see also* United States Steel Corporation
Carnegie Tech, 127
Charleroi, Pennsylvania, 118
Chatham College, 70

child care, 42, 86, 87, 98, 131, 139, 140, 165, 166, 173, 192, 195, 199, 201–2, 204
childbirth, 20, 28, 53, 63, 65, 71, 86–87, 97; learning about, 19, 93, 99, 107, 116, 117, 128; *see also* pregnancy
children, 32, 41, 67, 68, 129, 154, 155, 166–67, 204; care of, 53, 54, 87, 97–98, 107–8, 117, 118, 131, 139, 140, 165, 166, 173, 184, 192, 194, 195, 199, 201–2, 204; discipline of, 31, 32, 36, 58, 59, 69, 72, 129, 161, 180; responsibilities of, 24, 59, 69, 115, 124–25, 135, 160–61, 170, 180, 201; work of, 24, 59, 69, 115, 125, 135, 147, 160–61, 170; *see also* gender distinctions
childhood, 18, 24–25, 33–35, 51, 57–59, 80–82, 100–102, 124–25, 133–35, 146–52, 160–62, 169–70, 179–81, 186, 201–2
Children's Hospital, 128
citizenship. *See* naturalization
City Farm Lane, 12, 148, 156, 160
Civic Light Opera, 42
Cliff Street, 117
Colgate University, 39
Columbia Hospital, 184
Conroy School, 24
cooking. *See* food
Council House, 137
Council. *See* National Council of Jewish Women
courtship and marriage, 18–19, 27–28, 40–41, 52, 55–56, 62–63, 71–72, 84–85, 96–98, 107, 115–16, 127–28, 138, 154–56, 164–65, 172, 182–83; 138,

154–56, 164–65, 172, 182–83, 190, 203–4; second marriage, 55–56, 157; *see also* husband, marital relations

customs. *See* ethnic customs

dating, 40, 62, 63, 70, 72, 85, 92, 96, 127–28, 138, 189, 190; parental restriction of, 35, 36, 37, 38–39, 46, 182, 188, 193

death of: a child, 86, 117, 165; a father, 61, 137, 183, 198; a husband, 54, 130; a mother, 117; siblings, 167, 181, 183

Della Rosa, Italy, 25

Depression, 2, 12, 22–23, 127, 162–63; welfare during, 156, 161–62

Dinwiddie Street, 120

discrimination against Italians, 60–61; against Jews, 93, 121, 135; against Slavs and Slavic women, 152, 188, 190, 194

divorce and remarriage, 33, 71, 72, 155, 157

Dixon Street, 12, 153

Doctors Hospital. *See* Podiatry Hospital

drinking, 38–39, 154–56

Duquesne Gardens, 202

East End, 9, 10, 124

East Liberty, 9, 10, 52, 56, 57, 58, 60, 67

education: elementary through graduate, 18, 24, 27, 35–36, 37, 39, 60–61, 69, 95–96, 102–4, 115, 134, 137, 151, 170, 171, 175, 181, 188, 203; ethnic and class attitudes toward, 5, 6–7, 22, 23, 26, 31–32, 39, 55, 58, 66, 83–84, 102–4, 113, 115, 123, 127, 146, 152, 163, 175, 181, 185, 188–89, 203; religious, 36, 37, 59, 74, 83–84, 88, 91, 93, 134; sex, 19, 28, 68, 69–70, 93, 116, 126, 135–36, 154, 155, 171, 181, 187–88, 192–93, 202

Eighth Avenue, 148, 150, 163

employment of women, 2, 67, 73; effect of Depression on, 3; effect of World War II on, 3, 12, 30, 190–91; of immigrant Italian, 5, 24, 51–52, 54–55; of immigrant Jewish, 6, 84, 115, 124–25; of immigrant Slovak, 7–8, 152–53, 156; *see also* work; career and family

ethnic church, 9, 35, 56, 59–60, 68, 164, 166, 167, 180, 184; religious education in, 59, 74; *see also* names of individual churches

ethnic customs: Italian, 25–26, 44, 59–60,

68, 74; Jewish, 82, 83, 91, 117, 120; Polish, 180, 194, 200; Slovak, 151; Slovak/Hungarian, 167

ethnic identity: historical significance of, 207–8; Hungarian, 167, 172; Italian, 35, 56–57, 74; Jewish, 89, 94, 139–40; Polish, 180, 182, 184–85, 194; Slovak, 152, 159, 164, 167, 172; Spanish, 204; relinquishing, 68, 74, 159, 187, 193–94, 200, 201

family, extended: Italian, 18, 19, 20, 21, 24, 25, 29, 33, 34, 36, 43, 52, 68, 74; Jewish, 101–2, 113, 114; Polish, 186; fathers, 18–19, 24, 25, 26, 34, 35, 36, 38, 40–41, 58–59, 68, 71, 80, 90, 92, 98–99, 103, 108, 114, 133, 134, 148–49, 170, 179, 186, 188, 197; stepfather, 162–63

feminism. *See* gender distinctions, women, women's roles

Fifth Avenue High School, 120

Fifty-Plus Club, 65

Flamingo (club), 60

Florida, 96, 100, 101–2

food and cooking, 22–23, 24, 53, 88, 116, 158, 159, 160, 161; Italian, 18, 25, 34, 35, 44, 54, 68, 74; Jewish, 82, 86, 94, 116; Slovak, 146–47, 148, 151, 161, 164, 169, 175; Spanish, 204

"Forward" (newspaper), 115

Frick Training School, 195

generations, change and continuity over, 23, 32, 43, 46, 75, 123, 131–32, 174, 206; expectations for children and grandchildren, 74–75, 119, 123, 175; strong bonds between, 132, 141, 210

gender distinctions, 20–22, 33, 37–39, 43, 68, 91–92, 103, 127, 136, 174, 192; ethnic views of, 4–7; restrictions of females, 22, 27, 31, 33, 34, 35, 36, 37–39, 46, 52, 55, 69, 83, 84, 92–93

Girl Scouts, 132, 134

Glosser Brothers (department store), 101

grandmothers, 18, 24, 26, 91–92, 100–101, 147, 160, 161, 162, 174–75, 187, 201–2, 205; relationships with granddaughters, 18, 67, 91–92, 101, 141, 160–61

Greater Pittsburgh guild for the Blind, 42

Hadassah, 132, 133
Heisel Street, 12, 148, 154
Heths Street, 124
Highland Park, 60
Hill District, 8, 9, 113, 119, 124
Hobart Street, 128
holiday observance: Italian, 22, 25, 34–35, 43–44, 51, 54, 59–60; Jewish, 81, 87, 94, 101–2, 125; Polish, 180; Slovak, 151; Slovak/Hungarian, 167, 169
Homestead Hospital, 165
Homestead, Pennsylvania, 10–12, 148, 150, 154, 160; ethnic churches in, 11; industry in, 10–12; ethnic churches in, 11
Homestead Strike, 1892, 2
Homewood, 52
Hood College, 203
housing, 11–12, 33, 90, 114, 150
husbands, 20, 21, 28, 29, 30–31, 43, 52–53, 55, 63–64, 71, 73, 88, 98, 99, 115, 116, 118, 128–29, 154, 155, 157, 165–66, 167, 172, 173, 184–85, 190, 192, 195; second husbands, 55–56, 72–74; see also marital relationships

illness, 26, 57, 65, 70, 71, 86, 117, 122, 130; mental, 64, 65; old world beliefs and treatments, 26, 117
immigration, 19, 51–52, 113–14, 147–48
immigrants, 1; Americanization of, 3, 8, 23, 30–31, 35, 58, 108, 194, 200; living conditions of, 8–12, 52, 64, 80–81, 114–15, 124, 149–50
International House, 189
Irene Kaufmann Settlement, 134
Israel, 88–89, 105, 106, 138
intergroup relations: Jews and non-Jews, 92, 94, 121, 126, 134, 135, Polish with other nationalities, 180, 187, 193, 204; Slovak with other Slavic nationalities, 159, 164, 167; with non-Slavic people, 163
Italian Sons and Daughters of America (ISDA), 65
Italians, Americanization of, 35; family life of, 18, 33, 38, 43–44; organizations, 65; religion and attitudes toward, 21, 35, 41, 43, 74; social life of, 23, 58, 60, 65; second and third generation descendants of, 24–33, 33–46, 57–67, 67–75; see also

Depression, discrimination, employment, ethnic custom, ethnic identity, immigration, recreation with family, work

Jessup, Pennsylvania, 145, 160
Jews, Americanization of, 83; charitable activities and community life, 81–82, 83, 88, 98, 115, 117, 125–26, 134–35; family life of, 80–83, 86–88, 90, 98, 100–102, 113, 116, 124, 130, 133; newspapers, 83, 115; religion of and religious observance, 81, 82–83, 88, 89, 92–93, 94, 125; synagogue affiliation, 99; Zionism and, 88–89, 105; generations of American-born, 80–89, 90–100, 100–108, 124–33, 133–41; see also discrimination, education, employment, ethnic custom, ethnic identity, generations, immigration, recreation with family, work
Johnstown, Pennsylvania, 10, 12, 84, 87, 91, 100–101; 1936 flood in, 91

Kaufmann's Department Store, 22, 26
Kennedy, John F., 137
Kingsley House Settlement, 9, 53, 57, 60; see also Lillian Taylor Home
Kingston, Pennsylvania, 181

language: English, 21, 58, 83; German, 187; Hungarian, 169; Italian, 21, 35, 54, 56–57, 67; Polish, 83, 180, 182, 186–87, 188, 200; Slovak, 169; Spanish, 204; Yiddish, 83, 91, 115, 126, 134, 150; embarrassment at use of foreign language by parents and grandparents, 35, 91
Larimer, 9
Lillian Taylor Home, 53, 60
Lincoln Avenue, 169
Linden School, 99
lodgers, 114
Lubavitcher Movement, 89, 99
Lubove, Roy, 8

McBride, Judge Lois, 191
McKeesport Hospital, 195
Magee Hospital, 191
marriage. See courtship and marriage
marital relationships, 19, 20–21, 22, 27–28, 30, 38, 39–41, 52, 59, 71, 97–98, 100, 107, 118–19, 125, 129, 154–56,

157, 164–65, 166, 167, 168, 183, 192, 196, 197, 204
medical career, 190, 191, 194, 196, 200; difficulties of women in, 196–97; relations with other women in, 196; *see also* career and family
menses, onset of, 19, 126, 171, 181
Moga Street, 67
Monroeville, Pennsylvania, 183
Morningside, 71
Morningside School, 134, 135
mother, relationship with, 38, 42, 45, 66, 71, 87, 88, 108, 124–25, 141, 173, 199, 202; roles of, 24, 34, 42, 58–59, 92, 93–94, 115, 133, 135, 146, 148, 157, 161, 162, 168, 170, 179, 180, 198–99, 201
motherhood, attitude toward, 63, 68, 71, 94, 98, 107–8, 117, 128, 165, 184
Mount Mercy College, 37, 203
music, 51, 120, 172, 180

Nanticoke, Pennsylvania, 179, 182, 183
National Biscuit Company, 61
National Council of Jewish Women, 125–26
National Park Junior College, 95
naturalization, 157–58
Neel Street, 157
neighborhood, 8, 9, 10–12, 24, 33, 52, 53, 56, 57, 58–59, 67–68, 90, 99, 113, 119, 120, 121, 124, 128, 129, 148, 150, 154, 160, 169, 170, 180, 187
Nixon Theater, 128, 183
North Side, 8, 24, 33
North Versailles, Pennsylvania, 55, 56
Northwestern University, 39, 103, 104–5

Oakland, 10
Our Lady Help of Christians Church, 9, 56, 59, 68
Our Lady of Mercy Academy, 36

Paris, France, 129, 135
Park Place Elementary School, 184
Peabody High School, 134, 135
Penn Overall Company, 62
Penn-Ross Supply Company, 61, 66
Pennsylvania State University (Penn State), 96
Pittsburgh and Lake Erie Railroad, 183
Pittsburgh Coal Company, 163

Pittsburgh, Pennsylvania: employment in, 2, 10–13; ethnic neighborhoods of, 8–13; industry of, 1, 2, 10–13; Italians in, 8–9, 10, 52, 56, 60, 67; Jews in, 9–10, organized labor in, 2; Renaissance in, 3; Slavic peoples in, 10–12; *see also* individual neighborhood names
Pittsburgh Survey, 2, 11
Pittsburgh Symphony, 42
Pliscov (town in Russia), 113
Pliscover (society), 115
Pliscover Ladies, 115
Podiatry Hospital, 196, 198, 200
Point Breeze, 195
Polish: activities in Nanticoke, Pennsylvania, 179–80; church, 180; neighbors and friends, 181, 188–89; organizations, 184–85, 186–87
Polish Hill, 10
Polish immigrants: Americanization of, 187, 194, 200; education and, 180; family life of, 183, 186; organizations, 184–85; religious affiliation, 184–85; descendants of, 179–85, 186–200, 200–206
Polish National Alliance, 184–85, 186
Polish Women's Alliance, 185
pregnancy, 19, 28, 52, 86, 98, 107, 139, 155, 173, 202; difficulty in becoming, 41, 73–74, 117; feelings about, 63, 71, 98, 107–8, 117, 128, 165, 184, 191; feelings about mother's, 68, 94; *see also* childbirth
prejudice. *See* discrimination
Presbyterian Hospital, 120, 190
PTA, 132, 133

Radio Corporation of America (RCA), 39
Ravine Street, 165
recreation: self and/or with peers, 27, 38, 51, 60, 62, 65, 69, 81, 84, 86, 93, 153–54, 163–64, 166, 168, 170, 189, 203, 204, 205; with family, 21, 23, 32, 42–43, 52, 53, 55–56, 58, 68, 81–82, 86, 90–94, 129, 166, 169, 180–81, 183, 204
Reedsdale Street, 24
Regina Coeli Church, 35
religious conversion, 166, 190, 204
religious observance: giving up, 74, 94; traditional Italian attitudes toward, 21, 35, 41, 43, 74; traditional Jewish attitudes toward, 89, 91, 92, 94, 123, 125, 134; Pol-

ish attitude toward, 180; traditional Slavic attitudes toward, 165, 166, 167; *see also* education
Robert Morris College, 63
Rochester, Pennsylvania, 118, 124, 125
Rodef Shalom Temple, 99, 137

Saint Ann Church, 164
Saint Anne–de–Beaupre Shrine, Quebec, Canada, 165
Saint Bernard Church, 40
Saint Clair Hospital, 42
Saint Elias church, 166
Saint Francis Hospital, 137
Saint James Church, 184
Saint Nicholas Church, 164
Saint Philomena Church, 165
Scranton, Pennsylvania, 156
Shadyside, 203
Sharon, Pennsylvania, 118
siblings, 33, 37, 44–45, 61, 62, 68, 80, 87, 92, 93, 97, 100, 106, 113, 114, 115, 117, 127, 165, 166, 167, 181, 183–84
Slavic immigrants: American-born descendants of, 160–68; 169–75; Americanization of, 152, 157–58, 159; family life of, 160, 169, 173; religion and, 152; social life of, 153–54; *see also* discrimination, Depression, employment, ethnic customs, ethnic identity, immigration, immigrants, work
Slovak Hall, 127
Society of the Blessed Mother, 60
South Avenue, 195, 199
South Side, 10
Squirrel Hill, 10, 99, 121, 128
Stanton Heights, 9, 120, 129
Sunnyside School, 134
synagogues, 81, 91, 125, 134; ethnic, 8
Sypniewski, Casimir, 186
Syria Mosque, 36

"Tageblatt" (newspaper), 83
Tukston Street, 113

Unemployment, 2, 64
United States Steel Corporation (USX), 11, 12; *see also* Carnegie Steel Company
United Synagogue Youth, 135
University Catholic Club, 40
University of Haifa, 138

University of Michigan, 136, 137
University of Pittsburgh, 130, 133, 137, 188; Graduate School of Public and International Affairs, 130; Graduate School of Social Work, 137; Medical Center, 189; Medical School, 133–90; Nationality Rooms, 188; School of Public Health, 130
Utica, New York, 51–52

volunteer work. *See* work
Volunteers in Service to America (VISTA), 106
Vonnegut, Kurt, 136

Webster Avenue, 114, 116
Wednesday Mothers' Club, 53
welfare. *See* Depression
Westinghouse (Electric Company), 195
West Homestead, Pennsylvania, 162
West Mifflin, Pennsylvania, 165, 169
Westmount, Pennsylvania, 87, 90
West Penn Hospital, 194
West Point (Academy), 96, 97, 103
Wightman School, 99
Wilkinsburg High School, 188, 203
Wilkinsburg, Pennsylvania, 184, 186, 187, 195
Winchester–Thurston School, 102, 104, 107
Wohlfarth's Bakery, 162
women: impact of women's movement on, 45–46, 103, 106, 123, 131, 140, 174, 197, 205; impact of World War II on, 3, 63, 64, 67, 95–96, 119–20, 128–29, 180, 190; involvement in anti-Vietnam war activities, 104–6; involvement in 1960s counter-culture, 105–6
women's roles, attitudes toward, 123, 131, 168, 197–98
Women's Medical Society, 196
Wood Street, 187
work of women: paid, 18, 24, 26–27, 38–39, 44–45, 51–52, 54–55, 70, 106–7, 115, 130, 137, 146, 150, 151–52, 156–57, 158, 159, 163, 173, 174, 181–82, 191–92, 203; unpaid at home or in family business, 20, 24, 30, 55, 59, 70, 85, 86, 116, 135, 159, 167–68, 170, 205; volunteer, 42, 98–99, 131, 137, 158, 166, 167, 185, 205

WQED-TV, 106–7
Wyoming Seminary, 181

YMCA, 83
Young Judea, 135

Y-Teens, 170
YWCA, 168, 189

Zonta, 197–98

The Author

Corinne Azen Krause received her M.A. from Carnegie-Mellon University and her Ph.D. from the University of Pittsburgh, where she is currently a research associate. She is the author of numerous articles on ethnic, women's, Pennsylvania, and oral history.